FACE UP!

FACE UP!

Tenets, Techniques & Trends of
Public Relations for the
21st Century

Rita Bhimani

Rupa & Co

Published 2002 by

Rupa & Co

7/16, Ansari Road, Daryaganj,
New Delhi 110 002

Offices at:
15 Bankim Chatterjee Street, Kolkata 700 073
135 South Malaka, Allahabad 211 001
PG Solanki Path, Lamington Road, Mumbai 400 007
36, Kutty Street, Nungambakkam, Chennai 600 034
Surya Shree, B-6, New 66, Shankara Park,
Basavangudi, Bangalore 560 004
3-5-612, Himayat Nagar, Hyderabad 500 029

ISBN 81-7167-718-5

Typeset by
Nikita Overseas Pvt Ltd,
1410 Chiranjiv Tower, 43 Nehru Place
New Delhi 110 019

Printed in India by
Saurabh Print-O-Pack
A-16, Sector IV, NOIDA 201 301

To
Kishore, my omnipresent inspiration
and
Tapati and P.N. Mookerji, my creative parents who
shaped my writing and PR career

Acknowledgements

In the updation of a book, the parameters get more challenging; the expectations higher and the new developments a force to grapple with.

These became easier with the help, advice, encouragement from a number of sources.

A supportive husband is the first great power source. If Kishore Bhimani had not re-directed his adrenalin from writing his own novel on the political system to the making of my book, we could have been two people with obverse forces. He scoured my previous book, made his observations and suggestions and goaded me on whenever I had computer elbow. For giving me space, time, wisdom, he is the first to be acknowledged.

To D.P. Ghosh, management and corporate training consultant and long time friend, I owe a special debt of gratitude for his inputs with updating terminology, with reading all of the book astutely and giving quality time to the special touches and also to helping me grapple with net quirks.

I express my gratitude to Arun Chopra of Indigo Arts who creatively mentored the face of the book and the special title pages and Avijit Chatterjee for his humorous illustrations.

To the many people who appear in this book, the CEOs, friends and associates from Advertising and Public Relations agencies, fellow PR professionals and other business associates, I am thankful for their contributions. Whether it was interviews, case studies, inputs needed yesterday, they gamely came forward. Particular thanks to P.K. "Ronju" Dutt for his initial advice and to my brother Khokan Mookerji for all his judicious suggestions, both of them experts in their own fields of management.

I cannot thank my publisher R.K. Mehra enough for taking an instant decision to update The Corporate Peacock and giving me a stringent deadline to complete it.

Rita Bhimani
Kolkata

Contents

An Apologia from the Author

When this book was first published six years ago, in 1995, the very terminology and appellation of Public Relations was being described on the back foot. I mentioned how nobody queries lawyers or chartered accountants about what it was exactly that they did, but when it came to the profession of Public Relations, a lengthy explanation would always ensue. For a profession that is crafted around its very communicative skills, we queried, why do people end up making faces at PR-oriented jobs, when we should be putting a face to a corporation, an identity to a cause, a tactical plan to institutional intent.

In the new millennium, sadly, the general perception is still vague, misunderstood, with blurred edges to the definitions. The good news, however, is that in these few years, the new needs of a highly wired world of business and industry have demanded finely honed core competencies from corporate communicators to implement their strategic plans. There are also the environmental considerations and interests of the numerous new stakeholders of a corporation which are making new demands on PR practitioners' skills.

Just as companies are insisting on such expertise, the people who man corporate relations positions, as well as specialized PR consultants and advertising agencies with discrete skills area, are focusing on the new business requirements.

This new edition will examine the current needs and future trends where corporate communicators play a significant role. These are the areas of Corporate Governance, Human Resource Management, Customer Relationship Management, and the move away from Corporate Vision and Mission to Corporate Intent, Convergence. We will continue to focus on the traditional areas where Public Relations interacts with the universe of its publics, and also give updates on the management of crises, corporate philanthropy, the enhancing of image and identity. There will also be an exhortation to widen the knowledge base of practitioners.

This book aims at collating and catalysing a few new ideas to push the profession a little further ahead to play a role in advancing competitive advantage for the corporate world. The core mantra of course is creative thinking, which is the only real catalyst. This book is to be read quickly, and acted upon fast. It is not a conventional textbook, but meant as a little energizing pill for the strategic approaches to communication management.

Public Relations is a fast changing profession, which has vital ramifications in the volatile business scenario. The proactive field of Public Relations can make or break the company, be a catalyst in times of crisis, provide links in strategy for mergers and acquisitions, or be the big idea behind a mega happening.

Public Relations in my opinion is all about *five Cs: catalysing ideas, confidence building, credibility, creating perception* and *market share* and *capturing mind share*. I hope that sums up what the rest of the book will expand on.

Foreword

Yet another book about public relations and why not!

It is not only necessary to keep abreast of public opinion but one should always try to anticipate what public opinion will be like in the future. No period in recent times has undergone such radical change in public opinion and this book seeks to be of some help to those in this profession. I cannot think of anyone more competent than Rita Bhimani for expanding on its many facets.

Rita was born into PR and imbibed it from her father, who, many years ago, was public relations manager of Tata Steel and my colleague. She has inherited the gift of communication from both parents, her mother, Tapati, whom I remember well, having been a writer of consequence. And Rita's own deep insight into the subject for over a quarter of a century makes her competent to expand on the subject.

All our lives have been changed with the advent of computers and E-mail, communication—the essence of Public Relations has been revolutionized and it could become impossible to keep pace with the new trends in corporate communication. Which is why I feel a book like this by Rita will be of immense use for the new age public relations manager. Also, Public Relations is no longer the exclusive domain of the PR expert and will affect the corporate performance of every executive in the organization from the managing director downwards—all of whom have to adapt themselves to the changing face of PR in India. I say this because the public image of a company is going to be based more and more on its performance and not on how cleverly one can sell the image.

As in all spheres, honesty of presentation is likely to be the best PR technique. As you are, so shall you be judged. Rita has highlighted this.

I hope all executives and CEOs too will find the time to read this book which has been written with style and panache and a large dose of humour to leaven the topic which is a serious and ingrained component of corporate life today.

21 January, 2002
Kolkata

Russi Mody

BOOK ONE:

The Heart of PR

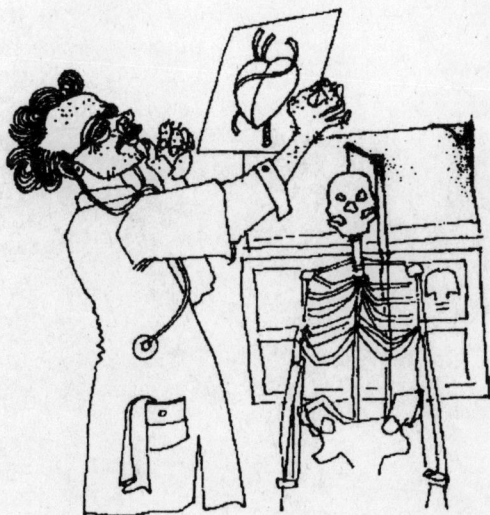

1

Wresting Credibility for the Corporate Communicator

We begin with old perceptions making way for new perspectives of the Corporate Communicator of today. More credible, greatly proactive, highly creative.

"What exactly do you do?"

I can't seem to remember when I last asked this of my chartered accountant or lawyer friends. And yet I find myself, along with my counterparts in this seemingly esoteric profession of Public Relations (PR), at the receiving end of these queries all the time. And we end up horribly defensive, always having to offer a two-para explanation every time we meet someone socially, in offices, on the road, in the air. CEOs ask it of us, as much as the man on the street.

Something is wrong, somewhere. Our profession is built around communication, and yet we end up with people making faces at us, where we should be putting a

face to a corporation, an identity to a cause. It is the one profession that has been widely misinterpreted, largely misrepresented by those peripheral to Public Relations and given Appendix status in any management strategic plan.

Some of it has to do with the name. "Public Relations" has about it a certain veneer of superficial bonhomie. If it had been called Public Affairs Management, Corporate Communications or Consent Engineering (Ed Bernays, the grand-dad of Public Relations, first coined the phrase Engineering of Consent to describe the profession), it might never have had to go through the ignominy of wrongful placement in the management structure.

But I do think these are mere semantic hurdles. In this book, the attempt will be to put Public Relations in its proper business context for prospective "users", whether they be heads of organizations, or executives in marketing, advertising, sales promotion, who interact with this discipline. It is also meant to reach out to those in administrative functions personnel management and Human Resource Development (HRD) who might have to oversee some part of this discipline. Students choosing a career path could find something in this to make them more streetwise and slot themselves more appropriately.

The day might come when some of the typical scenes played out so often could cease to be. Such conversations could become the wastebinned examples of the past:

Student graduating in English Honours: "I am a born communicator. I love the English language. Advertising's a bit too superficial for me. Journalism—I don't have the patience to go through hack reporting until the by-line descends on me years hence."

Student adviser: "Then, what are your other options?"

Graduating hopeful: "There's Public Relations. No special

talents required. The pay is good, the contacts to be made terrific."

Or

Company Secretary, in a note to Managing Director: "We are shortly going to the market for funds. Our image is not at its best, with the recent pollution control charges against us. Let's recruit the PR guy we had been thinking of inducting so he can tackle the negative image problem and help us with media projection."

Managing Director: "Good thinking. But please watch budgets. We can't afford the top people in the PR field. Get a middle-level chap who will toe the line."

Or

Finance Director: "Last year's publicity and advertising expenditure needs to be drastically curtailed. With the closure of our main unit, we have to cut back on all superfluous expenditure."

CEO: "I agree. But we still have to let the public know our future plans."

Finman: "Of course we do, I strongly recommend a short-term contract with that Public Relations consultant we were talking to. It would cost us a few thousand a month, but compared to the lakhs we could end up spending on my advertising campaign, the free column inches of space could prove to be highly cost-effective."

And finally:

Bank Manager to Area Director: "We need to start a publication to communicate with all employees in our branches all over India."

AD to BM: "I told you, no recruitments possible."

BM: "But sir, you don't need to recruit. Remember the wastrel in the credit section who was the hero in the office play staged last year? He can be put on this job and given an Assistant PRO designation. Let him have a bash at it anyway."

Four sets of stories that are enacted in numerous permutations all over the country in worse combinations all the time. But the writing on the wall is bold and unbeautiful for us professionals. The situations are reactive, show Public Relations in a secondary role and take the shine off professionalism.

Views of Corporate Commmunicators and Corporate Chiefs

The secret lies not in complaining about lost opportunities or about the old perceptions any more. The serious Corporate Commmunicator of today is successful because he is proactive. He is not cocooned into a single mindset function. When we talk of achieving boardroom status for the Public Relations manager, it is something that has to be won by precept not just aspired to in principle.

Where do we find such people? And what do they do to earn their status of credibility?

Sanjay Singh, Director of Public Relations at Tata Steel, is one of the star examples of a communicator I would term "line-of-fire" person. The kind of manager who gets out of his given mould and into the battlefield to tackle the large number of soldiers who form part of the stakeholder map of the company.

"The ability to communicate by the Public Relations Director" says Singh, "is directly proportionate to the trust placed in him." In the chapter on Rightsizing, we will talk about how companies like Tata Steel have set up their Performance Ethic Programme where the group that implements this has as a key resource, the Public Relations Director.

Singh finds that wresting credibility can happen if you seek and assimilate information at every step. He has in fact sought permission to sit in on most departmental meetings to be privy to information that would help him in dealing with the various stakeholders. Thus, media persons can be given an accurate briefing by competent PR people like him without having to refer back to the CEO or to a product manager, simply because he is comprehensively in the know.

He shares the example of the role that the Corporate Communications played when Tata Steel was setting up its Gopalpur project. For weeks and months before the project was to begin, a team of people, prominent amongst them the Corporate Communications personnel, had set up an interactive line of communication with the villagers of the area. A Herculean effort to convince them about the benefits that would eventually accrue to those whose lands would be acquired and traditional farming skills would give way to industrial work.

When the project was finally aborted, due to external circumstances, it was the frontline communicators who faced the music from the rural folk who said they were not fond of what the government had preferred but what the individuals, the corporate had promised through their grassroots one-to-one communication.

This ability and responsibility is given to a handful of Corporate Commmunicators. Not conferred, but a faith that has to be planted and nurtured for the roots of confidence to grow.

S.H. Venkataramani, the Head of Corporate Communications of ITC Limited is a role model when it comes to what a communications chief of a conglomerate ought to do. He monitors the flow of the information river that runs through such a company, sometimes stemming the tide, at other times controlling the flood waters and on yet other occasions directing it towards profitable use.

On a more down-to earth note, Corporate Communications gets a well-articulated grid in the way it is perceived, worked on and carried through in the totality of the ITC set-up. Venkatramani's previous long stint as a respected newspaperman surely puts him on a strong ground in terms of empathy to the needs of the fourth estate, which he combines with the maturity of in-depth knowledge and broadness of approach to the multifarious publics of this company.

To whom, and how does he communicate? What is the methodology? What is his interaction with the Chairman like? And with other departments of the Company? Is he the first point of contact for the internal and the outside world? Are there spelled out directives about how a Corporate Communications head functions, or does the personality of the incumbent cast his own set of objectives, guided by the wisdom of experience?

The first thing to note is that "communication" implies more than just talking, writing, interacting. It is the seeking of and assimilation of a wide base of knowledge and information; it is being a listening post, it is having the ear of the CEO, the confidence of colleagues, the respect of the other publics who constitute the universe of the company's business transactions.

At least this is what emerges in talking to Venkatramani.

When it comes to dealing with the internal publics, for instance, the CC chief believes in the strong exponential power of communication, in much the same manner as the famous mathematician Shakuntala Devi illustrates the reach of a piece of gossip in a village. So if one person talks to four of his family members and ten friends outside about the company, imagine the coverage through 12,000 employees—168,000 people receiving a communication within hours. A feat not possible through any news item or advertisement in a newspaper.

The stress on employee interactivity is matched by the focus on Investor communication which becomes a tremendous support service to the Finance function.

And with the media, who have the greatest access to a company's information through the stock market and investing community route anyway, the communication that goes out to the latter has to be in complete consonance with what is spoken and written to the fourth estate.

The same holds true with the relationship between the Corporate Affairs Department which deals with Government at the Centre and the Corporate Communications department. At ITC there exists an internal matrix of sorts, which ensures a common platform of communication when something is conveyed to the government or FIIs or academic institutions. Part of this happens because other departments often check back with Corporate Communications before they put out statements, the key being the healthy respect for the intuitive nature of the Corporate Communications function, which is both watchdog as well as the repository of right response.

There is also the anticipative aspect, the fact of, say, tackling press queries on sticky issues. A set of formulated responses to all possible queries is worked out, so that the CEO can give out the credible answers without having egg on his face. Media handling training programmes for the CEOs of different businesses are organized, to ensure right responses, how to face television cameras and also to be alert when accidents and other unforeseen events demand that something must be said.

Other imperatives are the garnering of information about the company through the presence of the Corporate Commmunicator at other functional meetings, at strategy sessions of other key divisions, at vision workshops, at discussions on important issues.

On that critical day when government issued a fiat banning sports sponsorship by tobacco companies, the Corporate Communications department, and its head had to be available the whole day right up to midnight, speaking continuously to the media.

You have to be accessible, return calls immediately, be responsive, and it is only then that the respect, the enhanced perception, the positive stories, and the long-term bonding with this key influence group happen. There is one more key element—the feedback on perception of the company. This, whether good or ugly, has to be conveyed to people at the highest level to enable corrective measures to be taken.

Two aspects must remain sacrosanct. One, the respect for the authority of the Corporate Commmunicator, and the other, the interaction, information sharing and transparency across divisions and also between different levels of management. A strong PR set-up is at the heart of successful projection of corporate performance. A complementary, advisory role, existing for the company as a whole in the guise of a dependable, credible resource cell.

The perception of Mani Sankar Mukerji, the best selling, prolific novelist who has been a close Public Relations Adviser to key corporations such as Dunlop and RPG, and is acknowledged for his deep perspicacity in management matters, is, as expected, a creative one. He takes the scenario back 1000 years and asks was persuasion necessary then? Did good causes really need urging? It is now imperative not just to get acceptability of concepts but also to make sure of the quality of those concepts. Today it seems to be based more on event and issues management, and less on the credence sought for new concepts.

In his newest book, "Sankar" as his millions of admiring readers know him, has become the first author in any Indian language to give shape to a whole novel based on a Public Relations company. The convergence of the novelist's ideas and his practical application of thought to his story should be a telling tale for practitioners of Corporate Public Relations.

We have talked about the people who have been closely interlinked with the Public Relations strategies of corporates. To look at it from the point of view of an Image Management Advisory like Perfect Relations, is to get a succinct, telling sum-up of a new concept in Public Relations or Corporate Communications.

The founder of Perfect Relations, Dilip Cherian, known to more people as a media person of calibre has this to say about his agency and the definitions of image management:

"Perfect Relations chose to define and then refine the concept of Image Management in India. This was because when we were creating our service menu at the time of our launch we felt that plain old vanilla Public Relations was not adequate for the evolving India."

"Since our market was going to be corporates—both local and global—we felt that the Indian economic environment required a product offer that was much more than the Public Relations that was available. Though global PR agencies were already in the Indian market, we felt that neither they nor the home-grown ones were able to look at the bigger perspective.

We defined Image Management as a dynamic interplay

between local requirements, global protocol and an appropriate mix between strategic consulting and flawless delivery. Image Management was fundamentally presented as a top management tool rather than an adjunct to a Corporate Communication division. Because of this it included many more aspects of corporate strategy, environment scanning and multiple audience addressal systems. We feel that the immense success of this "product" is best proven by the fact that, at least in name, it is becoming the basic offer attempt by several agencies that have now trodden the path we blazed.

"However the secret at the heart of image management is environmental dynamics. Today Perfect Relations has evolved far a field from where we started. And we intend to keep it that way."

The tandem development of having topflight Public Relations practitioners running the Corporate Communications departments of companies as well as the growth of agencies who have specialized in image, perception and crisis management, augurs well for companies. (Chapter 7 deals with the approaches of a clutch of the more prominent, proactive PR agencies of India.)

And finally, we look at the importance of corporate communication from the point of view of a CEO who runs a large conglomerate and also heads up the most prominent industry body in the country. Sanjeev Goenka has this to say about Corporate Communication and the responsibility he places on his own Corporate Communication chief.

"Corporate Communication is a critical tool. Every section of stakeholders has to be persuaded in order to reduce conflict or interests and to secure consent. I do believe that the quality of consent depends on the quality of communication. People can no longer be coerced and consent engineering is the only route.

The remarkable growth of the media and the complexities associated with it will call for the finest brains being involved in Corporate Communication. As I see it, the PRO can no longer limit himself to the role of an information courier, he or she has to constantly advise the people at the top not only that they should communicate, but also what they should communicate. Why, what who and when have become important questions.

If the Corporate Commmunicator is not empowered, the quality of persuasion will suffer.

Being a firm believer in Corporate Communication, I have no hesitation in confirming that our own Corporate Communication chief is one of my closest executives. We deal with him both at a formal and informal level. We exchange views almost daily wherever we are; there have been cases when we talk to each other late night, early morning, in fact at all hours of the day and night. Our Corporate Communication chief has the freedom to wake me up at midnight, if necessary.

Our Corporate Communication chief believes that our communications style should be flexible and an ideal CEO need not be a prisoner of his PRO. Therefore, both of us have the freedom to interact directly. I have a large number of friends in the media, but between my Corporate Commmunicator and me there is no tension. We keep on exchanging notes constantly and depending on the situation, we decide who will take the shot.

This has worked well, because I have the fullest faith in my Corporate Communicator, who feels that a big group like ours should not always speak through its spokesperson.

Communication is a subtle game, it must be humanized and care taken constantly to keep it "soft and warm."

The warmth of such supportive ideas and ideals should keep the fires of corporate communication proactivity blazing. Thus should spake more CEOs, and in this spirit must more Corporate Communicators wrest confidence in the profession and in themselves.

2

The ABC of Public Relations: Redefining the Approaches, Basics, Concepts

---

How does Public Relations serve the needs of today's business scenario? We re-examine the basics here and take a fresh look at definitions. And see Public Relations as the communications cornerstone of corporate strategy.

The redefining of Public Relations presupposes that some definitions exist. They do, of course. And these have been reiterated so often, that it would be tantamount to going back to basics. But we must do that before we move on to today's interpretations, sorely needed in order to firmly establish Public Relations as a strategic management function, which integrates itself into the corporate framework at the brick and mortar stage and is not the fire extinguisher that sits around waiting for that moment of crisis.

We ask ourselves the timeworn questions: Is Public Relations a division of the Managing Director's secretariat?

Is it a subsidiary of the marketing function? Is it a sub-division of the advertising set-up? Is it a selling conduit? Or has it acquired a relatively independent stand-alone status in strategic corporate communication?

Public Relations is a discrete function, and yet has a complementary role to all the functions of marketing, sales promotion, advertising and human resource development. But it is as an independent resource for the corporate process that we have to view the role of Public Relations today, and that is why we might have to resort to a few redefinitions to put the profession in its right perspective.

When the International Public Relations Education and Research Committee published a Gold Paper in the eighties in collaboration with the IPRA International Commission of Public Relations Education, a working definition prepared by Dr Rex F. Harlow was included. A Veteran Public Relations professional, Dr Harlow said:

Public Relations is a distinctive management function which helps establish and maintain mutual lines of communication, understanding, acceptance and cooperation between an organization and its publics; involves the management of problems or issues; helps management to keep informed on and responsive to public opinion; defines and emphasizes the responsibility of management to serve the public interest; helps management keep abreast of and effectively utilize change, serving as an early warning system to help anticipate trends; and uses research and sound and ethical communication techniques as its principal tools.

A lengthy explanation perhaps, but necessary to define the parameters of Public Relations and defend its niche status. For Public Relations today is at the cutting edge of the rapidly changing corporate scenario. With the shifting sands of takeovers, mergers, acquisitions, the rise and fall of the IT and dotcom sectors and hi-tech bowing down to bio-tech, the core communication competencies have to stay ahead of the business buzz. These changes, coupled with the exacting standards of a sophisticated media demanding accurate, analytical information on the double puts Public Relations under increasing pressure to perform proactively.

The definitions on these pages will serve to highlight that this is no static profession and show the evolution of the concepts from the very esoteric to the pragmatic. And how these concepts have been coloured by the very nature of changing business demands.

When a Vice President of General Motors talked about Public Relations as a "fundamental attitude of the mind, a philosophy of management, which deliberately and with enlightened selfishness places the broad interest of the public interest first in every decision affecting the operation of the business," he was possibly looking at the art of the profession, with a sprinkling of artifice.

Even Ed Bernays, the grandmaster of Public Relations was talking broad theory when he stated that PR was "the attempt by information, persuasion and adjustment to engineer public support for an activity, cause, movement or institution." Since then, the Engineering of Consent idea gained considerable ground.

There are candid definitions like this one about Public Relations as "finding out what people like about you and doing more of it, finding out what they don't like about you and doing less of it." Some basic truth in this, no doubt, but we need more apt interpretations. Like the pithy one by Sanat Lahiri, the first Indian President of the International Public Relations Association (IPRA) as "negotiating changes with the minimum of friction."

There is the overstatement of intent in the definition that "Public Relations is a combination of philosophy, sociology, economics, language, psychology, journalism, communication and other knowledge into a system of human understanding."

Through an inadvertent remark, came another definition by a company head when he talked about Public Relations adding to the "creditability" of a corporation. Now that is the essence we have been seeking! For Public Relations can make a significant contribution to a company's bottomline by enhancing credibility. What a cinch!

Ultimately, the less that is verbalized about it, the better it is for a clarity of understanding on the subject. It is overstatement that has made for some of the lack of credulity on the part of the general public about PR's needs or its efficacy in the larger corporate environment.

We need to emphasize what Public Relations is not, for one. It is not liaison and favour seeking with government for companies. It certainly is not the chairman's social events wing, nor is it the press relations facilitator of a corporation. It isn't even just the write-arm of a company.

Perhaps this is why the most popular definition, among the students, has remained a classic: "Public Relations is the deliberate, planned and sustained effort to establish and maintain mutual understanding between an organization and its public."

It has been assimilated because it is succinct and makes its goals clear. Stressing on two-way traffic in communication, on the need for planning and the necessity for sustained, not one-time effort. One more advantage of this definition is that it uses the word "establish" rather than "influence" public opinion.

Ideally, Public Relations can be termed the

communications cornerstone of corporate strategy. Not in a reactive way, but in a structured manner whereby a communications plan to interact with a company's numerous publics can be formulated in tandem with business plans.

Certainly, any institution, or individual, or club or university or corporation can survive without formal Public Relations. But can they actually expect to continue to be in the business they are in, without any formal communication channels? There is such a thing as a competitor, a decision-maker, a regulatory body, a buyer, a supplier, an employee, a man with a handful of shares in the company—all needing inputs about the organization which affects their business of work in some way.

What companies need to do is to refrain from some fundamental mistakes of viewing the process of Public Relations if they are to get the benefit of this corporate service. Public Relations must cease to be the forum to get miles of publicity minus the ad campaign. Its "effects" must not be evaluated vis-à-vis direct contribution to the bottomline. Public Relations budgets must be made beforehand, in cold calculation, not in hot pursuit of a sudden idea or a crisis situation. And finally the Public Relations department must be nurtured, nor grafted on.

Does Public Relations still convey what it set out to be? Most agencies, practitioners, and CEOs believe that the term should definitely change. Comprehensive Image Management is what Prime Point believes in. On the other hand, Ogilvy Public Relations Worldwide have no issues with the term Public Relations. "This has become a point of debate" they feel, because the term "acquired negative connotations during pre-liberalization days. However, the core of our business is to open up channels of communication with all the sets of publics that impacts or is impacted by a client's business, to provide them adequate and verifiable information, create an atmosphere of trust and emotional bonding. This goes way beyond perception or image management."

Dilip Cherian, Consulting Partner, Perfect Relations says "the difference between Image Management and Public Relations is the difference between marketing and distribution to retailers."

And it is not just terminology that is important. The issue at hand needs to be matched up with the way it is presented, the approaches involved, the professional tools used.

3

Careering Around Public Relations

We scrutinize the methodology and structuring of Public Relations departments, as also the qualifications for recruitment of PR personnel and consider a system of accreditation for enhancing professionalism

---

The biggest challenge today is the information revolution, which could make the Public Relations practitioner extinct. Or, perhaps, indispensable!

So, while we are looking at phenomenal progress in the world of business, industry and commerce, at the centre of which lies a key element of corporate communication, we also have to take stock of the position of this discipline in the new firmament.

A Public Relations person is created, not born. He is winnowed into the corporate management structure and does not, or should not go into the profession by default.

There was a time when the generalist who had not qualified for the more serious science subjects or engineering, who had not studied medicine nor gone into

A Public Relations person is created, not born

the finance line, but who wrote reasonably well, went into Public Relations. People with secretarial backgrounds, which means stenography and typing, have also been known to do extremely well in a Public Relations set-up.

Journalists have made the move to Public Relations because it is better paying and, they imagine, more secure and infinitely less deadline oriented. Advertising people seek out Public Relations when they reach a dead end in a particular slot. And most woeful of all, people are promoted and moved every day from personnel and other departments to Public Relations to effect an equilibrium in staffing.

For a profession that relies heavily on its communication skills, it should have better verbalization of the requirements of people in its own trade.

So, the issues today are based on three key aspects:

- One is the method by which companies structure their Public Relations departments and the way in which they set about hiring professionals in this field.
- The second is the configuration of Public Relations courses at undergraduate and post-graduate levels and in Institutes of Management.
- A system of accreditation must be put in place to ensure the credibility of the profession.

Methodology

1. Companies must evaluate the very necessity of having a full-fledged or a partial Corporate Communications or Public Relations or Corporate Relations set-up.
2. They must work out the line of reporting, depending on their individual structure. Ideally a Head of Public Relations who may be given the designation of Vice President or General Manager or Director will oversee

all Public Relations activity. He should report to the Chairman or the CEO. Under the Director, there could be several managers to look after Internal Communications, Media Relations, Issues Management, Advertising and Publications, Government Relations. The artists, photographers, visualizers could be outsourced. Many of these functions are rolled into one, something that can vary with the size of corporations.

3. If companies are into downsizing, or do not have budgets for large Public Relations departments, many assignments and large chunks of Public Relations activity can be handled by external consultants. The debate about the benefits of in-house Public Relations practitioners versus external experts is discussed in Chapter 6 of this book.

Recruitment

Advertising in a focused manner is what is primarily required. In the company I worked for before starting up a Public Relations consultancy of my own, we set about recruiting a Public Relations Executive by first advertising the position with our special requirements, which said five years in a similar profession—journalism, advertising, Public Relations of course and superior writing and analytical ability. Nothing fancier. The parameters of the job were also spelled out.

Despite that, a large number of unrelated and irrelevant applications came in, which were easily dismissed. Of the rest, it was easy to single out just five who really fit the bill.

How do you then pick the right one? Just a verbal interview is not good enough. So we structured a written test. A sample of the Director's Report from the Annual Report was given from which they had to make a Press

Release. They had to write an essay either on an industry of their own choice giving an overview of its current problems and prospects or on a topic of the management's choice. A section of the "question paper" had twenty short topics ranging from international issues to sport and music to test their versatility, which required short snappy answers. A section tested their proof reading abilities and their familiarity with printing terms and finally a one-liner on themselves was an indication of their ability to be terse, risible, creative. It took all of three hours. At the end, only one star emerged.

Qualifications and Qualities

So, the nuts and bolts qualifications of a new practitioner would start with a minimum university degree, which calls for a liberal arts background, combined with an MBA, would make for the right kind of candidate for a Public Relations post. This business administration qualification would make him better equipped to understand the company's financial position, its policies and its performance levels to be able to approach its communications strategy in a more mature manner.

Apart from this, an ideal Public Relations man (note, there is no gender bias, merely the use of the ubiquitous "he" for the sake of convenience!) is one who combines the knowledge of men and matters and communication expertise with applied knowledge of business. He should be intelligently conversant with the manufacturing, marketing, financial and legal aspects that affect a company as much as he is capable of conveying any deviations in these areas when the need arises. But while he should be the fountainhead of ideas, he cannot end up becoming the storehouse of lost causes and diverted problems of the secretarial or sales departments.

The typical and most desirable, qualities are a suave and urbane person, who is a voracious reader. He is a person with a feel for history and a desire to be current and topical and ahead of the game. One who can inspire confidence in superiors, peer groups and subordinates about getting a job done and tracking a situation ahead of its time. He has objectivity, risibility—the right peppering of a sense of humour. The kind of person to whom colleagues would gravitate to during lunch break or CEOs would seek out at the drop of a hat. For it is he who is meant to be the repository of information gleaned and the creative counsellor. Also, one who anticipates developments and plans accordingly rather than react to events.

According to Professor Sam Black, who wrote a number of pragmatic books on Public Relations (and cautioned me never to use the term PR which has a pejorative, adjectival meaning), students need a strong base in the social sciences to qualify. And to "understand how man communicates, adapts to change, behaves within small groups, organizations and social structures...in addition the student needs to understand political systems and government and management theory." There should also be skill development in writing, editing, speech and graphic design and maximum exposure to the full range of communication techniques.

To complete the profile of a Public Relations candidate, the additional qualities, apart from paper qualifications, are seen as abundant common sense, first class organizing ability, good judgment, objectivity and keen critical ability, imagination, calmness, an infinite capacity for detail, a lively, inquisitive mind, willingness to work long and unsocial hours, resilience, flexibility and the ability to deal with many different problems at the same time. More mundanely, some writing, editing, speech writing skills and exposure to graphic design and wider communication techniques.

There's something else, too, that we feel gives a good candidate the edge over his average counterpart. It is that empathetic style and personality, which many people feel exists more in women than in men. It has often been suggested that Public Relations is a woman's profession, a "softer" profession. We fail to understand why. This is a communicative and analytical professional like so many others of its ilk, and there is no reason why a woman is better suited to it.

Do people perhaps mean pulchritude? The fact that a beautiful, well-turned out woman can cut through red tape and influence decisions? I can think of better results, if it comes to sex versus sex, if a gorgeous hunk of a male were to be employed by me to get that difficult contract through, seeing that he would do it with éclat, given the assumed combination of "beauty", brains and brawn.

Statistics in this area do not throw up surprises or biases. It is still male-dominated. Which again does not mean anything significant, as more jobs go to men than women, anyway. The issue of the glass ceiling is not being debated here either.

What is happening, though is the trend in Public Relations courses, which sees more women than men entering, competing and going out and getting those jobs.

Ultimately, companies need to work out their own means of testing candidates, but I would recommend similar approaches to the one I have mentioned, adding of course, an interview with senior managers from various divisions to complete the picture.

Views of PR Agency Heads on whom to Recruit

To get a better perspective of what is expected of recruits into the profession, we asked a number of agency heads about their expectations.

Srinivasan of Prime Point, which is "the smallest PR agency in the world", feels that MBAs are not effective communicators and is not in favour of them. "In many private organizations, when MBAs hold charge of senior positions, they function more like private sector bureaucrats." The reason is that MBAs are not aware of the importance of communication through the curriculum that exists in business schools. That is why they have started their foundation to concentrate on those management students who need a new awareness of the finer points of corporate communication.

This point is reinforced by Ogilvy Public Relations who feel that most MBA courses do not have a significant Public Relations component in their curriculum.

When they started their PR division in 1985, they found they were recruiting from across disciplines—advertising, marketing and only a very few with hard-core Public Relations experience. This mix gave them a better insight into consumer minds.

Their stringent parameters for recruitment are— personality, writing skills, thinking ability, understanding business. Some of their brightest stars are people they have trained themselves.

"Career prospects are much better than what the industry usually offers." They said, "In most places a lateral shift is the only way to rise in the organization. In Ogilvy we have practice areas, which are like independent/ autonomous units themselves, entrepreneurial in nature and allows full personal growth."

With Genesis, the career prospects are, encouragingly, "enormous." The person must have, though, that "fire in the belly." People showing initiative and enterprise have great prospects naturally. Someone starting at the lower end as an Associate can go up to the level of being a Partner and even a Managing Partner of the firm. They look for people with excellent communication skills and more often than not prefer to recruit management graduates. People with domain experience, which could be in finance, healthcare, consumer and technology or from the services sector could have an edge, just as previous job experience is always an advantage for beginners.

Linopinion, the PR subsidiary of Lintas look for a combination of management and communication exposure and unlike some of the other agencies, do feel it is advantageous to have an MBA.

Perfect Relations outlines the career prospects very clearly. The Functional areas within PR are defined as: Client Servicing, Media Relations, Media Monitor, Internal Communications, Marketing Team, Research and Database, Seminars and Conferences. Internships are on an interesting rotational system as interns pursuing postgraduate degrees or diplomas get the chance to be trained in all major departments.

As far as education is concerned, mass communication and PR background is essential but not an advantage. Similarly MBAs are recruited, but do not appear to be craved for. All candidates do undergo a mandatory written test and interview procedure.

However as far as skill sets are concerned, candidates do require excellent communication and analytical skills and should be comfortable with multitasking and multi locational thinking. They should have an excellent academic record and a good understanding of the Indian business environment.

But what are the real qualities sought? Certainly a flair for lateral thinking and a proactive approach to idea generation. While experience in Public Relations is not essential, what is more important is consulting experience in the fields of management strategy, corporate planning, organizational development.

People are recruited from all walks of life, since there are specialist teams to look after sectors like Information Technology, Telecom, Pharmaceuticals, Consumer Goods, Travel and Tourism, Automobiles, Entertainment, Marketing, Banking, Finance, Infrastructure and Management.

This should give any aspiring young professional plenty to chew on, as the field appears to be extremely wide open and flexible, requiring only that the person be analytical, gifted as a communicator and be able to fit into many skill sets that are required by a vast array of businesses that PR agencies interact with.

System of Accreditation

If the Public Relations profession wishes to seize and retain its credibility and its position as a critical arm of management, a system of accreditation must be put in place. This is still in the process of being given final flesh and form by the IFPR.

Exhortations for the 21st Century Communicator

The corporate communicator in the 21st century has to move very fast to update himself. He has to be completely net-savvy, to have the power of information literally at his fingertips. The Internet is not just the preserve of a fortunate few: everyone from finance heads to farmers is accessing information through this medium. From the chairmen of companies down to the workmen—everyone can source data to educate, entertain and enliven.

In this kind of E-scenario, communicators, who pride themselves on being the purveyors of information and the strategists of communication technology, have a challenge and problem on their hands. For if knowledge has become this free and eternity is a 5-minute impatient wait for the net surfer, then where do their skills come into play? Is this profession in danger of extinction?

It is and can be unless they create systems and strategies by which this information is digested, distilled and channelled to the appropriate publics who make up the corporation's universe. They have the skills to steer the vast bodies of knowledge available to all and sundry. But it has to be done on the double.

Public Relations cannot be kept cotton-woolled in its comfortable corporate cocoon. It is a vastly interactive and proactive process with other professions. And PR professionals must join hands with the marketing experts to ensure that brand building is more closely linked with image building. For that is where the market capitalization of companies lies today—in their brand equity.

There has to be a greater degree of globalization in approach. The Internet must be used to reach out to PR systems around the world. This should assist the practitioner to borrow, exchange and swap evolving strategies from transnationals, other governmental bodies and NGOs for the new requirements of their companies.

Practitioners should preach what they practice. People who have spent more than 10 to 15 years in the profession should take a vow to give back something to the education and development of the younger group of practitioners. They should give talks, write articles, lecture at PR courses, create new short courses, farm out internships, so that their knowledge and experience can be shared to help the younger set to grow. Those at the vanguard of the profession should adopt a student, possibly, and give him or her the benefit of their head start!

Certifications and accreditations must be formalized and it must be ensured that an even large body of knowledge is made available to students.

This knowledge base must also permeate the higher echelons. Public Relations Managers must make more of a dent in boardroom decisions rather than in lower level managerial planning.

Let us not forget the ethics that should rule the profession. In this E and Dotcom dominated world of ours, it is all too easy to steal, pirate, and get to know the rival approaches because of ease of access. Practitioners must steer clear of conflict of interest, of the temptations of media manipulation and give the profession a cleaner, stronger, more proactive, more bullish image.

High-speed optical fibre networks for carrying digital data will put us on a faster track in IT networking. Internet technology-focussed curricula and advanced diplomas in web and e-commerce technology will open up vast areas of new activity. Computer users around the world can have instant bulletins and tailored e-mail bulletins. Will the Public Relations practitioner get sidelined? Quite the contrary. But yes, they will need to innovate, upgrade, update, and also start taking risks. And the challenges for Public Relations as a career will be better and more rewarding, if not more demanding.

4

Public Relations in Academia

How is the Public Relations practitioner of the future to be equipped to get into the profession? Some discussions and recommendations on where and how Public Relations should be taught. And the place of Public Relations in Management Education.

As Public Relations continues to evolve with the changing business needs of companies, nations and non-profit bodies, the people who come into these organizations as contenders for Public Relations posts must be armed with the basic qualifications. Although we have been advocating that there is no substitute for experience, it is still incumbent on Public Relations associations to ensure that the courses on Public Relations, whether they be degree courses, or diplomas or part of an MBA, continue to be offered, to be updated and upgraded, so that aspirants to the profession are able to get the grounding required to step into the profession.

However, we will be making a serious mistake if we feel that our one-year and two-year diploma courses, our

Masters degree and our crash courses in Public Relations will be doing the job of getting people on the practical road faster. These are useful courses, but we also need to have a full-fledged recognized undergraduate Public Relations course which will confer the degree of a B.A or a B.Sc. in Public Relations and will equip both the degree holder and company alike with a newly qualified professional to be given a specific job in a well-defined department.

The scenario the world over is wide and diverse. In one's association with IPRA as Chairman of the IPRA Research and Education Committee, we brought out a Gold Paper on Public Relations Education-Recommendations and Standards. While these Gold Papers are largely recommendational in nature, their content is an invaluable guide to the norms that people would seek out on subjects in Public Relations ranging from research to ethics to propaganda.

In Gold Paper 7, we decided to get inputs from a large cross-section of professionals in Public Relations and educators on the subject from the USA, Great Britain, Germany, Denmark, Finland, Japan, Belgium, Spain, Sweden, Switzerland, Malaysia, the Netherlands, and of course India. It was masterminded by Professor Sam Black in his capacity as Chairman, IPRA International Commission on Public Relations Education.

The views from so many different corners of the globe, rather than serve to confuse issues, made some things crystal clear. It emerged, for one, that Public Relations education at the post-graduate level was the most effective. In fact, following from this observation was the fact that with Public Relations education continuing to develop at the post-graduate level, we were compelled to look beyond to the development of doctoral programmes, without which we would not be able to develop the very educators and scholars who would further add to the body of knowledge about the profession and who would upgrade the intellectual characteristics of Public Relations.

But while there was a general theoretical agreement on the curricula for Public Relations education, there were found to be differing schools of thought about the purpose of programmes in the field. One school of thought was all for technician-based communication skills courses that are very similar to many basic first-degree bachelors programmes. Another view was that these programmes should go "beyond the skills approach and prepare students for roles as counsellors, managers, decision-makers." They believed that this required the study of Communication and Organizational Theory, Statistics, Research Methodology, Public Relations Management and Administration.

On the whole, the consensus and the recommendations were for Public Relations education to consist not just of Public Relations courses, but of study in all disciplines linked to the demands of the practice. It had been observed that in all the traditional professions, educators had found that students required a broad liberal education in the sciences, arts and letters before beginning their education for professional practice. In other words, the suggestion was that those who intend to study Public Relations at universities should first get a general liberal education.

From the final listing of recommendations, it looks like Public Relations should be taught as an interdisciplinary subject with both academic and professional emphasis. Also that it need not be uniform throughout the world. Rather, it is essential, that curricula should take into account local and national cultures, religions and indigenous conditions. New texts, yes, particularly those dealing with specialized aspects of practice and research. Public Relations departments of universities should consider it their duty to cooperate with national Public Relations associations in the provision of short courses at varying levels.

The Core

What should constitute the core of a Public Relations course that would benefit students as much as they would form a basis for suitable candidates for corporate Public Relations work?

Obviously, if it were possible to make do with one single course around the world, it would have happened a long time ago. There are variables to be taken into account in each country; there are also the variables of what students and professionals taking the courses want out of them. The time span is important. Give us a three-week crash course, they say. And if you do, and do it effectively, you might get more of the right people for the right job in percentage terms than from a two or three-year degree programme. Then there are the professionals who want to go through a year's study of the subject, for, to them the pleasures of work and study side by side make for a complete dedication to the profession, theoretically and practically. As for those students who want to do a complete undergraduate degree in Public Relations, it is a commitment to the profession from the beginning.

On these pages, we are setting out a suggested course context, which could be mixed, mashed, consolidated, extended as the situation demands. The duration of a course that would encompass all the sections and topics recommended here would be two to three years. However, a full one-year diploma can accommodate the key areas from these heads. There can also be condensed six-week to six-month courses, quite apart from intensive workshops that last a week.

The purpose here is to give a reasonably comprehensive idea of what constitutes the curriculum for a course in Public Relations that would equip a practitioner to have multiple options in Corporate Communications and related fields.

A Suggested Curriculum

A.   *Fundamentals of Public Relations*

1.   Principles and concepts of Public Relations.
2.   History and developments of Public Relations: The world scene and the individual country background
3.   The socio-political and business environment
4.   Behavioural sciences

B.   *Corporate Public Relations Structure*

1.   The structure of Public Relations departments
2.   The role of the consultant, Public Relations agencies and the Public Relations arms of advertising agencies.

C.   *The Content of Public Relations in The Management Set-Up*

1.   Public Relations as a communication arm of corporate strategy.
2.   The numerous communication targets of Public Relations:
    a.   Employee relations
    b.   Communications with labour unions
    c.   Media interaction
    d.   Community interface

      e. Financial communication
      f. Issues management
      g. Environment concerns
      h. Government liaison, including local bodies
      i. Dealer and consumer networking
      j. Business associates, including those in other countries

D. *Public Relations Planning and Research*

   1. Opinion polling, audience surveys, issue monitoring
   2. Evaluation techniques and feedback structuring

E. *The Tools of Public Relations Communication*

   1. Writing and production of in-house publications: Corporate literature, including corporate brochures, newsletters and house journals, speech writing and other internal communication
   2. Printing and production techniques
   3. Planning, scripting, production techniques for the audio-visual media, documentaries, films and in-house video and multimedia productions
   4. Interaction with the media: newspapers, magazines, radio and television networks. Use of media for advertising and writing for the media
   5. Internet training
   6. Trade fairs, road shows and exhibitions
   7. Photography and Computer Graphics
   8. Event Management: to cover special/sponsored events, workshops, seminars, conventions and in-company training and other programmes

F. *Ethics and Law*

1. Codes of Public Relations practice as well as ethics in business
2. Regulatory agencies
3. Public Relations law

G. *Evaluation and Feedback Techniques*

1. The measurement of Public Relations programmes and their effectiveness
2. Methodology, tools for tracking the effect of Public Relations campaigns

H. *Professional Public Relations Organizations*

The role of such organizations, both international and national

I. *The Study of Related Areas like Advertising, Marketing, Journalism*

J. *Case Studies & Internship*

Working professionals should be invited to share case studies and carry out workshops as part of this paper.

Arrangements should be made with companies situated in the area where the courses are being conducted to have students train for a specified period.

K. *Thesis*

The litmus test of students having absorbed their course material and beginning to think for themselves is to have them do a miniature thesis on a subject of their choice, under the guidance of one of the professors teaching them. The traditional "study paper" can sometimes be a mere chore to be gone through, by accessing the easiest material available to a particular student.

Our recommendation would be more to do a project where two or three students combine, research a particular "issue" that is relevant to society or to their environment and make a presentation where they will be judged on content, their defence of it, the thoroughness of their research on the cost-benefits of the project, the feedback system they may have devised and the totality of the creative approach.

Public Relations in Management Education

One final recommendation—that business and management schools at university and other levels should have Public Relations included in their management education programmes, taught by qualified faculty or experienced Public Relations practitioners on a visiting faculty arrangement.

In the reality of today's market-driven world, where MBAs not only command the best salaries and top jobs, but are also able to evaluate companies who come to them, things have truly come a full circle. Such a scenario requires the efforts of Public Relations practitioners and professors to tailor some meaningful courses into MBA programmes to be able to give students another dimension of a discipline that is a vital new part of the management process in corporations.

In fact, one would like to say that there should be specially designed intensive courses set up at such management institutes that could benefit people working in Public Relations in the following fields: Managements of merger and acquisition situations, issue monitoring, liaison and lobbying with governments and special groups, financial Public Relations, media monitoring, networking and global restructuring Public Relations and industrial relations oriented Public Relations

Such courses, along with opportunities to work on case studies of real life situations, complete the picture for an intensive management course. Are our Institutes of Management listening?

5

Who Needs Public Relations?

The diverse institutions and individuals requiring professional Public Relations go beyond the more traditionally defined corporate world. Who are they? And who are the "publics" of Public Relations?

In answer to the question, Who needs Public Relations, we in the profession would like to say, everyone. Although this might sound a little brash and simplistic, it is true. However, we will pinpoint a few specific institutions where formalized Public Relations practice is put into effect. This will also serve as a guideline for those entering the profession to see how a number of areas can open up for the aspirant.

A college or university. A Public Relations expert needs to defuse those crisis situations where student bodies could be in revolt over demands, where there is a change in educational policy, where something could go wrong with examination papers or simply when, in interaction with State and Central Governments, grants have to be sought.

A newspaper. What! For something that sells itself! Some of the better newspapers have Public Relations staff quite separate from the advertising department or the marketing people. *The Statesman*, actually had at one time, a Public Relations Officer who was not only good for liaising with some of the leading advertisers at a top level, but also, internally, started a communication system. It was almost a busman's holiday type of project—having a house journal for a newspaper—but it helped to bring about a family feeling and participation amongst newspaper employees who were always writing for others, not for themselves.

A non-profit body. From the point of view of the organization, whether it is Rotary, UNICEF, the Institute of Cerebral Palsy, the Red Cross, or any number of charitable and cultural and social service organizations, the setting up of a Public Relations cell is not just that of putting in yet another committee. It is an integral part of an institution, which has to interact with a number of bodies for its very existence, for the support of its causes, for misunderstandings that can crop-up as, at every stage it is public money at stake. And from the point of view of aspiring practitioners, these are the institutions where they can start, and even continue to make their mark. When a big salary is not the prime consideration, such organizations are the ideal places to apply all the learning from those colleges of mass communication.

An individual. An aspirant to a political post needs it, so does a person standing for president-ship of a chamber of commerce. So does an actor, a producer or a gallery owner, or a non-resident who is seeking to make a mark in business circles in the country of his origin. There is also the area of celebrity marketing which only a handful of Public Relations experts can get into, but which hold out the excitements of a proactive, ringside involvement in showbiz, politics and the buzzing world of big business.

A cause. The problems exist—AIDS, drugs, population explosion and other environment concerns, slums, poverty of every sort, child abuse, women's rights on abortion and property and marriage laws, the handicapped, the uneducated-and the champions and the doers for these causes are only in thousands, not in millions. All we can say is—communicators of the world, unite. You have nothing to lose but your inputs of time. And in the more formalized established institutions, a career can be carved out, which will be remunerated, too.

Corporate bodies

Corporate organizations constitute the bulk of recognized Public Relations activity involving numerous publics, each requiring an articulated approach.

Employee Interaction

The most important "public" of Public Relations activity in a corporation is the employee. He is vital in a more crucial way than people can imagine. A quick search in the Thesaurus revealed something astounding. The section which is devoted to Abstract Relations, Space, Matter has "Employees" shown under Volition. The power to decide for yourself. The element of choice.

So, if the contention is that volition is the element, then an employee could be viewed as a decision-maker, someone who cannot merely be a target for communication but who would also be dictating the direction in which a company moves. Which means that Public Relations practitioners cannot be mere purveyors of information, but have to ensure an involvement and participation of and direction

from employees. Employee aspirations have soared with soaring profits, mergers and conglomerates becoming bigger around them, they do not take a passive role any more, but are involved, concerned and not content to lie back and take what comes to them. Hence, in targeting the employee, Public Relations expert has to remember some basic tenets. He has to ensure the least amount of secrecy and holding back of information. He has to cater to many strata of employees, he has to convey the company's plans, ideas, projects, and vision, without platitudes and ensure better communication during a crisis. Remember! Effective Public Relations begins at home.

Shareholder Interface

Those who hold a stake in the company have been pandered to for years through just the statutory annual report and interim report. At the annual general meeting of the company, the immediate bonhomie has constituted the level of interactivity with a shareholder. And yes, some companies have institutionalized shareholder visits to their plants, which turns out to be a sort of annual picnic for shareholders and a massive organizational headache for the secretarial department.

Is this all that shareholders, particularly the smaller ones, deserve, for staying with a company, as many of them do, for years at a time, because they value their investment in it, as opposed to those who merely play the markets? Surely, they need to have a well-heeled plan made out by the Corporate Public Relations Department of the company in conjunction with secretarial department to share the company's plans and policies with a "public" which understands them and knows their financial story inside out.

A well-treated shareholder can do a lot for the company's image in terms of his feedback to his peer group. For, armed with his detailed knowledge of the company's financial status, twinned with the kind of "treatment" the company metes out to him in terms of goodies like shareholders meets and gifts and information, he can be a better ambassador of the company than the organization could ever imagine.

Aside from the corporate view of the shareholder, there are now new investor associations, which are championing the rights of shareholders. This is an issue which companies need to be aware of so that their interaction can extend beyond shareholders to these association, if even to safeguard their own actions. What these forums have done is to take positive action against companies whom they find charging unduly high premiums on their proposed rights issues, or companies who have neglected to give bonus issues and have gone on adding to their accumulated reserves. Apart from such watchdog action, they also educate their members on the intricacies of the capital market and have been even known to advise the Securities and Exchange Board of India. Companies should be able to keep in touch with such associations and have an ongoing system of informing them of their own actions to avoid censure.

Shareholder relations is such a key aspect of Corporate Public Relations, that we have known a close associate to have been put into the former function from being in Public Relations, because the company in question considered the day to day monitoring of shareholder grievances and queries as important as the company's other, more "creative" interfaces.

Today's imperatives are to leave no areas fallow where an opportunity to communicate exists.

Consumer Consciousness

There is often a tendency for the marketing experts to shy away from a direct involvement with Public Relations, as if the two were in watertight compartments. And yet in today's market-driven scenario (at least that is what companies are claiming they are), there is a lack of cohesion in a strategy where product identity, brand positioning and corporate image are tied in systematically.

Where Public Relations comes in, when marketing products is concerned, is in revealing the character of the company that is behind a product. It is a sort of value-addition of corporate personality to what a consumer would find in a product catalogue. A committed customer, and following on many other aspects of the product and the originator of that product—the company. In good times, this should work according to formulae. But if a product were to face a crisis *a la* Tylenol, or an airline were to have a crash, it is the earlier Public Relations efforts of a company which will provide the back-up to consumers about the innate stability of the company under fire. It could be summed up as the reassurance factor beyond the brand image.

Which is which? Can Public Relations be considered a tool of marketing, or is marketing the handmaiden of Public Relations? The reality is that in not conceding enough ground to one another, they continue to function in isolation, terminology included. If marketing is a function that harnesses corporate resources to meet consumer demand "at a planned profit and with mutual benefit", and Public Relations is the creation of a two-way communication between a company and its numerous publics, consumers included, then there is surely a case for an intertwined approach to the market segment in question.

To quote Llew von Essen from his Handbook of Public Relations: "The marketing person can use market research to help assess consumer attitudes, but this is really only part of the problem. Public Relations, by creating a two-way communication with the consumer, is often a far more effective aid in assisting marketing to appreciate and recognize consumer needs." He is of the opinion that Public Relations techniques can be effectively used to put the company's side of the picture across; to explain marketers' problems, talk about product complexity, review market conditions and pressures, show how good companies are in combating these pressures and, above all highlight how the consumer benefits from product improvement, research and keen competition.

Dealer Dealings

There is a further isolationism in the case of companies with large dealer networks. The people who are in touch with such dealers may rarely consult their Public Relations departments, except when they need specific gifts designed or if there is a dealer newsletter to brought out.

But beyond that, there is no integrated approach to communicate what we mentioned earlier in the case of consumers—the formulation of a corporate personality in the minds of the dealer which is quite distinct from the product that he is in immediate contact with.

But having said that, we cannot get away from the efforts of some—a handful of companies who have, through their Public Relations efforts, instituted even such things as financial funds for dealers that have served them well when they have required sums of money for, say, a wedding in the family or a crisis arising out of an accident.

In Book Four, Chapter 9, we focus briefly on a new

concept in dealer networking where Public Relations will have a new challenging role—Business Television.

Media Monitoring

The area which occupies considerable amounts of time for any Public Relations department is the relationship with the media. To many people, this is probably the only function of a Public Relations person. To the Chief Executive, this is the area which is likely to create the greatest problems. To the Public Relations expert, this is what brings in the best opportunities to communicate the product-policy-plan conundrum of the company through well-mustered techniques. To the journalist or the television producer, it is sometimes a reactive situation of reviving unsolicited plugs, but also one which could provide material for analysis, projection of industrial progress and background for potentially explosive stories.

Government Goodwill

When Public Relations was in its infancy, the strongest focus, and perhaps the need of the day, was lobbying with the powers that be. The words PR and lobbying were synonymous. Ivy Lee in the USA led the field with his efforts. Today, we have come full circle in the needs of a company to interact with the policy-makers, not just through their Government liaison departments, but also through the efforts of their Public Relations managers, who are expected to be able to study the Big Picture and present, not just a case for a license, but a total image package. What does all this add up to?

The diverse nature of the Public Relations exercise that organizations have as part of the running of their business. Nothing can work in isolation. This book talks about the intertwined and the multiplier effects.

These are some instances of the overlap of functions and the target audiences that require this team effort

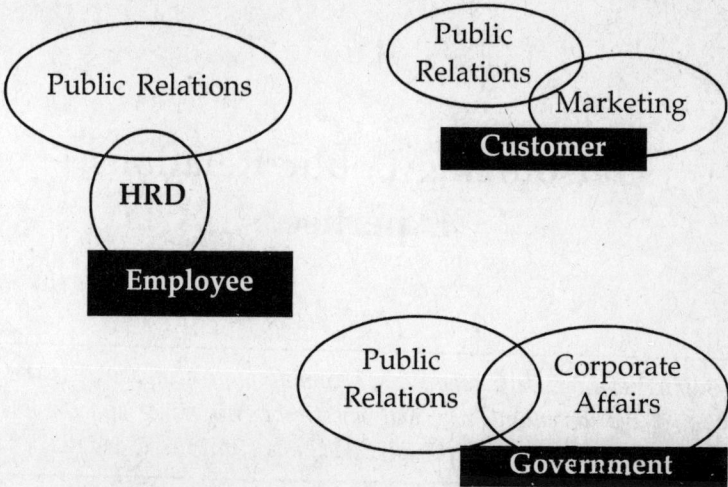

6

Outsourcing Public Relations Expertise

Public Relations departments are becoming more compact. It is the hour of the consultant, who will objectively give advice and counsel for the more complex Public Relations strategies of today.

When in doubt, hire that consultant. Because when in need, or in danger, it could be too late, and too expensive to do a repair job to your corporate face.

There is nothing new in the concept of consultants in relation to a corporation. I refer readers to a book by Professor John Galbraith—*The New Industrial Society*—that was *de rigueur* reading in the sixties when it was first published. In it, he brought out the concept of what he termed the Technostructure, which "changes our view of who runs the modern industrial enterprise; for the owners and managers it substitutes the complex of specialists and technicians who in fact exercise the decisive power."

Galbraith believed that there is a certain section of individuals like physicians, newspapermen, scientists and entertainers, who sustain, and are not sustained by the organization to which they belong. So they are not diminished in a separation from the umbilical, but can carry on regardless to re-establish their identities.

So, does this strengthen the case for the independent counsel, whether he is a PR consultant, legal counsel or financial adviser?

If the new technostructure of corporations points to the enhanced role of the specialist then there is surely an increasing case for expert slots in functions where internal departmental structures may prove bulky, and possibly bureaucratic.

Which brings us to the idea of the Public Relations counsel. Can the PR firm, untainted by the reach of big brother—the corporation—be the objective counsellor, which can advise, bail out, catalyse, determine and evaluate the corporation's many communicative requirements?

For a large number of us who have, following a long period of sustenance by corporations, decided to take on the role of counselling, the answer is a strong affirmative. We've taken the plunge into the icier, independent waters of the entrepreneur chiefly to bring our experience to bear on corporate situations in a dispassionate manner.

And this chapter shares the pros and cons, but mostly the former, of what a PR counsel can do to enrich corporate image and communications departments. It is a complementary role to the PR manager. We are not adversaries, although, when called upon, we could be the devil's advocates.

On a Personal Note

The temptations of snuggling in the silken threads of a corporate cocooned world are immeasurable. Your identity is assured, your infrastructure guarantees fingertip access to information and systems, your financial status is regularly refilled and what you lose by way of independence, under the umbrella of accountability, you gain through experience where the larger financial stakes may not be yours. Thus, when I decided to take to the dirt road not travelled before, to set up a PR consultancy service, the opportunities seemed boundless, but so did the problems of individual initiative in the high-expectancy world of business and industry.

"What will you gain going out into the big bad world of entrepreneurs? Surely, we've looked after you, haven't we?" said my managing director, who didn't accept my resignation for a long time. It was a great feeling—individual Vice-Presidents took time off to "counsel" me against leaving. Sure, the company had looked after me, and I regarded it as a large joint family. But when you decide you want out, not because there is any conflict with the organization, or because you seek a couple of extra perks, but because you genuinely wish to start something new, it is not a simple process.

Fortunately, the transition was much more pleasant than I had imagined. Initially, the discipline of home as workplace saw many compromises for the family, as unfamiliar faces and situations were the order of the day rather than the exception.

But the most rewarding aspect, profits apart, has been that, when you have been in a field and a discipline long enough, and people know you for what you can contribute, you don't have to solicit business. It comes to you!

Offer a specialized service, and the people are there to receive it. Compete with large players and you could end up with quite a few bruises. Remaining in your own league is important, but I must caution that this could smack off complacency and the one thing we cannot afford in the PR line is to go out of currency.

It is a constant process of updating. Keeping up with new management tomes, constantly gleaning information form newspapers, magazines and professional bodies, lecturing at conferences, participating in seminars, talking to students, writing papers on the subject, helping out with situations for non-profit organizations and frequently emoting the subject with all and sundry are all part of this process of Being There. Of Staying On. Of maintaining an authoritative foothold in the profession.

Lest I be accused of sermonizing at this stage, let me say in self-defence that my remarks are meant to be experience sharing. I detest secrecy and most of us consultants should shun the client who holds his cards too close to his chest. Don't expect us to bake a good plan without supplying us with the basic ingredients. If we have to go hunting for these, the cake may never rise.

The Size and Shape of PR Consultancies

PR consultants come in numerous sizes ranging from a man and a computer operation to huge conglomerates that are swimming the international seas to find the smaller fish and swallow them. They form even larger set-ups that are geographically and multiculturally impressive for demanding clients across the globe. Their field of work covers industrial houses and consumer goods companies, non-profit institutions and trade bodies, government set-ups, political parties and even industrial personality build-ups.

They advertise themselves in diverse, quaint ways, just as the christening is done either using the person's full name or partners using surnames—possibly because this is a highly person-oriented profession. People come to you because they know your capabilities as an individual practitioner. It has greater impact when you present yourself to a potential client saying that you are, for instance, Murad Baig of Murad Baig Associates, rather than A.K. Bhattacharya of Corporate Communication Consultants.

The Name Game

When we were setting up our consultancy, we went through a host of names, some rather flippant like Preen Public Relations, others too general like Communication Consultants that could well be a telecommunication set-up. Choosing Ritam was an avoidance of the direct onslaught of Rita Bhimani Associates, and it was a personal name given by great grandfather, from the Sanskrit meaning purity, truth. It always calls for an explanation with people, which isn't all that bad really, except when the bolder ones take a potshot at the truth bit since the downside of the profession has seen lies and cover-ups.

However, on the subject of names, there are the doing ones like "Outright PR", "PR By Design", "Portfolio Communications", "The Public Relations Business" and the descriptive ones which include words like accolade, acumen, blitz, contact, action, attitudes, profiles, wavelength, adjust, adaptation—all of these in their titles. Most carry the names of their founders and partners, and these, in terms of poetic justice, are the ones which do succeed over the gimmick names. In India, agencies have been clearheaded and straightforward in their appellations—Genesis PR, Perfect

Relations, Good Relations (that's because they capitalized on the name of founder Tony Good, advantageously), Integral PR, Fulcrum Communications, Accord, Prism, C2C Online, Knowledge Management Group, Connections, Excellent Relations.

We have covered the activities and focus areas of a few of these Public Relations companies in the next chapter.

Worldwide, the numbers are phenomenal. Going through one directory, from amongst the numerous sought-after ones in the world of PR, we would like to mention the Hollis Annual, because of a personal interaction with the founder of Nesta Hollis, who, along with her husband, Robert, has been running this well-fed bulky book that contains over a thousand pages, and is a "classified guide to press contacts, Public Relations departments, news and information sources, Public Relations consultancies worldwide and services to communications and the media."

We in India do have the INS Year Book, something that no agency nor advertiser can ignore, but for every compilation, there is always a justification for another, more specialized one and we do feel that with resources of the Public Relations Society of India, the Association of Business Communicators of India, the Advertising Club and other organizations, and with the communications wires ever hot, that a directory of listings with names, billings and capabilities of agencies in Advertising and Public Relations and Market Research can be useful with the numerous businesses coming to India and with our own domestic businesses needing image side by side with investment.

Sure, this is the age of Internet and people can access information a lot more easily without resorting to listing tomes, but such bibles are still necessary and useful and can be done by a group of young people who are at their entry point in these professions.

Books of reference in the cyber age are essential for the networked connect-up, handy tools which become useful points of information and also serve as a medium in which advertisers can find a professional forum for their pinpointed ads. Directories and compilations do run the risk of getting outdated, but then the tools once again are more sophisticated than ever before to keep the information ahead of the game.

7

PR Agencies: Reputation Managers, Communication Catalysts

The new breed of Public Relations agencies and consultants are becoming proactive partners in business strategy. They lead the way with fresh ideas, workmanlike agendas and the ability to cope with crisis situations that beset many industries and institutions today, ranging from mergers and acquisitions, communication imbroglios to firefighting and foreseeing the impact of situations that could affect companies. The strategies—to take evasive, corrective action well ahead of those events, on the one hand, and also to go beyond what advertising can offer into areas which build reputation, energize brand image, follow flexible approaches and provide integrated communication solutions.

When we wrote to a large number of Public Relations firms in India and in other parts of the world, with a questionnaire and a special personal letter for inputs, the idea was to be able to get a cross-section of approaches which students, the Public Relations initiate and so many others in industry could benefit from. The questionnaire was based on five or six points: the size and reach of agencies and their affiliates, some of their key focus areas, their major clients, any relevant case studies, career prospects with these agencies and how they looked at the whole terminology of Public Relations.

Unfortunately, responses from the very agencies which aim at stimulating creative thought has not happened. So the ones who took the trouble to give their inputs stand out as examples of the professionals in communication who mean business and get it too.

Genesis PR

One of the outstanding inputs has come from Genesis PR. It is a full service communications consultancy firm with a strong national network. It is one of the largest independent Public Relations firms in the country, and has global affiliations with Brodeur Worldwide and Edelman PR, helping them benchmark their systems and practices internationally. While these agencies have access to the wealth of experience and case studies gained by them in different markets, Genesis PR gives them a solid base in one of the fastest growing and most important markets in the Asia Pacific region.

The Genesis philosophy is: "Effective Public Relations is synonymous with good communications and good communications means keeping the lines of communication open and direct." It certainly kept many lines open in providing us with an insight of how it understands the environment in which a business has to operate and translates that into achievements.

Its team of professionals (over 120 associates and staff) come from diverse backgrounds, which makes for providing comprehensive communication solutions across various sectors of the industry—healthcare, services, consumer technology, consumer and entertainment and corporate. Its research-based approach is unique, leading the agency to "devise strategies and base counsel, keeping in mind the primary and secondary audience and markets. The resultant PR campaign is a focussed road map, and executed in a sustained manner leading to measurable results." Genesis clients cover the Personal Products Division of HLL, Seagram's, IBM, Ericsson, British Gas, Max Healthcare, BBC World, National Geographic Channel, Accenture, Max New York Life, Hutchison, Tata Teleservice, SAP Labs, Mattel, Symantec and IDA Singapore among others.

Three focus areas of the agency stand out:

- A strong tradition of research-based communication planning to get an insight into the strategic and tactical goals of clients
- In its endeavour towards knowledge collaboration, it is the first Public Relations company to establish its own knowledge portal—myGPR.com
- Its Research Advancement Programme aims at advancing the knowledge, skills, competencies and improved behaviour of people within the firm for both their personal and professional use.

Obviously, this last-named area of focus shows the kind of career prospects with an agency of this sort. It has one major requirement: "fire in the belly." People who have started out as an Associate can go up to the level of being a Partner and Managing Partner too. Students note: if you have excellent communication skills, you could be taking a shot at a job in such a firm, but management graduates do have an edge as do people with domain experience, which could be in finance, healthcare, consumer and technology or the services sector.

Ogilvy Public Relations Worldwide

O&M is already a half-century into the advertising scene in India. It set up its Public Relations division, Ogilvy Public Relations Worldwide in 1985, with key focus areas being Public Relations and Direct Marketing.

Ogilvy PR today has 5 practice areas: Corporate and Finance, Strategic Marketing, Health and Medical, Technology and Public Affairs.

Always believing in offering full services to its clients, Ogilvy PR has translated this into what they call integrated communications where different disciplines have been brought in to address all the communication needs of clients.

Their 360-degree communication approach is a seamless multi-discipline offering. In anticipation of client needs, it has set up Ogilvy Outreach to get to the rural consumer and reach media dark areas. Ogilvy Interactive is yet another division.

Some of their major clients are Nokia, HLL, IIM Kolkata, ICICI, USAID, Kodak, Britannia, Cadbury and Cartier, World Gold Council, Fosters, Nasdaq International, apart from Yahoo India, 3M, Glaxo, SmithKline, ANZ Investment Bank.

Prime Point Public Relations Private Limited

"Comprehensive Image Management Solutions" is what is offered by this Chennai-based Public Relations and Image Management Advisory promoted by K. Srinivasan. Before he started his agency, he was with Corporation Bank, when he was closely associated with the building up of the image of the bank and at that time founded the Public Sector Public Relations Forum.

What is unique is the Image Management Community on the net which he manages with nearly 100 PR professionals globally.

Most significant is his Image audit, which studies and evaluates perceptions of various stakeholders like employees, customers, general public, media, statutory authorities about an organization. Correcting perception is done using various communication tools and techniques. This Image Audit has been done for the Indian Bank, the Bharatiya Janata Party, Laser Soft Infosystems, one of the leading Banking Software solution providers. They are retained by educational institutions like Anna University, one of the leading technical universities in India, for their comprehensive image management solutions. Prime Point is the first organization to be outsourced by any Public Sector organization in India.

Apart from its regular activities of media relations, internal communication, sponsorship, media monitoring, and Internet content management, another unique feature of this set-up is the Prime Point Foundation. A Trust for creating Public Relations awareness amongst Management students and corporate executives.

Perfect Relations

Dilip Cherian, managing partner of Perfect Relations defines Image Management as a dynamic interplay between local requirements, global protocol and an appropriate mix between strategic consulting and flawless delivery. Image Management, he says was fundamentally presented as a top management tool rather than an adjunct to a corporate communication division. Because of this, it included many more aspects of corporate strategy, environment scanning and multiple audience addressal systems.

"We feel that the immense success of this "product" is best proven by the fact that, at least in name, it is becoming the basic offer attempt by several agencies who have now trodden the path we blazed."

The term "Image Management Advisory" which Perfect Relations uses to define itself is a modern, pragmatic method of projecting the core communication competence that this agency possesses.

LINOpinion

The PR subsidiary of Lintas goes by the name of LINOpinion. Interpret it in more ways than one—break it up in two as the Opinion arm of Lintas, or keep the first four letters in caps and the second word is Pinion, upon which an idea rests. Their focus areas: integrated marketing communication, which includes mass media advertising, research, DR, CRM, PR, rural marketing. Apart from this, they concentrate on media buying and planning, social advertising and marketing, events and promotions and in-film product placement and promotions.

With the advent of liberalization and a lot of multinational companies coming into the country, the business of Public Relations opened up in a significant way. The opportunity therefore existed not only to add value to clients' communications needs by offering an integrated communications platform, but to also enhance revenue and experience in a new area.

Their major clients range from Arthur d'Little, Convergent Technologies, Futuristic Medical Technology, to Raymonds, Archies Greetings and Gifts, Ravissant, Alfred Dunhill, Siemens, Cox and Kings.

IPAN

In the pre-liberalization days, when a young whizkid from USA came back to India, we remember talking to Rajiv Desai to find out what he was really all about. Today, thirteen years after the setting up of IPAN, we can look with respect at one of India's leading public affairs and consulting firms.

During this period, Desai counselled some of the most significant international and Indian companies including STAR TV, Rolls Royce, British Telecom, Hughes Network Systems, Microsoft, Nokia, Intel, Goldman Sachs, Citibank, the HCL Group and the Escorts Group.

IPAN has been in step with major business developments in the country consequent to the opening up of the Indian economy. Among others: the entry of Pepsi in the face of a concerted campaign against it, the launch of Citibank's consumer banking business in what was then a highly regulated environment; the entry of foreign telecom majors, the clearance of the Enron project in the face of orchestrated opposition.

There are a host of agencies located in small towns who have a positive agenda for their clients. We share the example of Saprom, a Pune-based Public Relations agency, which believes that Pune, "yesterday's pensioners' paradise, is poised to be the Detroit of India" in this millennium.

To practice Public Relations in Pune, you must understand the people of Pune, which an agency like Saprom does, going into their minds and psyche and offering a package of services ranging from press conferences, product launches and financial information collation, to event management for enhancing image. They offer services to emerging cities like Nagpur, Aurangabad and Kolhapur, apart from networked services in chosen metros.

Kolkata-centric agency Progressive Consultancy Services says that "instead of going in for a quick-hit advertisement or a Public Relations campaign, they insist on a long-term commitment towards educating and influencing target audiences. "

The focus of such agencies is necessarily different from those in larger metros, by dint of their being reactive to the situations that demand the inputs they are providing.

These agencies have been quoted in the Chapter on Careers, as the student of Public Relations could gain from a view of what the agencies expect in their recruitment.

Having looked at the Indian scenario, where many agencies today are tied up with the bigger players worldwide, let us see what the picture is in the other parts of the world.

The Reputation of Management worldwide

"In a world in which businesses operate on a 24/7 global basis, where the media has instant access to information and consumers have access to round-the-clock news feeds, the PR industry must also move at top speed to help clients effectively meet new challenges. This environment requires the leadership of a new type of agency, one that can

- Manage communications not only with the media, but also among key stakeholders;
- Combine global experience and strategies with a deep understanding of local markets;
- Provide specialized areas of expertise—or "hyper-practices"—to meet very specific client needs;
- Meet consumer demand for in-depth information in entertaining formats".

This is why two leading communications agencies—Shandwick International (a global leader known for expertise in public affairs, consumer and entertainment PR) and Weber Public Relations Worldwide (a technology leader) merged to form Weber Shandwick Worldwide, creating the largest Public Relations company worldwide. Adding to the largeness of their resources is the fact that they are a member of the Interpublic Group of Companies, a $7 billion advertising and marketing conglomerate including McCann-Erickson Worldwide and SSC&B Lintas, thus giving them access to a vast array of resources across a multitude of marketing disciplines.

In our attempts of giving a worldwide perspective to the Public Relations industry today, this instance emerged as a positive signal about how the large Public Relations agencies can meet the demands of global businesses through their entrepreneurial approach and networking expertise, huge base of knowledge and the best ammunition to tailor their know-how to a vast array of client predilections.

It is this entrepreneurial spirit which has motivated a worldwide reach company like the Weber Group to "reshape the Public Relations practice with the application of new technologies and approaches that allow us to work smarter, faster and more effectively for our clients."

They have, in this era of e-commerce, demonstrated "the know-how, insight and energy to transform blue chips to 'new chips' with an Internet leadership position, establish 'new chips' as here to stay mainstream business leaders and successfully re-ignite excitement for traditional tech brands and unsung infrastructure heroes."

One of the issues that we wanted to study from a Public Relations counsel's point of view was the business of transparency of business practice. Ray Argyle, the CEO of Argyle Rowland Worldwide, who is based in Toronto, and whom one had met a decade ago at a Public Relations conference, was quick to respond to the current set of queries.

On the transparency front, he mentions that they have seen significant movement in both the US and Canada towards greater and more equitable disclosure of corporate information, especially that impacting on shareholder values. Both the U.S. Securities & Exchange Commission (SEC) and in Canada, the various provincial securities regulators, now prohibit the selective disclosure of relevant financial information, he maintains. An instance that Argyle shares with us is that of Air Canada who were fined US$ 1 million by the Ontario Securities Commission (OEC) for disclosing only to a few analysts via a conference call, instead of making general public disclosure (via a press release or any other means) of forward looking information about their financial performance.

Argyle feels that in an environment where corporations are being held so accountable by government, investors and consumers, there is an ever-growing role for the Public Relations practitioner in counselling and in effecting communication with key audiences.

Businesses today are looking for "image enhancement in the three areas of good corporate citizenship, financial leadership and as preferred employers." Their own client, Hewett Associates, recently completed a study of Canadian employers which identified the characteristics of the best employers. Exchange of information between employer and employee was considered an important attribute.

But "to meet our profession's full potential", Public Relations practitioners must "further enhance their business understanding and skills, in order to present themselves to employers and clients as strategic business advisors or management consultants who are specialists in communication, rather than merely as tactical executioners of functional disciplines such as media relations activity, for example."

Argyle is clear about one thing—companies are not downsizing corporate departments in favour of outside consultants, but rather are supplementing their internal expertise with external knowledge specialists.

An amazing array of strategies emerge from looking at what a number of other worldwide agencies who are in Reputation Management are doing.

The Founder-Chairman of Edelman Public Relations, Daniel J. Edelman says, "In 1952, I dreamed of a firm dedicated to the practice of Public Relations and committed to client service. Today we're one of the five largest firms in the world, but our focus has remained the same— delivering outstanding results for clients." They pride themselves on being the "only independent global Public Relations firm in the world."

Euro RSCG, which consists of 25 premium consultancies around the world, all with a global approach and a strong local presence, says, "our agencies belong to a new generation, a generation that has grown up in the digital age. We are leading participants in this transparent and intercultural world. We don't talk about the new economy—we create new ways of communicating in every changing economy."

Fleishman-Hillard is an international communications company whose "reputation for quality, creativity and results" is the foundation of their distinguished status in the industry.

The firm of Manning, Selvage and Lee says, "Commitments are made by people. And it is the 400 people of MS&L that set us apart. Skilled, imaginative people, dedicated to providing the highest quality of work and service."

Burson Marsteller, using the "knowledge and insight" of a couple of thousand people spread across 30 countries, operates in multiple functional and industry practice specialities. And adds value to clients through the use of Perception Management. "Our goal is to ensure that the perceptions which surround our clients and influence their stakeholders are consistent with reality and our clients' desired business objectives."

The UK-based Corporate Culture focuses on branding and reputation, on corporate social responsibility, while a firm like Porter Novelli of New York has been given an 'A' grade by "Inside PR" who considered their Health Care and Technology practices the best in the country.

Other global companies that have a long-established reputation are Hill and Knowlton, with 50 wholly owned office worldwide and Rowland Worldwide who now call themselves a regionally focused internationally integrated strategic communications/Public Relations consultancy, apart from the GCI Group, the youngest amongst the top ten, but with one of the largest wholly-owned networks.

We have touched on just some of the many networked and individual groups of agencies to show the range of services that are available to companies today. It is an ever-growing world of building public opinion, creation and retention of perception, and building and maintaining reputation.

8

New Trends

Today's multi-enterprise corporation is expecting to be serviced by either niche PR consultancies, or multi-discipline specialists in the communications field. Gearing up to these aspirations, Public Relations trends are all about turning ideas upside down and viewing it from a shirshaasana position. This chapter will touch upon a few trends as we perceive them.

Virtual Organizations

We are at an era in civilization when Virtual has many connotations, from the creation of a newcaster on television to the games people play in computers to simulate flights to the realities of today's world. When the Virtual Agency could be the New Millennium's answer to facing up to the big competition, through shared resources which can give traditional full-service agencies a run for their money.

What is a Virtual Agency?

Those who are part of this new world call it a way of doing business, a way of life, not just of communicating. They say not everyone with a computer and the ability to communicate is virtual. One of the earliest consultancies of this sort, NetGain, is a loose consortium of consultants each operating his or her own business and banding together when it suits them. In such a case, the business brief simply is this: Whoever brings in the business is the lead consultant on that particular project.

What are the advantages of Virtual Agencies in Public Relations?

Certainly, low overheads, translating to lower fees. Also, more flexibility, greater efficiency and a more experienced pool of people with complementary skills working on accounts. The downside is often finding qualified people, staying ahead of the software and of course, the loneliness of not having the face-to-face contact.

And people still look for a shopfront, a personality with whom they can interact.

Sumit Roy, who pioneered the idea of a "learn-by-earning" university (Univads) and changed the perceptions of ad agency commissions to a percentage on the sales they generated for clients, has created a Virtual Organization, LocoNotion Idea Studios. Incorporated in Washington in 1999, the CEO, Diane Garrod, lives on Whidbey Island, near Seattle, Nanette Kelley, the Creative Director and COO, lives in Fresno, California and Sumit Roy is now based in Kolkata, where compulsions of children's education have called for a re-location, but without any diminution in business revenues.

None of them have met face to face, yet they have several writers, web-masters, idea architects, graphic artists, photographers, e-PR specialists, translators and net-based marketing experts over 5 continents. Clients range from established transnationals to garage start-ups happy to pay them handsomely for " creating and implementing ideas that help them magnetically attract consumers and keep them loyal."

They operate from their homes and every month celebrate as "revenues keep leap frogging."

Yet, in this new-wired world, is the Virtual Agency working well?

Roy sees at one end of the spectrum, large full service, integrated brand communication consultants who offer communication services through a plethora of specialist divisions and subsidiaries. At the other, he endorses the small, flexible, independent and specialists boutiques, who "maintain creative independence and focus on the client's customer." But he cautions that, being headquartered in USA and working out of Kolkata, the US projects have been thrown into a tailspin because of the dotcom crash and following the September 11 events, business could be further affected. That is the downside of the global village.

Samule E. Bleecker writing on The Virtual Organization outlines several factors which are driving businesses toward virtual enterprising.

"Pace. As Alvin Toffler predicted more than two decades ago, businesses now run at warp speeds, demanding immediate responses anywhere, anytime. Today, 'it's survival of the fastest, not the fittest,' he notes.

Cost. The cost of the market entry is often smaller than previously, especially in the information services and other technology-driven industries, where even undercapitalised startups can have an enormous impact on innovation.

Personalization. Computerized manufacturing has made it economical to produce assembly-line product runs of a few dozen items instead of a few thousand. This has meant that corporations are now driven more by customer demands than by internal needs. Today, the customers get what they want or go elsewhere.

Globalization. Businesses no longer compete only with their nearest rivals, but internationally."

He caps his observations with this piece of virtualspeak: "Once we've accepted the pre-eminence of communication rather than location for winning enterprises, we will have come a long way toward reshaping corporations. Virtual enterprises will develop not in the image of the factory floor of 100 years ago, but as a new business ecosystem characterized by flexible relationships formed electronically at a moment's notice."

Virtual PR agencies in USA, UK

In USA several of these virtual Public Relations organizations have come up, which are more than just casual coalitions. IABC Independents is a network of Public Relations professionals in Washington. The group's name stems from the founders' affiliation with the International Association of Business Communicators, an organization of PR and marketing professionals. (The Indian version of IABC is the Association of Business Communicators of India—ABCI). They feel that clients get a lot of experience without the high cost, and being a network, IABC members tend to hire each other.

More such Virtual Organizations of independent communicators are Communications Centre based in Bethesda, Maryland and PR Pros based in Vienna, Virginia. The members in the group range from 12 to 20.

In the UK, a large number of such agencies exist, many of them focused on the IT and entertainment sector. For instance, KMP Associates is a Virtual Agency, which is a full service cyberspace Public Relations firm, while Text 100 is Europe's Number One technology PR consultancy offering a complete range of PR course to many of the world's most exciting technology companies. X-Press Press are pioneers of e-news release distribution business, supplying PR communities a same-day customized distribution network.

We have picked only a handful of examples, but the lists are growing daily.

Infomediaries

In an article titled "The Coming Battle for Customer Information" by John Hagel III and Jeffrey F. Rayport, published in the Harvard Business Review, the focus is on the fact that as consumers take control of information about themselves, companies will have to pay for it.

This belief is based on the fact that people have started to realize that the "information that they have divulged so freely through their daily commercial transactions, financial arrangements, internet surfing habits and survey responses has value and that they get very little in exchange for that value."

They anticipate that "companies we call infomediaries will seize the opportunity to act as custodians, agents and brokers of customer information, marketing it to businesses on consumers' behalf while protecting their privacy at the same time. Only a handful of companies with unique brand franchises, strong relationships with their customers, or radically new strategies will be positioned to become infomediaries; but they will be the catalyst for people to begin demanding value in exchange for data about themselves."

As more customers purchase goods and seek information over networks, or as they begin to use smart cards or other forms of electronic cash (which preserve their anonymity) it may become harder for those businesses to obtain information without the assistance of infomediaries. The authors believe that companies will have to manage partnerships with their customers to ensure continuing access to information. Particularly banks and high-end retailers, who collect detailed data about their customers, will come under more pressure to offer their customers increasingly more.

CRM

Public Relations practitioners would do well to keep in sync with Customer Relationship Management strategies. Today, CRM enables the enterprise to develop an effective multi-channel business communications strategy for the e-Business age. "It provides a foundation that integrates and enhances all communication channels such as personal contact, wire line telephone communications, wireless, fax, email and the Internet."

It also enables enterprises to build up synergies, while eliminating potential conflicts between direct, indirect and on-line sales and marketing strategies. It strengthens product and corporate branding by realigning business processes with customer needs. CRM is likely to become the most powerful tool towards ensuring customer loyalty in these days of parity products, where no amount of conventional advertising and other methods of brand building seem to protect the market shares of any marketer.

Crisis Management

Although we have dealt with this subject in some detail, the trend of having specialized crisis management firms dealing with today's world of increasing disasters, takeovers, accidents, failures, is a step in the proactive direction. Crisis forecasting is a specialized area, and firms such as Lexicon Communications in USA are an example of how an agency can even be pre-qualified by one of the world's largest insurance companies to provide emergency crisis management counselling and crisis communication services to select policy holders.

They also conduct advanced training seminars, workshops and full-blown crisis simulations to hone the skills of managers and executives who may at some time be called upon to serve on a crisis management team or respond to the media in a crisis-filled environment.

Developing Mind Power

Esoteric though this may seem, yet the use of innovation, creativity and an off the beaten path outlook are being seen as the new prescriptions for both individual advancement and for corporate feel-goodness and betterment.

The gurus of grassroots corporate thinking are reaching out to companies and individuals through their books, workshops and structured sessions. People like Deepak Chopra and Shiv Khera are amongst those who have made a mark internationally, while industry groups have even included in their business agendas, discourses by the vocal modern-day messiah like Shri Ravi Shankar who has propounded The Art of Living.

A consultancy based in Chennai called *Mindspower* run by Rekha Shetty, originally a Public Relations and advertising professional, is now the base for a number of programmes aimed at enhancing creative thinking and unleashing the abilities of sales, marketing and people from many other disciplines. Whether it is to increase the profitability of hospitals, or of younger minds, there is a package for all sections of society.

Specifically for the corporate world, the package offered is one where the objective is to develop individual and group creativity skills, understand creative problem solving and basic implementation skills, learn about managing uncertainty and risks, team building and knowing about competitive advantage and applying the tools of creativity in business.

"You are helped to expand your mind and train it to its qualitative best through the use of elegant Thinking Tools. You are presented with the mathematics of creativity. This unique mental tool kit will change the way you look at your company and your team," says Shetty, who claims that many companies have increased revenues and reduced costs using these tools and techniques, globally the ones who have used it being companies like Du Pont and IBM, Shell and NASA.

Image Audit

Important as it is to communicate ahead, there is also the need to rewind, to assess, get feedback on perception created. Agencies with a vision are looking not just at the beginning of the project—the market surveys and the brand research—but also at the conclusions reached after an image audit to improve upon wrong perceptions, correct certain actions taken and recommend new methodologies to steer corporates back on the right track.

New areas of communicative thought which corporates are incorporating, not just when everything else fails, but as an add-on to creative empowerment.

BOOK TWO:

Concepts:
The Art of PR

1

The Corporate Vision:
A Mission of Intent

Is the Corporate Mission Statement a roadmap for Institutional Intent or does it become a monotheistic whim of a CEO? The trends today point to consensus communication reached with top-level brainstorming. There is also a new attempt at shared vision across the board and implementing the essence of the Mission Statement.

All of it needs articulation. Vision—the limitless view, the prophetic parameters of corporate strategic thought on its goals and directions. And Mission—the concrete, corporeal entity that is the written down rite of passage of a company for further guidance and actioning. One blends into the other to form the roadmap for companies to have as their guiding principles of business.

To the corporate communicator, this is not an exercise to which he is privy only at the end, but in its very formative stages. Or so it should be.

In reality, where does it start? To what extent can a Corporate Communications specialist be a facilitator in the

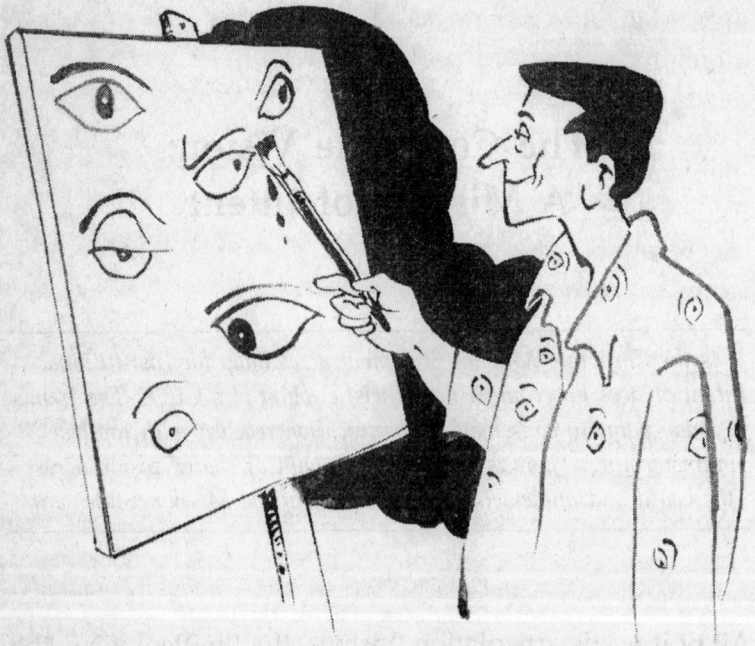

creation of the Mission Statement? And how much is it the purview of the CEO?

We asked this question of Paul Kirkham, Managing Director of British American Tobacco, Bangladesh. This 47-year old head of BAT was totally candid in his views when he said that the vision was always driven by the CEO. And done in a haphazard manner with too many heads, could lead to a mishmash of objectives. Consultation and consensus, in the case of his company, however, had happened with a 30-member team of managers who had been asked to take a broad look at corporate strategy. The net result was an understanding of the issues that affect the company in terms of the markets they relate to and also of where the people wanted to be. Which, translated, meant their desire to be part of an organization of world-class standards and the ambition to be bigger and better.

Hence their simple philosophy of Doubling Net Revenues in five years and the phrase Winning in Our World have already set the company apart from its peer group and in the larger context of their own parent company, as a performance oriented entity. One that is working in an open plan system of total transparency, which CEO Kirkham put into place against all odds in an environment determined by tradition and old values. So much so that a 2-year collective agreement has been settled in just two months. The beacon in its 10-year corporate strategy was its "Social Responsibility of being the Number One Company in the Country". Focussed, disciplined, well managed.

All of this arising out of a steadfast vision, and a pragmatic mission to boot.

It can be top down. But the exercise can also start from the communicator. At Indal, years ago, we wanted to formulate a Mission Statement based on the one that the then principals, Alcan, had done. It was a well-drafted policy statement, but there was no way we could copy it verbatim. That would be impertinent in the Indian context. However, we drafted an initial statement so that senior management could then be aided in the initial planning process of the Mission.

Our intention was not to clone the thoughts derived from the parent but rather to have a specific motivational document for employees, incorporating the goals set by the leadership in the company. Although that particular document now exists as an archival necessity, it did serve to get an involvement from employees at all levels, a "look-in" into a managerial statement of intent process. It was like putting their hands into a large trough of dough and getting a chance to give it a punch or two. It also, in its own way, got employees to think about the direction in which the company was heading and how they were a part of it.

The more workable aspect of this document was a shorter, more concise Mission Statement, which was then reproduced in Annual Reports and in the house journal and circulated to the employees in many other ways.

While this is not the ultimate word in the same manner as the directive Principles of State Policy would be, the Mission Statement is a kind of concretised spelling out of intent which is company-specific and goal-oriented. It is ideally possible to distinguish the personality or approach to work culture from a Corporate Mission Statement.

Agencies, even if their common mission is service, need to have a well-defined mission statement. One which highlights aspects like creative thinking based on a deep understanding of consumer behaviour, business acumen, technological expertise, leveraging knowledge for clients.

Similarly with companies, it is no longer a must-do add on, but rather something that could make that vital difference between apathy and commitment, between disinterest and a dynamic, positive reaction amongst employees about the motivations of the company they work for.

In their book on Strategic Management, Gregory G. Dess and Alex Miller specify that, "A Vision becomes tangible as a mission statement." And the fact that it can identify what is unique about the character of an organization. The authors believe that mission statements do attempt to answer several of the following questions:

- What is our reason for being? What is our basic purpose?
- What is unique or distinctive about our organization?
- What is likely to be different about our business 3 to 5 years in the future?
- Who are, or who should be, our principal customers, clients, or key market segments?
- What are our principal products and services, present and future?
- What are, or what should be, our principal economic concerns?
- What are the basic beliefs, values, aspirations, and philosophical priorities of the firm?

Three major benefits, the authors feel, accrue to an organization by writing a formal mission statement:

They establish boundaries to guide strategy formulation; create standards for organizational performance along multiple dimensions and suggest standards for individual ethical behaviour.

In examining some key mission statements of Du Pont, Reynolds, Dow and GM, it was found that the focus varied from the importance given to stockholders, customers, employees and even to the community at large.

What does Peter Drucker, the best-known management thinker of our time, have to say on Mission Statements? He takes a leaf out of the book of non-profit corporations, seeing in their statements a practical example for successful business groups to emulate. He feels the Mission can focus the organization on action. Apart from the obvious things like defining specific strategies to attain crucial goals, the Mission, he feels, "can prevent the most common degenerative disease of organizations, especially large ones." Which is: "splintering their always limited resources on things that are 'interesting' or look 'profitable' rather than concentrating them on a very small number of productive efforts."

The best non-profits, in his opinion, give a lot of thought to defining their organization's mission. "They avoid sweeping statements full of good intentions and focus, instead, on objectives that have clear-cut implications for the work their members perform." He is also all praise for the focus of non-profits on the environment and the community, whom they start with as targets, unlike businesses, which have an inward looking stance-seeking within the organization or looking purely at financial returns.

Bob Rosner, author of Working Wounded, highlights four possible missions and gives an example of an organization that operates with each.

Customer focus: The example is from Wal-Mart, whose mission is: "We exist to provide value to our customers." Their focus is on doing whatever they can to keep prices low and selection high. The Hewlett Packard **employee focus** mission talks of respect and opportunity for HP people, including giving them an opportunity to share in the success of the organization. A **products and services** focus for competitive advantage is the basis of Ford's vision. At a time when the quality of American cars was in decline, Ford's efforts went a long way to putting quality back into the vocabulary of American car producers. And with Sony, it is the value of taking risks, focusing on being a **pioneer**, not just following others, but doing the "impossible."

Rosner adds: "Once each of these companies established a core mission, that mission became the driver of all operations. It was promulgated in Corporate Communications; it became the basis of employee promotions and evaluations; it guided corporate goals, objectives and strategies."

But James C. Collins and Jerry I. Porras, in their paper on "Organizational Vision and Visionary Organizations" warn of the need for organizations that think of mission as their purpose. They ask: "What does the organization do once it has completed the mission? Without a broader, more enduring purpose from which to derive the next mission, there will be a crisis of direction once the mission is accomplished."

Read on about how some of our CEOs have articulated their mission, and leveraged those ideals.

2

Corporate Vision & Values:
A View from CEOs in India

---

*In this chapter we present the observations gleaned from CEOs
about how they drive their companies with their Vision*

Bajaj Auto

Rahul Bajaj, the high profile very vocal Chairman and
Managing Director of Bajaj Auto, is crystal clear about what
gives Bajaj identity and how they communicate this
identity and how their Vision is translated. He says that in
Bajaj a "few principles have evolved that have become
central to our being. They are not even written down in one
place but I believe have a pervasive influence on our
conduct."

These are:

"1. A passion for volumes and lower costs and hence
continuous improvement in quality and productivity.

2. A commitment to stick to our chosen business and to excel in it. This has led us to developing our own products, pursuing exports.
3. A deep commitment to ethical business behaviour.
4. A policy of being fair, but firm with all our stakeholders."

All these have naturally come to be associated with their "Value for Money for Years" by-line which is well known by most people.

Bajaj goes on to explain that the principles come from various influences: the nature of their business, their family traditions, his own predispositions. Even the character of the town (Pune) that they are located in. It is as if they were "almost born as a company with these values."

Bajaj feels that "Identity of a company is a very important asset. It influences our customers, dealers, suppliers, employees and shareholders and whoever we deal with." He also warns of the importance in all this of being credible. "Like an individual, a company has a distinct personality and it must ring true.

"We have a fairly stable set of employees. Even our managers, so the process of acculturation is slow and sustained by these values being reinforced by the dozens of decisions that are taken every day, at all levels, and what we do when things come to a crunch. Do we walk the talk?"

Tata Steel

From Dr. Jamshed J. Irani, former Managing Director of Tata Steel, we get yet another perspective. When Tata Steel which had always been seen and perceived to be doing things the "old way" decided to change, the process was termed "Turning the Titanic." Why this analogy? Irani's explanation: "If the Titanic had turned, it would not have sunk."

In fact, "Turning the Titanic" is the story of the complete change in the attitude and approach of a company like Tata Steel, an "old economy company" into occupying the premier position in the world steel industry.

And here we must talk about the Vision statement that Irani decided to create, a document that it took six months to draft. The Vision statement states:

"Tata Steel enters the new millennium with the confidence of a learning organization; knowledge-based and happy organization. We will establish ourselves as the supplier of choice by delighting our customers with our services and our products. In the coming decade, we will become the most cost-competitive steel plant and so serve the community and the nation. Where Tata Steel ventures... others will follow."

The Vision statement (some commentators say "Vision" is an unending journey, while "Mission" is a roadmap) has a very definite customer focus, something that has been followed to the letter, to the extent that Irani once asked the company to stop the supply of steel to a customer because he had complained about Tisco's inefficiency. Such complaints just do not happen any more, because of the intent to serve having been explicitly spelled out and further carried out.

Tata Steel's Vision and Mission is deeply rooted in its sense of values which it enunciates at every stage and its commitment, not only to the customer, as mentioned earlier, but to employees as well. Reinforcing that part of the Mission statement, which talks about a "knowledge-based, happy organization." When the new Managing Director, B. Muthuraman took over, a simple handwritten letter went out to all employees, saluting the beliefs of his predecessor and confirming, that, despite the slowdown in the economy and sluggish demand for steel and other constraints, the motto should be: "We will succeed under any circumstance."

Talking to Sanjay Singh, the Director of Public Relations of Tata Steel, he highlighted the Vision Statement as being one where Tata Steel takes a leadership stance for others to follow. In his view, when we wanted to know about the process of creating a Vision and Mission statement, Vision is what you see when you open your eyes, Mission is the immediate objective that propels you to the Vision and strategy is how you will win in the journey. "What is shared Vision?" he says "but the fact of something that is coined by one but shared by 50,000. Irrespective of which window you open, you see the same landscape."

RPG Enterprises

Sanjiv Goenka, Vice Chairman of RPG Enterprises and current National President of the Confederation of Indian Industry (CII) articulates the Vision for his Group thus:

"I am not involved with a one-product company. As a group, RPG is interested in a number of activities, the current focus being on consumer services—i.e. retail, information, communication, entertainment, power, while we continue to be deeply involved in tyre, life sciences and a few more businesses.

Naturally, our Vision for each company is different, but the basic game plan is that we should be amongst the top three operators in every business; the size of our operations should be internationally comparable and we must be able to face outside competition without a protective wall.

My close association with CII has taught me a number of lessons. We have a lot of strengths and India must pick up the best practices from every country which enjoys leadership in a particular business. We are very fortunate in having excellent manpower, but we must also learn to change and change quickly. Chasing change, instead of leading change, is a liability. However, India is opening her doors at a difficult time, which will lead to a lot of failures. As President of CII, I also realize that a nation can win the battle in the marketplace if only there is an excellent understanding between entrepreneurs, employees and the government."

We also wanted to know how he views the business of communication. This is articulated in Book One, Chapter 1, on Wresting Credibility for the Corporate Communicator.

Balrampur Chini

When asked about whether his company had a well-defined Mission and Vision statement, Vivek Saraogi, Managing Director, Balrampur Chini, states: "The Company has Vision to become the most efficient, profitable and one of the largest sugar manufacturers in the country with strong focus on forward integration through value addition/utilization of by-product. The Company has been making regular acquisition and expansion and has also moved into power and alcohol through utilization of bagasse and molasses respectively. "

The key point that he makes is that the Vision and Strategies have been formed through a process of brainstorming amongst key people in the organization. "Strategy development has also been done by discussion with professional consultants." He adds that his personal Vision and Mission is also to make the company the most admired and well run sugar company not only in India but also in the global sugar market.

The Balrampur Chini Stretch document is among the unique Corporate Communication tools and has been highlighted in Book Three Chapter 6.

SRF

Arun Bharat Ram, Chairman of SRF, who has also demonstrated singular industry leadership as CII Chairman, shared with us the methodology of his Corporate Mission and Vision Statement. The focus, he says, was "stakeholders—shareholders, employees, customers and society. Several discussions were held at the top level, followed by suggestions taken from other management levels, which were incorporated and were finalized by general consensus. A key statement which Bharat Ram makes is that "even at the individual level the goals of the employees are set in alignment with the organizational goals derived from these statements."

And best of all is the fact that the document does not stay cotton-woolled. All their presentations, both internal and external always start with the Mission; the CEO and Group Head and other top management make special mention of these statements in every forum; they are displayed throughout the units in meeting rooms, boardrooms, the workplace; the first few pages of the personal diary of employees carries the Mission/ Vision statements and at all communication meets, emphasis is laid on the Mission and its linkage with Corporate goals.

Gujarat Ambuja Cements

"The law of diminishing return does not apply to people." This was the pithy statement that led into the advertisement about Gujarat Ambuja Cements Corporate results. It was not a parading of better operating figures, but more a salutation to the spirit of excellence in employees. The advertisement continued: "Year after year, our people have continued to increase standards of efficiency. This year was no exception. In a market with surplus capacity and negative growth in demand, they've pushed operating margins to a record 36.5%. (The industry average stands at half that figure.)

Thanks to their efforts, cement production is up by 5%, while power and coal consumption are down by 3%. Proof once again, that while machines may have limitations to productivity, our people don't."

It is this same people and values orientation that manifests itself in the statements of Managing Director Narotam Seksaria who has made a phenomenal success of a very young company and taken it to a 1400 crore company. He says simply, when asked about whether their company has a well-defined Mission: Yes, we do have a Mission statement, so to say. It's more a reflection of our values and the work culture that evolved over the years at Ambuja. Our values are homegrown which we learnt in our families. As newcomers in the business, we had no expertise or experience to base our decisions on. Only the lessons in being fair and good human beings were used by us to guide our people in the business. And they seemed to work.

Luckily we have people around us who believed in the same values as well. Today, we have been able to define them and have been able to focus on them. They have become so intrinsic to Ambuja that we do not have to preach them. Only bring them back in focus in our day to day work now and then."

Jet Airways

Naresh Goyal, the charismatic owner-CEO of Jet Airways talks about the pragmatic Corporate Mission that Jet Airways has. It was formulated at the time of the airline's inception in early 1993. Inputs for this were given by the Board of Directors and Senior Management. "This has been our blueprint for progress and development," he says, adding that it is "regularly reviewed with employees at all levels and used to benchmark our services."

The Corporate Mission reads as follows:

"Jet Airways will be the most preferred domestic airline in India. It will be the automatic first choice carrier for the travelling public and set standards, which other competing airlines will seek to match.

Jet Airways will achieve this pre-eminent position by offering a high quality of service and reliable, comfortable and efficient operations.

Jet Airways will be an airline which is going to upgrade the concept of domestic airline travel—be a world class domestic airline.

Jet Airways will achieve these objectives whilst simultaneously ensuring consistent profitability, achieving healthy, long-term returns for the investors and providing its employees with an environment for excellence and growth."

Apart from all this, Goyal emphasizes that "there is total transparency within the Company with regard to sharing of information."

SPIC

Ashwin Muthiah, the 35-year old son of industrialist AC Muthiah, who is now at the helm of affairs of agri-business major Southern Petrochemical Industries Corporation (SPIC), incorporates agenda, time frame and sound implementation in his Vision for success of the corporation. On the one hand is his insistence on team building and bringing about "change in the way people think" by equipping them with better skills, bringing in new blood and talent. And on the other, to look at the hard facts of running the business—finding ways to increase income from marketing, reduce cost of inputs and overheads and even outsource cost centres. It appears to be a no-nonsense practical approach where Vision and Mission and purpose all meld together with a new immediacy.

Exide

S.B. Ganguly, Chairman of Exide Industries Limited sees the scenario in a broad, value-based way, probably in conjunction with his belief in The Art of Living, which has given the Corporate world some great homespun thoughts to mull over. He says that the Exide Corporate Vision Statement is a well-defined one, an exercise in which all Senior Management including Corporate PR was involved and the final statement emerged as a consensus out of a Workshop held for that purpose.

"The Vision Statement remains what we as a Corporate would like to be viewed by the world at large and to that extent presents a road map for the company's activities. Dissemination of the Vision Statement is ensured by its display across the head office, factories and branches which are spread all over the country."

The sharing of specific Vision and Mission statements has been done to demonstrate how today's industry leaders are talking of specific, credible and achievable goals for their companies. The statements are backed by their ability to be communicated down the line, and to be able to transform the higher thinking into a tangible framework of a roadmap.

It is vital for the Public Relations practitioner to be involved at all stages of the creation and ideation of a Mission statement. First, through the articulation of it, and then through devising a methodology of having it percolate to the intended audience.

3

Corporate Governance:
The Transparency Mantra and PR

What constitutes goodness, honesty, transparency in a corporate set up? This whole process of accountability and the greater obligations that are being placed on companies to abide by the codes of Corporate Governance, are also becoming the concern of Public Affairs departments. Not in the worst sense of lies and cover-ups, but in the way in which the communicator understands its implications and applicability in the divulging of information, the disclosures to shareholders and in the very essence of ethical credibility. As PR professionals, their role lies in using communication skills to realign reputation.

The risk as perceived by some people in hyping up a company, which follows the codes of good Corporate Governance, and is efficiently managed, is that the image could supersede the real facts. The truth lies in the fact that in the overall context of the role that Public Relations plays in corporate strategy, its awareness and tracking of the

issues concerning codes of Corporate Governance cannot be ignored any more.

It is all a matter of interpretation and also of actual implementation.

Transparency demands many things of many levels and layers of management and of all divisions, and is not just the responsibility of the Board. In specific terms for us communicators, it is an imperative not to continue to belt out management platitudes to employees and to a vast number of publics who feed on a company and make up the corporate universe.

What are the implications of Corporate Governance? Why did corporates have to be governed under the rules of Corporate Governance?

"Corporate Governance came to the fore due to a spate of corporate scandals that occurred during the first flush of economic liberalization," says Omkar Goswami, Chief Economist, Confederation of Indian Industry.

He goes on to elaborate:

"The first was a major securities scam that was uncovered in April 1992, which involved a large number of banks, and resulted in the stock market nose-diving for the first time since the advent of reforms in 1991. The second was a sudden growth of cases where multinational companies started consolidating their ownership by issuing preferential equity allotments to their controlling group at steep discounts on their market price. The third scandal involved disappearing companies of 1993-94. Between July 1993 and September 1994, the stock index shot up by 120%. During this boom, hundreds of obscure investment companies made public issues at large share premia, buttressed by sales pitch of obscure investment banks and misleading prospectuses. The management of most of these companies siphoned off the funds, and a vast number of small investors were saddled with illiquid stocks of dud companies. This shattered investor confidence, and resulted in the virtual destruction of the primary market for the next six years."

"These three episodes led to the prominence of Corporate Governance within the financial press, banks and financial institutions, mutual funds, shareholders, the more enlightened business associations, the regulatory agencies and the government."

As we traverse the path of globalization and a market-oriented economy and with heightened competition, corporates have to devise, develop and implement structures and systems that enable a core of values against which actions are measurable and frameworked.

Some telling clarifications have come from Pesi M. Narielvala who is former senior partner of S.R. Batliboi and Co. and is on the committee that recommended the instituting of the Study Group appointed by the Government of India in 2000 to operationalize the concept of Corporate Excellence. An expert on Corporate Governance and a former president of the Institute of Chartered Accountants of India, Narielvala is however, a realist on the terminology used and on the attitudes of corporates to their expected ethical behaviour.

To him, a Company Board is more like a Cabinet in the Government, for he feels a cabinet minister swears an oath of secrecy, in comparison to his Member of Parliament counterpart, who merely swears an oath of allegiance. So, in effect, corporations are by their very nature meant to keep in information rather than freely divulge it. To him, it is not mere Corporate Governance, but decisive governance that is the key. Democratic governance is not either good or transparent. In fact, in comparison with

India, China is more honest, perhaps because of its punitive measures, but this certainly puts it on the path of decisive governance and therefore progress.

So good governance is effective management, and a well-managed company will obviously have a better market capitalization. More than the ethics of management, it is the ethics of success that he is concerned with. A point at which Public Relations, attempting to reflect the successful behaviour of a corporation, comes in.

The structuring of systems of excellence is what concerns the communicator. At this juncture we have to look, not just at large corporates using Corporate Governance, but what really needs to be done, according to Narielvala, is to enlarge the scope to embrace schools, hospitals, any institution where transparency means a melding of accountability, motivation, identification of goals and efficiency for better management.

Thus it is that we see the role of Corporate Public Affairs in its own wider role and in the larger context of governing a host of institutions as being the facilitator sector. Not just on the narrower issues, as was done recently, to make provision for adequate representation of women on the Boards of Companies to remove gender bias and for better Corporate Governance. Rather, the Public Relations role will be to proactively use the tools to reach out to those with whom information has to be shared.

For Public Relations practitioners, it is not the why of Corporate Governance codes, but the how, the implementation, of it, that can serve as a complementary role in adding to the culling and dissemination of vital information, and possibly even saying more than less as we have seen in the new rash of Intellectual Capital Reportage and Ambassadorial Reports that some companies have adopted.

Many of these have been created by Mudar Patherya, who has given Corporate India a new benchmark or financial and non-financial reportage under the aegis of his company Trisys, long before the Corporate Governance codes were meant to be implemented by companies, and disclosures published in annual reports, Patherya's company, Trisys had started the process of Creative Annual Reports, and has also most recently, spearheaded another area of activity through the production of Intangibles Statements and other analytical documents. The chapter on How Creative PR can enhance Shareholder Value discusses these transparency documents. (Book Three, Chapter 6)

Narielvala warns of the dangers of the Public Relations practitioner making people look more for image than fact. If Public Relations gives a mirror image of a company, it depends on how good the mirror itself is. There is no harm in presentability or image building, which he feels is legit, in the manner of dressing up for a photo session, or in the way a sportsman would tone up his muscles. The warning signs are when the sportsperson takes steroids.

This is where the whole point of ethics comes into the picture. Or the mirror. "The key to good Corporate Governance" Narielvala emphasizes, "is knowing it is good for the company, without which you cannot succeed in a competitive environment. It should not merely appear to be good for the shareholders." It is simplistic he says to talk about transparency leading to better management. "Transparency is important to clean up the place. Just as in a forest, things get cleaned up by just being exposed." What will really constitute good and effective Corporate Governance will be a confluence of clearly identified goals, motivation, ethicality, efficiency, accountability, all of these topped off by a large dollop of "attitude".

At every step, new measures are being taken. Ernst and Young have tied up with IIM Kolkata to jointly create a code for Corporate Governance in India. The code acknowledges that Corporate Governance is not a prescription pill of regulation, available over the counter. It has to be enterprise-specific. Ernst and Young would attempt to ensure customisation to conform to the best international practices.

The government has sanctioned Rs.25 crores for an Institute for Excellence in Good Corporate Governance. Experts like Narielvala who are on the Governing Committee of this centre recommend that certificates should be issued to companies who comply and meet the standards and conditions set out in the Centre's parameters. The Report of the Study Group set up by the Department of Company Affairs intends, in its own words, to "operationalize effectively the concept of excellence in Corporate Governance on a sustained basis to sharpen India's global competitive edge, foster further and develop corporate culture in the country."

Among its key recommendations:

- Setting up of an Independent, autonomous Centre for Corporate Excellence to mainly accord accreditation.
- Introduction of a formal recognition of Corporate Social Responsibility
- Introducing measures for greater shareholder participation
- Clearer distinction between direction and management that would ensure that the executive directors are held responsible for legal and other compliance and the non-executive directors are charged with strategic and oversight responsibilities for the company's business

- Highlighting directorial commitment and accountability
- Suggesting application of Corporate Governance principles to PSUs.

How do companies like ITC look at Corporate Governance?

"The challenge of governance for ITC lies in fashioning a model that addresses the uniqueness of each of its businesses and yet strengthens the unity of purpose of the Company as a whole."

"Since the commencement of the liberalization process, India's economic scenario has begun to alter radically. Globalization will not only significantly heighten business risks, but will also compel Indian companies to adopt international norms of transparency and good governance. Equally, in the resultant competitive context, freedom of executive management and its ability to respond to the dynamics of a fast changing business environment will be the new success factors. ITC's governance policy recognizes the challenges of this new business reality in India."

ITC defines Corporate Governance as a systemic process by which companies are directed and controlled to enhance their wealth generating capacity.

ITC's Corporate Governance initiative is based on two core principles. These are:

(i) Management must have the executive freedom to drive the enterprise forward without undue restraints; and

(ii) This freedom of management should be exercised within a framework of effective accountability.

ITC believes that any meaningful policy on Corporate Governance must provide empowerment to the executive management of the Company, and simultaneously create a mechanism of checks and balances which ensures that the decision making powers vested in the executive management is not only not misused, but is used with care and responsibility to meet stakeholder aspirations and societal expectations.

From the above definition and core principles of Corporate Governance emerge the cornerstones of ITC's governance philosophy, namely trusteeship, transparency, empowerment and accountability, control and ethical corporate citizenship. ITC believes that the practice of each of these leads to the creation of the right corporate culture in which the company is managed in a manner that fulfils the purpose of Corporate Governance.

Other companies like Gujarat Ambuja Cements have been following the principles of Corporate Governance for more than a decade. Well before any SEBI stipulations came into being, their reporting had been open and extensive. Not only did their balance sheet and annual report reveal information, but also a separate booklet attached with the balance sheet gave insights into their efficient operations.

CII's Omkar Goswami, whom we quoted earlier on the background to the emergence of Corporate Governance, is confident of the scenario of corporate India where the next few years will see a flurry of activity, "driven by several factors."

We summarize his observations in point form. The first and most important is the spirit of competition, which has forced companies to drastically restructure their ways of doing business. Second, business groups that were on top of the pecking order have been relegated to the bottom. Simultaneously new aggressive companies have come to the fore which represent young modern outward-oriented professionals who place a great deal of value on Corporate

Governance and transparency, if not for themselves, then as instruments for facilitating access to international and domestic capital.

Third, the growth in market capitalization, where creating a distributing wealth has become a more popular maxim than ever before. Fourth, with well-focused well-researched foreign portfolio investors, the demand for better Corporate Governance and greater disclosure has become paramount.

He also feels that the pressure on Corporate Governance will intensify with the entry of foreign pension funds and, indeed, in the next five years, the biggest pension funds will invest in India, and some of them will, put Indian companies on their Corporate Governance watch. Sixth, India has a strong financial press, which has induced greater degrees of disclosure. Seventh, despite serious lacunae in Indian bankruptcy provisions, neither banks nor DFIs will continue to support management irrespective of performance. Penultimately, Indian corporations have appreciated the fact that good Corporate Governance and internationally accepted standards of accounting and disclosure can help them to access the US capital markets. The examples of Infosys making its highly successful Nasdaq issue stand out, apart from ICICI, Satyam Infoways and ICICI Bank.

Goswami says: "The message is now clear: it makes good business sense to be a transparent, well governed company incorporating internally acceptable accounting standards. In a couple of years, India will move to full capital account convertibility. When that happens, an Indian investor will seriously consider whether to put his funds in an Indian company or to place it with a foreign mutual or pension fund. That kind of freedom will be the ultimate weapon in favour of good Corporate Governance. Thankfully for India, the companies that matter have already seen the writing on the wall. Thus it may not be wrong to predict that, by the end of 2005, India might have the largest concentration of well governed companies in South and South-East Asia."

And for the Public Relations communicator, more challenges and a larger, open canvas.

It is not the intention, in a discussion on Corporate Governance, to make new practitioners feel they are entering an area, which is strictly not their purview. What existing professionals and new entrants alike need to know is the extent of its influence in the shareholder-relations activities. An awareness of its implications, the leveraging and application of information and some of the methodology discussed could be useful for taking a fresh, mature, holistic approach to shareholder interface by all manner of companies, be they service organizations, large corporates, institutions of education and of medicine, financial institutions. The responsibility for transparency will not just rest with the disclosure of financial information, but will have to be taken cognizance of by the corporate communicator in the attempts to retain credibility and confidence vis-a-vis a growing community of involved publics.

4

The Corporate Philanthropist

The involvement of companies in their communities is something that most corporates are doing with a sense of purpose and a depth of involvement. The patronage is no longer an enlightened self-interest, but rather a real concern for setting up institutions in every field of activity and also in making large projects happen from small beginnings, through creating a sense of involvement amongst employees

---

When a working mother spends eight hours or more a day away from her child, her inputs when she gets back come in the form of doubled affection and hyped up planning for what she can do to have fun time with the youngster. It is, as psychologists will say, an innate guilt that makes for overcompensated behaviour.

It is a similar behavioural pattern with companies. They set up factories where they are polluting the atmosphere and mucking up the agricultural ambience around. They recruit people and exploit them to the full. They get the necessary concessions from government so that they can maximize their profits. They hold back on a bonus issue so that reserves can grow. And then they ask themselves. What have I given society in return?

Guilt is just one small factor. Philanthropy also has its tax-saving motivations. Moreover, there is the need to rise beyond the image of a brand to becoming a company that is cultured; the big-hearted, concerned corporation which ogles at art, listens enraptured to a rare raga, widely cheers those soccer goals and doles out volumes of unavailable, reprinted books, all this while putting up a diagnostic centre and peeling off cheques for civic bodies hellbent on improving a city.

What is the real motivation behind all this corporate sponsorship?

We looked into the methodology of some of the companies which have joined the ranks of the patrons. The ulterior motives are really not that severe. For today, in some cases, it has become art for art's sake. The sponsors are truly involved and entrenched in the causes that they started out to support as a means of defraying advertising and promotional budgets to prop up brands of image at the opportune time.

It is so simple to point a finger at a company and say that there are strings attached to its sponsorship of the arts. That they are doing it mainly or only to enhance their reputations and image. Could this be a simple case of looking a gift horse in the mouth? Haven't whole institutions of learning in music come up because of the money injected into them? Aren't there more sports events which are throwing up champions and heightening an interest in sports where there might have been a limited following? Is there a single theatrical show where there is not either a souvenir brochure, a hoarding, tickets, post-play or pre-play publicity which has not come out of funding by an advertiser from his limited publicity budget?

We are in a strange dither today. There's one section of the public ready to condemn a company for getting so involved with its social projects that the main business it is in gets mired in the slush of publicity it generates. And yet some members of that same public will rush with a begging bowl to the company if there was a cause needing the vital funding that they would not be able to raise otherwise.

Having said this, what position should a corporate body take on its sponsorships?

We will share instances of companies which have long ago risen beyond any criticism that could be hurled at them simply because of one critical element: a well-defined project.

The reason why some of the big names in the business are so successful and why the newer entrants in the game are so stretched to get the same warm reception to their plans is simple. A me-too approach in sponsorship can be a somewhat unstable way of getting into the game. This thing of "Let's get into racing sponsorship" or "How about supporting the next set of music or drama conferences" is a sure recipe for expenditure without commensurate returns.

Hence the urging to state your intention, find a "cause" that the total management feels wildly committed to and one that the Board will readily ratify, and to then have a plan of appropriation for the next decade or so. One-time sponsorships are like one-night liaisons—titillating for the moment, but with an unsure tomorrow.

The companies which can join the honour rolls of commitment to an art form or a sports slot are so few in number, that the average person on the street could rattle off their names in one go.

This is therefore the very thing that companies have to aim at—to get their image entrenched into the public perception as being patrons of a particular "cause" that is their very own, almost a part of their business scene.

A Chairman views other Philanthropists

In this context, we would like to mention that there are various ways of viewing corporate philanthropy. Get corporates to put out their own stories, look around and report what is visible, or ask a corporate chief to comment on how he perceives others doing their acts of benevolence. This last-named route we consider somewhat unique and the point of view comes from the highly respected vision of the Chairman of Gujarat Ambuja Cements, Suresh Neotia, who is a philanthrope himself, but would rather talk about the rest of his peer group. His perspicacious views:

"Since the beginning of the twentieth century there were enough donors who were prompted by their own sense of philanthropy for community welfare. Many business families either through the Hindu Undivided Family (HUF) or through partnership were engaged in businesses of a substantial size. To those HUF and firms people donated money for social objectives, for the creation of hospitals and schools, among other things. In Kolkata, many Bengali landlords left their properties in Trusts. A few Marwari families joined together to contribute to many social assets like Marwari Relief Society, SVS Hospital and School, Amherst Street Hospital, and the like.

Only two families developed business under a corporate banner which were Tatas in the West and Birlas in Kolkata.

Both these houses established large Trusts and contributed individually and through their corporate entities. These Trusts became the catalyst of substantial charities in various parts of the country. The corpus of these Trusts continued to grow due to their investments in stocks of their respective companies which appreciated in value over a period of time. Even now, the Trusts of Birlas and Tatas play a significant role.

Corporate Houses in India have not yet matured and the story of corporate growth is only 20 years old. Most of the companies either were subjected to high taxation or they were engaged in making fresh investments each year to increase their size. Hence, very little was left which could be diverted to charity. Strangely, very few large social assets have been created by the Corporate Houses.

It is significant to point out that the Pai family at Manipal during the 60's generated funds out of which they are creating hospitals. Among the Birlas, the most notable is G.P. Birla, who is a very withdrawn and private person. My impression is that he is the single rare individual with philanthropic thoughts. It is said that through his various Trusts he continues to contribute to so many causes which include reconstruction of temples, creation of schools, and scientific museums, to name a few. The charities through G.D. Birla run into hundreds of crores of rupees and the man never projects to any one what he does. The beauty is that no one really knows how much and where he contributes.

Corporates are caught between two problems for which they have not been able to find an answer. On one hand, their responsibility to shareholders, who may not approve large funds to be diverted for philanthropic activities. The other is the Institutions who hold the shares of have extended loans, the FIIs may not welcome such large charities out of the company's funds. Apart from this, very few people in high positions of the company have great motivation to create large social assets.

At present it is limited to the fringes of philanthropy. Most of the Companies including Gujarat Ambuja carry out several social welfare measures like creation of schools and hospitals, etc. around their plant areas. Perhaps this is more to fulfil their social obligations of running an industry rather than an act of charity. There are companies who even do not contribute in this limited way.

The basic problem in India is our ancient thought of inheritance. In Western countries, when a person dies, a large portion of his assets goes into various institutions as bequest. In India, the heir inherits a large portion and only a very limited portion goes for charity."

But many good luck stories can be found, some of them showing corporates involving their own staff, some reflecting simple philosophies which have flowered into big projects and yet others showing how service organizations who normally cannot generate funds internally, also go out and give a helping hand to the community.

Involvement: Companies wanting staff to get involved in philanthropy and work in plant peripheral areas

When the devastating earthquake took place in Gujarat on 26 January 2001, the fascinating fallout was the extent to which corporate India rallied around, adopting, as Reliance did, whole villages, while other companies flew out their key personnel along with huge reinforcements to set up temporary shop for solid succour.

We quote here one such example of a company's voluntary and quick-response commitment to this earthquake.

Jet Airways

Jet Airways was the first private airline to land in ravaged Bhuj, the very next day after the devastating earthquake, armed with doctors, paramedics and medical and relief supplies. A Crisis Coordination Committee was constituted in the wake of one of post-independent India's unprecedented calamities to monitor operation of special flights.

750 temporary shelters were set up by them for over 700 families of Ramvav village in Kutch. This relief and rehabilitation operation was undertaken with active support from the French aircraft manufacturer Avions de Transport Regionale and the NGO Nivara Hakk Suraksha Samiti which has vast experience in social organization and housing. This assured the company of reach out better.

A detailed social survey was organized to establish a close relationship with the quake-affected populace and also to involve its participation in the project. Nearly 50 volunteers from Mumbai worked with the villagers for ten weeks to set up quake-resistant accommodation for Ramvav and tented hostels for staff and students of three schools in the nearby Nilpar. Fabricated in Mumbai and Ahmedabad, the tents do not require a change of canvas before two years. Designed to provide shelter till the villagers are able to reconstruct their homes, these tents will also serve as emergency shelters during any future calamity.

We have other inputs from Jet as well of other areas of social responsibility, given to us in detail by their Corporate Communications chief. The airline is well known for its Magic Box. Through the collections on this inflight programme, a project called SPARSH (Sastur Project of Action Research Services through Hospital) came into being in Maharashtra after an earlier earthquake. Through the funds collected, medical care is dispensed to inhabitants of 257 villages. Jet has carried huge amounts of relief material to a village in Ladakh after the Kargil conflict, has a **Save the Children** programme, which has in its purview both rehabilitation of urban slum children, a special care for the mentally retarded and an integrated development service for the earthquake victims.

The lesson in this: the swift communication and response, the involvement of employees and the long-term goodwill generated for the airline.

In a different kind of move, a company called KPMG, which is a chartered accountancy and consultancy group in UK, has organized and institutionalized an education-related initiative. It has invested some £3 million in community volunteer work, because it believes in encouraging employees to do their bit for the community, they are rewarded by better job performance and higher morale. Basically the scheme is meant for mentoring head teachers, providing leadership and management to them, and it has spun off 500 similar schemes since the start in the mid-nineties.

To some extent enlightened self-interest.

Education, for Self and for a Wider Community

One of the excellent examples of the founding of a school which is serving a large cross section of students, not confined to a company's own, is the Assam Valley School . Established by the Williamson Magor Education Trust and surrounded by some of the most beautiful tea gardens in Assam, this 95 hectare campus has reached out to boys and girls to hone their intellectual, physical, cultural and artistic skills in a free and stimulating environment. There are 25 students to a class, making for a greater climate of intellectual enquiry and it serves students from Class IV to Class XII.

This is an initiative started in 1995 and is a jewel in the crown of non-business achievements of the Williamson Magor Group.

Other companies like ITC's factories involve themselves with welfare schemes in their communities. In many places, their education scheme which began as an employee-oriented venture has grown to serve the local community as a whole. Similarly the Tribeni Tissues Vidyapith in West Bengal started as a primary school for employees' children and has now grown to be a Council for the Indian School Certificate-affiliated institution.

On a larger scale, ITC has pioneered the first private sector Institute of Hotel Management which is acknowledged as a centre of excellence by the hospitality industry. It is also a founder member of the IIM Ahmedabad, the IMI, Delhi, the Academy for Management Excellence, Chennai and the newest players on the scene, the Indian School of Business, Hyderabad which has a strategic alliance with the the Kellog and Wharton Business Schools, USA.

Dr Reddy's Laboratories

Naandi: The Power of 10

Who said small is ungenerous? Not when the initiative is a master-plan like the one emanated from Dr. Anji Reddy, Chairman of Dr. Reddy's Laboratories. We quote from the letter that he sent out to his employees:

"I am writing this not as Chairman of your company but as a citizen of this country concerned about the need for concerted action to improve the quality of life of the millions of our brethren who are suffering from abject poverty and deprivation.

Naandi, an autonomous not-for-profit development organization was set up on November 1, 1998 by the coming together of four corporates in Hyderabad viz., Satyam Computers, Global Trust Bank, Nagarjuna Group and

Dr. Reddy's Laboratories. The Government of Andhra Pradesh is a proactive facilitator to Naandi.

Naandi's goal is to channelize resources, human and financial, from all parts of the world, to support projects which will lead to lasting improvement in the quality of life of our most deprived sections of society. The focus is on providing better access to basic education, health and livelihood opportunities.

For Naandi to realize this objective, it is imperative that each and every socially conscious citizen wholeheartedly participates in this movement. Keeping this in mind, Naandi has come up with the Power of 10.

I, as Chairman and Founding Trustee of Naandi, appeal to you to ensure that each and every member of the DRL family willingly take part in this noble endeavour by contributing to the Power of 10."

Did it work? We asked Dr Reddy about the scheme. Basically it is a target setting exercise. The method is: targets should be multiplied by ten every year. For instance, their livelihood advancement program started with 125 children and is now over 1500 strong.

Dr. Reddy's Foundation for Human and Social Development has "become the laboratory for catalysing reproducible, sustainable, innovative experiments for social change. For social metamorphosis to be faster and sustainable, we realized the need for collective ownership (stakeholding) and identified our role in catalyzing and precipitating these (re)actions aimed at abetting the cause of the urban poor in their struggle for a livelihood."

In their Alternate Balance Sheet, they have shared the philosophy behind the work of the Foundation, which has as its cornerstone innovation and involvement of a wider stakeholder group to make for the success of their project models aimed at having a lasting effect on the poor.

Corporate philanthropy, they maintain, normally refers to the practice of corporates and businesses making cash contributions to a variety of causes as part of their overall corporate citizenship strategy. Dr Reddy's Foundation for Human and Social Development has taken a slightly different route—"innovating to involve the stakeholder participation of others including constituent community employees, NHOs, advocacy groups, government, media, national and international donors and network agencies.

It is a move from mere grant-making to a more people and expertise oriented supplement: technical support, management expertise and a host of other resources and services.

There is a 4-tier model that Dr Reddy's Foundation follows: At the first level is to develop new, sustainable models. Under this, there is a Street Kids Business School, a programme that helps rag pickers turn into entrepreneurs. It also has under its purview a market-oriented employment training service. At Level 2 is an amazing Child and Police Project, a programme that aims at ending child labour with the involvement of police as mentors. This one gets in institutional funding like UNICEF, CRY, National Child Labour Programme and the Agha Khan Foundation. At Level 3, there is the Rural Health Studies, SHARE, a society that extends credit to sections of society which have been considered "unbankable" and a Guild of Service which encourages women to commercialize their tailoring trade by introducing market-oriented programmes.

Service Organizations as Mentors and Catalysts

Thoughtshop Foundation

Most people perceive agencies as being in the business of serving their clients, creativity in one hand and profit motive in the other. We do not cavil at this, because the scenario is as it should be. But what motivates an agency to go beyond its calling, to spend that extra bit of time, which is precious to it anyway, to take on community initiatives where the pat on the back is being perceived well. And in imparting something of significance to the community.

The concept of the Thoughtshop Foundation, by the creative agency, Thoughtshop, gives you the feel good factor that an agency's resources and skills are being used to "educate, motivate and initiate change." The people behind this project are Mira Kakkar and Mrityunjoy Chatterjee, partners in the agency and the key people involved in developing "behaviour change communication packages" with two alumni from NID, Himalini Varma and Santayan Sengupta.

What are some of these packages that are making a mark on the community? One is the development of educational packages for target audiences in both rural and urban areas on reproductive health issues. They keep in close touch with field-based organizations and based on their feedback, have improved the quality of their products. Short training courses help organizations and educators to better use these packages. Interestingly titled the Champa Kit, Paro Kit and Shankar Kit, these have been respectively developed for rural adolescent girls, for slum based adolescent girls and for rural adolescent boys. There is a Kit on Pregnancy, Delivery and Family Spacing for rural women and their families and also on Puberty and adolescence, contraception, safe sex and STDs/HIV/AIDS.

The moot point about the usefulness of these kits is their story telling ability, with characters whom the audiences can relate to. A number of other aids have been developed like card games and board games and little curiosity books and flipcharts. There is also a tele-counselling service for young people, their parents and teachers and a radio programme *Gyaner Alo Zindabad*. The newspapers are also vehicles through they have an interactive monthly feature called ASK to answer young people's questions on HIV/AIDS and reproductive health.

A 30-minute feature film Akrant, was a touching, telling story that made a great impact on industrial workers.

Kakkar feels that every human being has the potential to do more than he or she is doing. And that each of us is responsible for not just our action—but our inactions as well. Freedom is to know that we create the world in which we live—and are therefore responsible—and therefore accountable for our contribution—or non-contribution! There is no tomorrow. *Any good thing that we can do for any human being, let us do it now...*

The Earthworm Society

Another agency that believes you cannot ignore the people around you, and that your involvement in projects should be completely hands-on, literally, is Trisys. The motto of its founders: Think Small! "The amount of work you can do when you are small is not inconsequential." A further exhortation: Don't just delegate, do.

Despite their 24/7 schedules, the employees of Trisys got together to shoulder the responsibility of restoring and beautifying the Lakes, which is adjacent to their office. A banner there must be, and the agency have formed The Earthworm Society in the belief that the earthworm keeps a low profile, does good work and doesn't get noticed himself!

Taking up shovels themselves, they have cleared rubble, tons of it, and trailblazed the way for groups of residents to go broomstick in hand to make the greens cleaner. Seeing this, slum dwellers of the area were quick to lend a helping hand, cutting bushes, cleaning the stretch and planting saplings, on the stretches bordering the lakes, and all along the pavements.

None of this work is done in isolation. They get the local residents, NCC cadets, students in a cricket academy nearby and even urchins to "dig and shovel" with the ultimate aim of beautifying the entire area. Supportive bodies include the Horticultural Society, chipping in with their technical know-how of what and how to plant, what to source, how to landscape, and do the earth-filling, and protect the embankments. It isn't entirely smooth sailing, the greening and the bettering of the environment does come up against bureaucratic hassles. Nothing that a grassroots brigade cannot conquer.

Just as they have done with the cause of education in the area. Even if it is a more difficult one to coordinate, handle and keep going. Whether it is to hire teachers to teach them English, giving computers to schools, mobilizing money for them and suggesting that they get on to the committees of a nearby school to get projects going with the children—the team from Trisys are involved and eager to up and help. They give the children surprises as when one of their suppliers dressed up as Santa and distributed gifts to children. Giving them such treats is one thing, but their bigger concerns are to give them better standards of training. Their resources are perforce limited, but they look to involving clients to involve them in action, as they are doing with Aptech who will give computers and continue by imparting computer education to the underprivileged too.

It is a hand-holding exercise, combined with commitments of invaluable time to keep the environment uplifted. And when the five saplings they have planted, grow into trees, which will be named after famous cricketers, they will see a greater flowering of their efforts. The community will too.

5

Establishing Corporate Image

---

*Beneath the logo and beyond the letterhead lies the creation of the
corporate personality, the company character, the institutional
reputation. What does it take to establish corporate culture or build
a corporate identity programme? Corporate identity is not just a
matter of intuition, but is something that is carefully contrived and
developed.*

Mostly About Image

A flag, or a pennant, is a country's most conspicuous cue.
Many of us Indians have seen the evolution of the national
flag from the time it had a *charkha* in the middle to its current
form and it has always been dinned into us that the colours
stand for various qualities that we ought to be emulating.

But beyond that, a flag, whether it is the tricolour, or
the stars and stripes or the red circle on a white background,
is something that does not strike the average person as
being a work of painstaking research. How can the student
of history forget, for instance, the searing effects of the
blood red swastika on the flag of Hitler's Germany, which

Albert Speer, Hitler's chief architect, described as being more effective than any flag "divided into three stripes of colour."

But for even these strips of visual effect and nationalistic drama, there is a large chunk of expenditure on conceptualization and execution. We closely followed the redesigning of the South African flag, having become regular visitors to that country. The process was not simply one that concerned a flag for the new post-apartheid South Africa, but was part of a total search to possibly strike a new chord amongst a populace seeking to get international approval in the same measure as they were trying to bring about amicable multi-party rule.

Vexilologists had to contend with 700 proposed designs for a South African flag, some of which were outright rejects like Bart Simpson at the beach, or a banana and an assault rifle substituting for the hammer and sickle. Reporting on this, The Los Angeles Times-Washington Post News Service said that when the Commission of National Symbols recommended a new national motto, coat of arms and national flag, it was the national anthem that proved to be the most difficult to choose. There were 119 songs submitted in 11 of the country's major languages. The flag itself had to go through emotional quotients and national issues before becoming the multi-hued symbol as it is today.

But quite apart from the hallowed institution of the national flag, it is the international airlines which are probably playing a much larger role in carving out an identity for their country of origin than ever before. Whether it be their colour combinations, their logos, or the whole face they present through massive advertising in all media, airlines have made a fine art of image creation.

However, with the large number of airlines competing

not just for air space, or for media space, but for nicking out a little niche in customer consciousness, the problem no longer is one of blitzkrieg advertising, but of establishing a personality. It is an identity that has the two-fold job of not only projecting an international airline in all its efficiency and epicurean claims, but also in maintaining the special flavour and character of the country of origin.

This is where even something as basic as a symbol can be a crucial identity factor. Look what happened to Air-India when, a few years ago, it went into a multi-million dollar exercise to change over to supposed contemporaniety The maharajah, long-established, and an endearing figure who could be made to do and say what no sterile symbol would ever do, was suddenly dethroned and a costly and non-passionate sun made its appearance in his stead, draining all warmth and wit from the airline's identity. Thankfully, the maharajah is back bestriding the advertising, cocking a snook at all those who believed that they could substitute today's formless images with yesterday's timeless personality.

This isn't the only instance of the fact that money can't buy your personality; leave alone the fabled love that the mopheads sang of. If anything, the one I am about to cite brought ignominy to an established TV network and even more, to the firm that was hired to produce a corporate identity programme for it.

In his book, *The Corporate Personality*, Wally Olins describes what happened when this major design consultancy firm came up with a symbol for the National Broadcasting Company—NBC as it is popularly known—and it turned out to be exactly the same as another symbol created for a small television and radio network in Nebraska. In one instance, the design firm had expended massive amounts of money and time on producing the symbol, while the other one for Nebraska happened with hardly any expenditure, and was the brainchild of just one person. It created waves in the international media and one of the comments that ultimately came out of it was something that designers even today, two decades after the event, find hard to grapple with.

Abstract symbols continue to be the order of the day, as does plagiarism, especially with publication of books that reproduce the major work on symbols in India. Small-time designers merely have to pick up a particular design manual showing a large range of graphic symbols of causes and corporations. They then rework some of the author's ideas into their computers. And presto! You have a new symbol for a merged company and a massive bill to boot.

It is a sorry reflection on the companies who want them, that the whole approach, in a large number of cases, is a superficial one. It is one that emphasizes more on the graphical aspects without giving too much thought to the real mission and character of the corporation. Many companies look upon the generation of a symbol as an arty exercise, an assignment flung at an agency with the same casual air as the request to do a quick trade pamphlet. Even worse are the numerous instances of the son or daughter of an employee, just out of a commercial art course, being requested to design a corporate symbol. It is assumed that an academic exposure to commercial art is enough to produce something which can have a profound, perhaps perpetual, effect on corporate image.

One company asked three sets of designers, which included a large agency to submit a set of logos for a new subsidiary. When the logos came, they were all scrutinized eagerly, but ultimately rejected and a new one, drawn by hand by one of the finance heads, was put on the market. Needless to mention, none of the designers were paid for their efforts. And the same symbol which had been fashioned before our eyes, by hand, got used, one fine day, for a recruitment ad without even a mechanical finish to it!

Giving Image Creation its Due

If a designer were to suggest that he be paid a few lakhs of rupees for the creation of a logo, corporate reaction would be that the guy is probably pocketing 90 percent of it as grossly inflated profit. In reality, it is not a very large sum if the designer has been retained to study the needs of the company, its type of business, the milieu it is in vis-à-vis other companies in the same industry, the position it holds in terms of turnover on the corporate ladder, the reason for its seeking a new image, and the use it will put this symbol to in everything from its basic stationery to its buildings and its brands.

Ideally, it should not stop at that, but there is a further expenditure involved. Which constitutes the publishing of a Corporate Identity Manual for the benefit of those within the company who will be printing it on all company documents, painting it on company vans, etching it, forming it, enlarging and contracting it, adapting it to package design and utilizing its character in exhibiting and communicating the company to a number of involved publics.

Ultimately, a symbol and logo freshly devised must make an immediate statement, a simple, straightforward, elegant, well designed and well-thought-out single message, which does not need to be annotated, explained at length, but which will give the consumer and customer of the company a good feeling about it. Gimmickry must be replaced with dignity, but the sobriety should not snuff out the creative tilt.

This game of patenting corporate identity continues to have two sets of players at two extremes. At one end of the scale is the long-established company which has carried on its business for decades, usually with considerable success, but without any distinct stamp of personality. A company like that would probably approach consultants like us when they suddenly discover that they have gone into a number of diverse businesses, saying, "Why don't you re-do our company logo and give some thought to a quick corporate campaign to announce it?"

Just like that. The slapping on of a symbol to redefine a major shift in the company's operational structure and relocated philosophy! As we've said earlier, the fact that it would cost them time in terms of research, money in terms of conception and major board-level decisions for the whole exercise to be meaningful in the long term does not occur to them at the time of making their simplistic request.

There was this company that dissociated itself from its parent in the UK, wanted to devise new logos and announce the name change, but within severe budgetary limitations. Nothing dramatic or earthshaking was finally done. They have quietly slipped into using a straightforward letterhead with no announcements and have more or less said-let's get on with our work, we've mere engineering guys after all and do not require the fanfare.

But for one such company which has perforce to tone down its deeds to suit its pocket and its compulsions, there are other players in the business like ITC, RPG, HLL, Modicorp to cite just four examples of multidimensional companies who have gone to great lengths for their corporate identity programmes.

Where there is a need, there is also a service to back it up. One specialist in corporate identity claims that this has not received sufficient attention along with corporate culture. Although "identity is to culture what cause is to effect." Identity in his lexicon is still too often thought of as "image" instead of being recognized for what it is at the bottom: the very heart and soul of an organization.

Yet, the building of an identity is left to chance or to sudden spurts of advertising brilliance. It takes tougher bricks to build identity than the projection of clever pictures and words. In this case, Advertising and Public Relations would have to work together on researching the whole problem, go through the design and development stage and ultimately come up with more than just a logo and a handbook. The communicators will need to examine many variables. Is the company going in for diversification in a related and synergistic business or into new areas? This will determine one set of messages and approaches about how it wishes to be freshly perceived. Does the company merely want a new lease of life? Or is the competition doing new tricks that it has to counter with a new face?

The process is fraught with as much excitement as it is with hazard. The planning and teamwork between management and the business centres and the communicators will be vital in the process of formulating, projecting and maintaining corporate image.

6

New Dimensions in Corporate Identity

Corporate image, identity, culture, intent, soul. Many terms. Newer ways of branding image. The emergence of corporate personality. The multifaceted corporation needs to project distinct traits, combining innate competencies with specific segmentation.

Identity is Ingrained Image

The creation of identity through a logo is just one pulchritudinous part of corporate personality. The most visible part. But relating identity to logo is like referring to a person's name without alluding to his other characteristics. Companies all too often do a one-time expenditure on the creation of a new logo with its itinerant advertising back-up. But once done, there is never a thought for how that company should continue to be embedded in the public mind.

The reason why we are embarking on the finer semantic interpretations of corporate image, identity, culture and even soul, is because today's corporations are competing in an environment when, with the numerous brands on offer and the multifaceted operations that a single company is going into, there is a need to assert a distinct personality for each corporation.

Sometimes, it is easy enough with the founders, or strong chief executives steering the way in which companies behave react, interact and even retort when pushed to the wall in times of wrongdoing. Most Indians will always be quick to cite the example of the Air-India Maharaja as giving the airline its special character and even the links with its creator and with JRD are easily recalled and established. Sometimes, a brand overrides its company of origin.

Speaking on this subject to the Public Relations Society of India some years ago, Subhas Ghosal, a top calibre advertising professional and philosopher of that calling, talked about the fact that when an organization has a complex mass of businesses or brands, or both, the creation of the value system and, therefore, the emergence of the corporate personality is much more complicated. "The company, then, has to face a situation where it must assess the extent to which the corporate personality dominates or endorses its component parts or is dominated or endorsed by them."

In fact, he argued, today's competitive world makes it essential for a corporation to be a better manufacturer and marketer, and it must have better managers and be a better corporate citizen. As an employer, it has to be more benevolent; as a dispenser of dividends, it has to be generous. And its brands have to be superior, too.

This is where, we would imagine, that on the one hand there would be an ingrained identity or corporate style, while on the other, there would be the perception by the public of the corporate image, one built probably by management and the leaders of a corporation, the other by their Public Relations experts.

Why is it so important to identify? Are we as practitioners once again urging the spending of huge sums of money on frothy exercises? In the new context of changes in legislation, in attitudes of government to business, as is happening in India, the increasing globalization and the cross-transactions between corporations, it is not only wasteful, it is imperative for companies to project distinct traits, combining innate competencies with specific segmentation.

What it all boils down to is, primarily, to establish a corporate image, internally, for the employee to relate to. And then, to effectively portray the corporation the way it would like to be positioned to its external publics.

Internally, there can be many benefits, particularly during a merger or acquisition, when the identities of two disparate companies have to go through a single route. The synergistic projection is one area which could be a particularly challenging one for Public Relations departments along with the HRD department. Externally, through a well-orchestrated campaign of projecting such a company, the benefits of attracting more capital, better employees, having a larger customer base, cannot be underestimated.

It is easy enough for an agency to be given a brief to project a strong image of a company before a share issue, for instance. Our business magazines and newspapers have seen thousands of attractive advertisements which emerge in a series to air the competences and the character of a corporation. In many cases, it may be possible to make an immediate impact; in most instances, consumer recall can be poor and the fundamental point about a company missed unless solid research has gone into the projection, and management themselves have thought about how they wish to be seen and known.

Germane to the discussion is how corporate personality or identity cannot be flung on like a shawl, but needs deeper contemplation. Otherwise a corporate mission becomes mere lip service, in the same manner as corporate intentions can misfire, if there were well-thought-out intentions at all.

New dimensions in Corporate Intent

The designing of logos and symbols have taken on new dimensions in the new millennium, facilitated no doubt by the multimedia ease with which people can create these through computer-aided design. The demands, concomitantly, from companies to leverage logos for new brand strategies in the competitive environment is growing. This is making for a doubly focused and highly creative approach that is being taken by specialist groups to meet the heightened expectations of corporates.

One such company, Shining Strategic Design, has as its founder the colourful Shombit Sengupta, a Paris-based brand strategist. He has been instrumental in giving a new makeover to clients like Nestle, Unilever, Remy Martin, P&G, Nivea, Reckitt and Coleman. And we have seen how brands like Britannia, Wipro, Lakme and Eveready have impacted on public consciousness.

His strategy has obviously worked effectively, as the general public has responded to the new graphics and messages—reflected in the hiked sales or some of these products, on the one hand, and the creation of the visual mnemonic for Wipro, which, through one rainbow flower, could reinforce a group identity. When Wipro commissioned a consumer research programme, investing over a crore of rupees to ascertain consumer perception of the group, it found that with its diverse interests in IT, consumer and health care and lighting, the visual imagery was fragmented and lacked a common identity.

That is when efforts to communicate its values through a symbol happened. Their Corporate Brand Manager, P. Anirudh said, " The idea was to use a visual mnemonic to say what we are and what we want to be, that we stand for things like warmth, laughter, dynamism and represent a young, growing organization that is open, approachable fair and down-to-earth."

The logo was subsequently popularized with generous ad and sales promotion budgets, the focus being on products that carried the Wipro brand name. Efforts were also made to orient employees to meeting the values that Wipro stood for. In the end, there was a huge swing in perception of the human values that Wipro represents.

The *Eat Healthy, Think Better* slogan and the changed visual has made for a huge jump in awareness and sales of Britannia biscuits, and other food products.

With Eveready, the idea was to further its brand image in a battery market clustered with various players. They needed a changed perception to provide a sharper focus on the products of the company. To ensure better success, the company, apart from its imaging exercise through the interaction with the design group, Shining, has also gone through a brand evaluation exercise in tandem, with Ernst and Young.

Shining's creative thoughts on their strategies: "The corporation is almost like a tree, the root is the concept or vision, the trunk is the infrastructure for production marketing and the fruit is the brand, the trade and shareholders." Advertising agencies are experts in nurturing the fruit and the strategic consultants are best at keeping the trunk in proper shape, and Shining's methodology is to look at the root to align the trunk and the fruit with the vision.

To taste other fruits of successful brand design outfits, we looked at the work of Pentagram, probably the best-known design consultancy in the world. A survey in the Financial Times London had them rated by their peers as the "Rolls Royce of Design."

In their Compendium of work, some of their philosophy is summarized thus:

"Knowledge begins with interest, and never ends. Knowledge may tell you why there are twenty-six letters in the alphabet, or how a seventeenth-century theatre was built, even who put a moustache on the Mona Lisa. It may also tell you which shapes are aggressive and which are passive, how different colours affect perceptions of space, or what paper to use for letterpress printing or litho.

But knowledge in itself is only enough to equip the commentator or critic. The designer needs method as well, also learned but arguably finite. A repertoire of techniques is at the designer's disposal, some formal and universal, some more esoteric—a designer's personal tricks and short cuts.

Representing experience, knowledge and method combine to give the designer insight and a sure understanding of what is possible and what is not. Equipped thus, the designer can advise with authority, judge with conviction and persuade on the right course if action, even in the face of solid preconceptions and prejudices. And when the body of knowledge and method is shared, the power and thus benefit to designer and client are greatly compounded."

As they do, in designing and creating everything from corporate logotypes, book covers, magazines, calendar graphics, figurative design, designs for hotels, shops, theatres, restaurants, in short, graphic architects in a multitude of situations.

There are many consultancies today which have been formed just to deal with corporate image and identity—a vast and fascinating subject which holds challenges in equal measure for designer and strategy sifter alike—quite apart from the recipient, the corporation, which can get the full benefit of professional personality build-up. That is, if it has the will, the heart to spend on a good identity programme and the innate oomph to actually make it stand apart.

BOOK THREE:

The Ramparts of PR

1

Information is Power and Presence

The canvas is vast for sharing information with the publics of companies. The written word, the visual projection, the wonderful world of websites. All of these are magnificent tools in the hands of corporate communicators. Here we talk of corporate histories, multimedia presentations, website creation and periodic publications, which exist in a variety of combinations in organizations as vital communicative elements. The Annual Report, more than a mere statutory document, is another important communication device which is discussed in detail in Creative PR to enhance Shareholder value and the House Journal is given a separate chapter as an all-time classic communication implement.

Corporate Histories

The weaving of a corporate story has a number of dimensions. The trumpeting of tales of success, the documentation of family sagas, the egocentric focus on modern day maharajas, the picturebook unfolding of a business baronage. They come in various shapes and forms, from the more impersonal commemorative books that

communication departments put out to the humanized tales that read like novels of adventure and romance.

Many of these are commissioned works, and require deep research and involvement from the authors. Some of these are taken up by leading publishers and become commercial successes, like the book by Bachi Karkaria (To a Grand Design) on M.S. Oberoi and the whole saga of the group or like R.M. Lala's Beyond the Blue Mountain eulogizing J.R.D. Tata. Some of them are done to record for posterity the tribulations and the successes of a corporate group and the individuals who drive it, and here we record the impressions and comments of a leading corporate historian, Sujoy Gupta, a full time editor and author and part-time academic, who has six corporate histories to his name.

We publish this in the form of a question and answer session that we had:

Corporate Histories have moved away from the more impersonal corporate profile documents into a personalized, humanized approach: how have you been instrumental in persuading companies to do this, or has the initiative come from companies, too?

Yes, it is true that corporate histories have moved away from being a dry documentation cum narration of chronological events to, as you aptly put it, a 'humanized' story. While the initiative for each of the six corporate histories that I have written came from the respective companies, the approach to content formulation was entirely mine.

A company's destiny, after all, is moulded by the people who lead it; therefore, if one can get under the skin, so to speak, of these leaders, one can understand the 'how' and 'why' aspects of the unfolding corporate decisions and events far better. The history must, after all, seek to ask and answer far more than just 'what'.

Some of them highlight individuals, others salute the total enterprise: how have you blended the two?

There are two things happening together. One, there are outstanding individuals who provide leadership, vision, imagination and so on. Two, there is the aspect of a team spirit leading to cohesiveness of corporate purpose. In one's anxiety to highlight the former, which is obviously easier to do—and, I may add, more 'tempting' simply because it is likely to 'please' those in corporate power—one mustn't lose sight of the latter. Without the latter aspect in place, no visionary leader can achieve anything.

Indeed, if I may refer to my latest book titled 'Four Mangoe Lane' on the Williamson Magor Group, I have tried to portray the anonymous planter-manager as the 'hero'. True, brilliant individuals like John Trinick (who invented the Trinick sorter) and Prabir Das (who invented the Das weigher) are given due credit, but the focus really is on the anonymous planter. In fact, the book is dedicated to him.

How much objectivity can be maintained in such corporate histories? Are they just a means of puffery or can they become enduring documents for particular industries, while also serving as inspirationals about personal rags to riches lives?

I think the histories I have written are objective for the simple reason that I have made sure that the company management wants it so. The reason is selfish: I have to keep my reputation as an objective, credible author intact!

Jokes apart, to explain my point and to answer your important question, let me quote at some length from my prologue to the history of the JK Organisation to be published soon by Tata McGraw-Hill. It will serve to aptly answer your question:

One of the first things that JK Organisation chairman Hari Shankar Singhania told me was that it was not his intention that a hagiography be written. As entrepreneurs, he explained, successive generations of the Singhania family have doubtless made many mistakes. Business risks are notoriously difficult to prejudge, and it is but expected that notwithstanding the astuteness or the acuity of their sense of judgement, the Singhanias erred, despite the application of customary prudence. Hari Shankar was firm that none of these mistakes was to be brushed under the carpet. He was clear that at the eclectic level, a raison d'etre of this book is to help the present and future generations of society learn what lessons they will from the story of JK's experiences in entrepreneurship. And in this story, successes are as relevant as failures. Therefore, both must be told.

"This book does not commemorate any particular landmark event: a centenary or an anniversary, for instance. Indeed, the JK Organisation has no desire to use this work as a publicity tool. The house of Singhanias has long believed in the virtue of self-effacement, and although it probably needs some effort nowadays to keep to this philosophy in a dog-eat-dog competitive world, scions of this house continue to gamely adhere to this tradition.

"Rather, the idea behind expending the tremendous cerebral effort that goes into an effort like this one, is to contribute a mite to India's nascent bank of management literature to help others benefit from the rich JK experience in entrepreneurship over several generations in widely varying economic and political environments.

"In the current post-liberalisation scenario, Indian business is fighting for a toe-hold in world trade in circumstances that are daunting, to say the least. There are hardly any role models for the practising entrepreneur or manager or professional to turn to for sustenance, even if he has the time or inclination to do so in the middle of his perpetual battle for survival! In this context, JK offers itself as a case study of an Indian business house that has faced an unprecedented gamut of vicissitudes in the course of its eventful existence."

Which are the Prominent Corporate Histories?

I have written and published the histories of BOC India, Andrew Yule, Coates of India and Williamson Magor. The manuscript of the history of the JK Organisation is complete and hopefully it will be published soon. I must place on record that I also completed the manuscript of a history of the Indian Aluminium Company Ltd in 1998 but the company went through ownership changes just then and the history was consigned to the shelves.

As a business house, the Tatas·are about the only one in India with a keen sense of history. More than one book on JRD Tata was published during his lifetime. Recently, ACC has published its history albeit, in my view, the narration is too dry and factual for pleasant reading.

What is the time span required to create such histories? How much freedom are you given to write? Do you find enough transparency of information-sharing when researching these?

Between one to two years, usually. Since the approach and work methodology are discussed in advance and agreed upon mutually, the freedom is well nigh total. There is no bar to asking searching or 'embarrassing' questions and to examining past records, so the transparency level is high, too. I guess all these are precisely the factors that lend a book its credibility.

Are corporate histories sold, or sent out as gifts to important business associates, the press, friends, etc.?

Both, although I dare say far more are sent out as gifts than are sold. If the company is itself the publisher, then the book is unpriced and meant as a gift. But if a well-known publisher publishes the book, it carries an ISBN number and is catalogued and is a priced volume available at bookstores. They can then also be ordered and bought via the Internet.

This was an attempt to bring a personal view from a corporate historian to bear on this form of Corporate Communication. A genre which will grow and endure, as long as there are good luck stories to be told and shared and perceptions of great corporations to be projected.

The Creation of Websites

Another initiative which the corporate communicator has as an area of opportunity for creating perception management is a company's website. No company worth its salt can be without a fairly comprehensive website, which tells the corporate story, which goes into some details about products and technologies and enables the surfer to get more than adequate, transparent information.

The content creation is one where you need a combination of solid research, good writing ability and a large amount of creativity. The company must stand out and be noticed. In the creation and design of such websites, there are now many content providers who do the job. But the important thing to remember is not to sacrifice quality for an economical quote from small developers, unless, of course, price is the consideration.

We asked Abhijit Roy of Price Waterhouse Coopers, who have a separate division for website creation, to comment on the trend and offer suggestions. To quote him:

"The days of pretty websites and fancy text are over.

"People want a site that is content rich, downloads fast, is easy to navigate, functional and has well defined targets. Of course websites must be pleasing to look at, but beauty should not be skin deep.

Though it is tempting to get a site up quick and fast, but it will be worthwhile to work out a detailed plan on the target audience and the functionality that the site will have.

It is utterly foolish to overlook backend technology if you want a robust site that can handle a large number of visitors who would like interactive facilities and perhaps wish to transact some business as well.

While developing content, it will be good to remember that sharp crisp text that tells the story quickly is what surfers want. Do not ramble and try to flout your command over the language. Keep your site focused.

People often forget that updating a site is mission critical. Would you like to read a newspaper that has the same news every day? Of course not. Just remember that visitors would come back if you have fresh content every day. Therefore, site maintenance is priority one.

Invest in technology that makes maintenance easy.

Don't penny pinch in selecting a good Web String Service Provider that supports the software you would be using to build and maintain your site. You will find that there are hosting service providers who offer inexpensive packages, but you will later discover that they do not support a number of software that you would like to use now or in the future as your site grows.

Keep your site scalable so that you can handle large traffic without minimum fuss. It is like keeping provisions for widening the highway so that as and when traffic increases the road can grow wider.

Continue to register your site in as many search engines as possible regularly as otherwise you will find that your site comes in the third or fourth page of a search engine which is of little use."

The Growing World of Audio-Visuals and Multimedia presentations

Websites are one of the necessary corporate information means of doing interactively and with regular updates, what has been the more static corporate brochure route.

How do we view the rest of the tools of multimedia communication? For an insight into what is happening today and how the future can be grasped, we requested one of the younger generation of multimedia experts to share his thoughts and vision. Tapas Sen Gupta, at 35, is a management graduate who dallied with the corporate world for a short while, before branching out into corporate films, audio visuals and multimedia productions for trade fairs, corporate houses, chambers of commerce, advertising awards and television channel signatures.

In his view, to use a Dylanesque phrase, which cannot be overemphasized—the times they are a-changing. And the biggest move is the change in attitude and perception, as well as the mindset of corporate decision makers towards audio-visual Corporate Communication.

The trends as he sees it are:

- A recognition of professional packing in audio-visual Corporate Communication modules;
- Audio visuals perceived as a need-based function rather than an image-based activity;
- The use of technology to score points and deliver messages beyond the traditional tedium of

transparencies and endless talk to sleeker means of communicating;

- Recognition of the Small is Beautiful axiom in deliverance of corporate sermons through audio visuals;
- The small is big syndrome. Which means, look corporate-think big concept being put into practice by small business—saree traders, cinema hall owners, sweet shops and jewellery shops, all flaunting communication modules through interactive CD presentations and being sent as direct mailers to friends, associates, foreign agents;
- Reaching out through the World Wide Web;
- Young people with far-reaching ideas doing value-for-money jobs;

A look at today's trends:

What are the mass communication devices being used? Mass communication devices like: Brand advertising across all media; Help Desks—IVRS (Interactive Voice Responsive System); Direct Mailers' Websites/Portals; Public Interactive kiosks; Syndicated PR; Events and Promotions; Telemarketing; Outdoor innovations including video vans. Targeted communication has in its purview corporate films, training videos, multimedia presentations and multimedia catalogues, touch-screen kiosks, digital billboards.

A view of tomorrow's scenario:

Tomorrow means e-mail junking, interactive billboards (giant outdoor screens with online release supports), interactive television, multi-city video-conferencing, SMS Advertising, WAP-based mobile communication for salespeople, intelligent office building concepts and robotic communication—development of artificial intelligence.

To quote Sen Gupta: "Perhaps this is the beginning of a different world of communication. Sci-fi may now mean scientific fidelity. Rapid communications adaptability might trigger future shocks...but nanoseconds are the future and it is here already. Look around. It took 25 years to graduate from AIR to Doordarshan. 5 years for the cable boom. 2 years for the Internet explosion. And look around at your gatekeeper or even the fishmonger. Mobile and ATM savvy. Surely those days are gone of relaxing in front of a socialite piece of furniture called the computer."

To know how we have come a full circle from this high tech world, let us go back to how, in all this mad whirl, we need, once more to be read to.

I-Read-We-Learn: Pre-digested Reading for Today's Managers

The corporate *sutradhar* is back! In today's mad, mad, cad, fad world, where actioning concepts are of paramount importance for managers who have no time to read, or sit and stare, getting required reading in digestible, pill form seems to be the answer.

There is so much being produced by way of management thought, but so little time to flip through those tomes because of pressures of the competitive environment, that something needs to be done.

Coming up with a solution to this modern-day malaise is Pradeep Dutt, who is widely known in corporate and government circles as a turnaround expert, and has, during his 30 years of corporate experience, been CEO with large multinationals, including Lipton India and Bata and headed up the Bengal Chamber of Commerce and Industry.

Dutt has devised what he calls the IRWL (I-Read-We-Learn) Programme, "based on the current scenario where managers hardly find the time to read management books to further their learning." He feels that new concepts, practices and ideas are coming forth at a fast pace in the global arena of doing business. "To be able to update human capital is therefore a formidable challenge for any organization, big or small."

The programme envisages narration, interpretation and learning in one module without the individual manager having to read a given book. It is Dutt who does the reading and the subsequent regurgitation, in highly interactive sessions that last around four hours. The sessions conclude with a summary of learnings that you take out of the book.

To give an example, some of the books that have already been decimated and discussed are Gary Hamel's *Leading the Revolution*, Scott M. Davis' *Brand Asset Management*, Robert Slater's *Jack Welch and the GE Way*, Stephen Covey's *The 7 Habits of Highly Effective People*, *Managing Radical Change* by Ghosal, Piramal and Bartlett and *Brand Warriors* a book edited by Fiona Gilmore in which corporate leaders share their winning strategies.

The sharing of knowledge through such means is a much-needed step in a fast paced world where books are often bought by busy managers because they have read reviews of them, seen them in airport bookshops, or browsed through them in bookstores in cities other than their own and picked them up to read on a rainy day.

Converting rainy day reading into a reality is the task of such IRWL programmes, and companies might start having in-house practitioners who will concentrate on just this kind of knowledge disbursement.

2

Crisis Communication: More than just Debunking the Damage

Crises happen without a plan. What corporate communicators need to be armed with is a plan of action, in tackling the media and in anticipating the effects of crises on their companies. A few instances and observations.

The scene: a calm studious morning in a Florida second grade class. Eighteen smiling, young innocent pupils are going through a set of reading and pronunciation drills. Listening to it is the President of America. The date: September 11, 2001. There is a brief interruption as his chief of staff comes and whispers something in his ear.

The news is thunderous. But instead of causing further panic amongst the young, the reactions are to observe a moment of silence, ask for divine blessings for the victims' families and for the country and then go on to tackle the humungous national tragedy.

Media reactions and coverage are instantaneous, extensive, and fearless.

An important announcement...
Our beloved xxııox has opted
for a new abode more
heavenly.

Transport this very set of events on to a corporate crisis of the Bhopal and Chernobyl types and you have a different methodology of reaction. While reporters dig out information, companies seek to temper what is to be told to the media, how much to let go, and to what extent to hold back.

Today, apart from putting in place experts to be the first point of contact for media, relatives and others, to deal with queries, and earlier, to anticipating disasters, companies are turning to other set-ups, which specialize in Crisis Management.

We communicated with one such organization—CMS or Crisis Management Specialists, who are a new organization in Canada with a hand-picked team of experts in contingency planning and continuity management. Their team combines the expertise of an array of disciplines, so that they can deal with floods, forest fires and train wrecks, just as well as they can tackle terrorism and civil unrest, maritime and aviation disasters. An integral element of the team they claim, is "our technology, communications and systems engineering specialists who can work with our clients to ensure a full integration between crisis planning systems and their daily operations."

The way they do it is to go into risk analysis, threat assessments, business intelligence, crisis communications training, disaster planning, executive protection, even covering in their purview kidnap and ransom policies. A Crisis Management software system has also been developed by a company and is now in use by corporations and governments around the world.

Another aspect which is less disaster-based and is more focused on re-engineering and on mergers and acquisitions is handled by an agency called Paragon, also based in

Canada. They help organizations through the difficult steps of re-organization, strategic planning and maintaining effective communication with staff at all levels.

Altering Misconceptions

In India, some Public Relations agencies and independent consultants are doing just that.

Some examples of advertising management have been culled from agencies who have shared this information with us. When pictures of Pepsi bottles with fungus in them were splashed in newspaper, their agency, Perfect Relations launched an intensive media awareness campaign with the objective of reassuring customers and prevent spreading of misinformation in the media. How did they do this? They highlighted that 40 percent of Pepsi bottled in India was spurious, established that the bottle reproduced in newspapers was not an original bottle, and then suggested Government needed to take a firm stand on enforcing laws against spurious manufacturers of consumables.

What happened in the end was that many illicit plants were raided and closed down, Pepsi emerged as the aggrieved party and the case was dismissed in court.

Averting Takeover Bids

A different kind of crisis was faced by Indian Aluminium, a leading diversified aluminium company when it became the subject of a hostile takeover bid by Sterlite Industries, a company in the primary businesses of copper trading and smelting and jelly filled cables. The agency handling the Public Relations of Indal, Genesis PR, came forward with the kind of Public Relations support, which became an integral element in warding off the hostile bid, particularly as most of the action was played in the press.

Indal had not been performing too well over the previous couple of years and the scrip was at an all time low. Sterlite took this opportunity to launch a bid for Indal, claiming that they would be able to better manage the company.

Alcan, its original Canadian principals, who had gradually decreased its shareholding, was perceived as a disinterested party. However when it decided to launch a counter offer and it essentially became a bidding war between Sterlite and Alcan. Obviously the idea was to thwart the Sterlite hostile bid.

The Public Relations support, we are told, consisted of putting out the required messages during the various stages in the take-over bid process with a view to ensuring that the shareholders did not sell to Sterlite. Although price is the key governing factor, communication with the various stakeholders plays an equally critical role. At each stage in the Bid process, various activities were undertaken to communicate with and influence the target audience. Everything from press statements, constant interaction with the press on a daily basis, press conferences and briefings and presentations to large shareholders, not only about the bid process but also positive stories about the company's future growth strategies were also communicated to instil confidence in the investor community.

At every stage, being an extended crisis situation, says Genesis, the strategy was dynamic and consisted of tackling each new situation as it arose. For each new development, a particular strategy was devised and implemented to target the various stakeholders, which included employees, unions, customers, shareholders, financial institutions, government, opinion leaders and influencers from industry and the public.

The satisfaction was in the objective being achieved through a prolonged difficult phase. And the main achievement of Public Relations was in dramatically changing the perception of Indal, which was negative when Sterlite launched the bid to one where Indal came to be recognized and accepted as the leading integrated aluminium company in the country.

Using the Net to Deliver Messages During Crisis

BSMG Cyber PR in USA where Debbie McGinley is Managing Director maintains that "while crisis communications is a standard component of most traditional corporate Public Relations programmes, companies too often neglect to include the online arena.

McGinley feels that the Internet affords companies a luxury like never before: an immediate, unfiltered, direct channel to consumers and media. Something that is never more important than in a crisis. The method: have a crisis response template ready. A crisis website template will serve as a guideline for where and how the information on the company's website should look, so all you need to do in a crisis is to plug in the appropriate response information. A standard posting template for newsgroups should be in place and of course you have to establish an online crisis chain of command.

The three points that are noteworthy for this as a crisis communication vehicle are:

- It allows a company to immediately communicate a response to the crisis
- A broad audience can access the response from anywhere in the world at any time
- Addressing the issue online underscores the company's concern to its key audiences and helps convey the

diligence with which it is working to rectify the situation.

McGinley recalls the situation with Intel's Pentium microchips thus:

"A few years ago, a teacher in Lynchburg, Va. noticed a flaw in one of Intel's Pentium microchips. After contacting Intel, which confirmed the flaw, the teacher waited for a response from the company.

Receiving none, he sent an e-mail reporting the "bug" to colleagues, who, in turn, posted the message in a CompuServe forum; the first public disclosure of the flaw. Intel still did not respond.

Stories of the flaw soon migrated from Intel-specific newsgroups to more highly trafficked areas of the Internet. Soon, mainstream media picked up on the problem and made it front-page news, resulting in Intel's recall of all chips with similar flaws at a cost of a half-billion dollars, and undercutting the company's image and credibility."

The virtues that make the Internet so unique also make them very valuable during a crisis. The Internet allows for quick and accurate dissemination of a company's information to customers, investors, the media and other important constituencies. Moreover, as the Web matures, these audiences often turn to a company's Website as a primary source of information on a crisis. Companies that do not use the Internet during a crisis risk undercutting the relationships they've invested so much time building.

Companies learn largely from experience and there are a few who actually put together a strategy to encounter crises. The ones who do so are companies that deal with processed food products and pharmaceuticals, airlines who have the responsibility of public safety, companies manufacturing products that could present hazards of explosion and pollution. Such companies have to live with a certain preparedness and in fact, already have contingency plans in place for tackling crashes, contaminants, explosions, sabotages.

What we would like to see, ideally, is for every company to have, in place, a communication strategy for eventualities. It isn't only a mining company that can face a cave-in or an airline that has to anticipate the action following a crash or a hijack. Every organization has a potential devil of a crisis. A bank can have its hold-ups. A corporation can have a fire that claims lives. A healthy company could suddenly become the target of a corporate raider. The crisis permutations are many and varied. The action is just one: preparedness.

Just as many companies go through fire drills if they are located in high rises, they should also have crisis situation dry runs and simulated emergency situations. Communication experts need to address crisis handling through structured manuals and programmes in as assiduous a manner as they address their promotional plans for a company.

Airline Crisis Management

All airlines have Crisis Management manuals in place today because disaster management has assumed a critical role for the airline industry. It affects the communicator, particularly, because there is heightened media attention that is associated with airline crashes and hijacks, with maximized media focus when it comes to unprecedented events like the hijacked airliners crashing into the World Trade Centre in New York and causing major international repercussions.

From studies conducted by academics, it has been found that "because of the vast amount of media attention that surrounds aircraft disasters, most people do not realize that airplane accidents are actually rare occurrences." The authors of this paper on Airline Crisis Management maintain "historically, disaster-response plans have been insufficient, and consequently there is a need for intensive crisis training in order for the airline to deal professionally, effectively and courteously with the passengers and crew involved. Crisis Management in the airline industry specifically includes prevention of the disaster, highly extensive contingency planning, rapid response, and prompt delivery of information to the public."

And, we may add, greater transparency of this information to the press, the Next of Kin, to the general public. Putting a massive responsibility on the Public Relations personnel of airlines who are under pressure and scrutiny.

A Media Relations 2-day course prepared by an agency in USA—Paragon, can be applied to airline disasters and other Crisis Management. It would be useful for corporate communicators to put manuals in place and also use such models in their companies should disaster strike. The first day in this module is divided into several segments, which consist of talks, discussions and demonstrations. They have in their purview perceptions of the media, learning the structure of the media, learning about types of interviews, setting up of interviews, personal preparedness in terms of dress, mannerisms, and actually going through dry runs. The second day is live interviews, critiquing, debriefing, problem-solving.

Preparedness and planning are the key words for communication modules to be set up.

3

Out of Adversity: Post-crisis Communication

Bhopal and Chernobyl will always have the Pavlovian reaction from people of unmitigated disasters. The aftermath has not been palatable. But it is taking the initiative of bestselling authors like Dominique Lapierre and industry groups like the British Nuclear Industry Forum to rescue some good out of adversity.

Dominique Lapierre: Re-engineering an old crisis to reap new rewards

Why rake up something that happened 17 years ago? Many of us wanted to throw this question at Lapierre when he was sharing his personal account and signing copies of "It was Five Past Midnight in Bhopal" at Oxford Bookstore in Kolkata. What purpose could it serve?

Many people want to "turn the page" and move on, claims Lapierre. But it is the will and the empathy of this amazing author that has made him spend three years in Bhopal, interviewing, researching, getting into people's minds and hearts, to seek the truth, to offer redressal, to document and celebrate the spirit of survival. And through the writing of a racy, well-researched and human story, to send out a message—"never forget Bhopal, but never let it happen again." Lapierre has already set up a gynaecological clinic in Bhopal, and intends to do more in terms of medical assistance through the royalties garnered from the sales of this book.

Lapierre's 370 page book, an extremely racy and readable account, is told like a novel, built up with beauty, myth, the music of *mushairas*, the smell of flowers and nights blessed by stars through most of the recounting, and only dealing the disaster blow in the last hundred pages.

Publisher Shekhar Malhotra was also present at the book reading, and gave us his own graphic account of a Parisian cab driver's donation for Bhopal when he overheard the story from Lapierre and Malhotra. Also telling was the recounting of their visit to Bhopal and a citizen of that town coming up with the statement: " It needed a *firang* to come and help us." In publishing their book, the mission is blatantly clear: It is a mission to see that Bhopal is not forgotten. The idea is to stimulate corrective action by others. As the French Premier did after reading the book. He had a small town which had gas shells strewn all over, evacuated, to avert any further tragedies and had the shells removed and deactivated.

If Lapierre intends to milk post-crisis sympathy from this book, he will get it. But more so, the book will serve as an excellent reference work for the background to the pesticide that initially held out promises of plenty and then went sour. The facts that go back to the beginnings have never been presented so succinctly, for most people have looked at the dreadful event in the heat of indignation and passion, and not in cold retrospect, when many new lessons can be learnt.

From the adversity, Lapierre's book and his impassioned writing should "give a voice and a face to the people of Bhopal" as he himself puts it. Why did the dream project of Union Carbide turn into a Titanic? That is why Lapierre felt like telling the story and then following it up with a measure of philanthropy.

He holds back nothing. The US$ 470 million that was given to the government by UCIL was tantamount to silence money. Some of it went into a Bhopal Memorial Trust Hospital, an elitist hospital which the poor cannot get anywhere near, and which has a poor rate of occupancy anyway.

The contribution both from the renewed awareness created by this most readable tome and also the donation of royalties from the book will make it an example of a communication initiative that could never have been sponsored, initiated or commissioned by any company. It had to happen with an author's passion for ferreting out the real story and for writing it to carry a strong warning and a plea for preventing further disasters.

Chernobyl and After

A novel waiting to happen is the story of Slavutich, a town 50 kilometres east of the Chernobyl plant. Before the accident, the workforce from Chernobyl lived in the town of Pripyat, close to the plant. After it, the families were evacuated from their homes, temporarily re-housed and they now live in Slavutich, built by eight former Soviet Republics. Estonia, Latvia, Lithaunia, Belarus, Azerbaijan, Armenia, Russia and Ukraine.

In an informative set of stories put out by BNIF, whose activities are mentioned in the chapter on issues management, the prettier picture to emerge about the people of this town gives the same kind of feeling as that conveyed by Lapierre about culture-rich Bhopal. Each of the eight former Soviet republics brought its own workforce and materials and built houses and flats in the style of their own republic. So the town has eight different sectors, as varied in style as they are in personality and character. The population of Slavutich is around 25,000 of which more than one-third are children. It has the country's youngest population, highest birth rate and lowest mortality rate.

The families of Slavutich enjoy a relatively high standard of living and have access to some of the best stocked shops in Ukraine. There are excellent schools, sports facilities and one of Ukraine's best schools.

In putting out the positive information about this town, the effect has been to reduce terror, panic and rumour. And create an understanding of the problem in retrospect.

What people, meaning experts in their fields, are saying about Chernobyl today have been documented thus, and we bring five such comments:

Dr. Keith Baverstock, Radiation Scientist, WHO, Rome in a letter to The Times, London in June 1995:

"The claim that one million severely deformed children are the result of exposure to Chernobyl radiation is not credible, and is damaging to public health itself. Without in any way minimizing the health effects of exposure to radiation, little good and much harm results from exaggerating them. Already the psycho-socio effects of the accident are diminishing the quality of life and well being of millions of people. Over 2000 children are born in Belorussia each year with severe deformities and disabilities which are due to birth defects and hereditary conditions and have nothing to do with radiation. Similar rates occur throughout Europe. Between 40 and 80 such cases will involve severe limb deformities."

Piers Paul Reed, author of Ablaze—the Story of Chernobyl, writing in the Spectator on 17 April 1993:

"A leading campaigner against official secrecy over Chernobyl Professor Dmitri Grodzinski, told me that the stories of hospitals lined with gaunt, dying and deformed children, as reported in the Sunday times in 1990 were nonsense. He showed me magazines that had used photographs of thalidomide children to illustrate articles on Chernobyl."

Dr Alexander Lutsko, International Sakharov Institute of Radioecology, Minsk, Belarus and Dr Alan Flowers, Kingston University, June 1995:

"Any glance at general health trends in Belarus during the 1980s shows a continuing increase in cancer, leukaemia, perinatal mortality and many other health defects prior to the Chernobyl fallout. (It is) an unfortunate error to link the undeniably poor health of the population of parts of the Former Soviet Union to the Chernobyl accident."

Dr Robert Gale, US bone marrow specialist who operated on heavily contaminated individuals in the immediate aftermath of the accident, interviewed in Nuclear Europe 5, 1987.

"The replacement of nuclear by fossil fuel (in the former Soviet Union) would result in approximately one million deaths in the next 50 years. In the (former) USSR about 20,000 deaths might occur because of

Chernobyl. So if there were no more nuclear accidents in the (former) USSR then the comparison would be 20,000 versus a million lives."

Professor Richard Wilson Mallinckrodt, Professor of Physics, Harvard University, in 21at Century Science and Technology, Summer 1993:

"(The two-headed animals reported in some newspapers), from what one can gather, come from the farm areas—the collective farms—and they are almost certainly due to over-fertilization. If you just put nitrates down without measuring, its easy to put down 30 times too much, and have these animals getting 30 times too much. Then you start getting those genetic effects."

Other facts that have been put out are comparisons with deaths from other accidents/disasters thus:

"Chernobyl is the worst civil nuclear power accident to ever occur. It killed 31 people directly and it will cause cancer deaths in the long term, through these are unlikely to be detectable compared to cancer deaths from other causes.

To put the accident in context, the following comparisons might be helpful:

- The International Atomic Energy Agency has worked out that 40,000 deaths are caused each year in the USA by people inhaling the fumes from burning fossil fuels in coal-fired power stations.
- In 1984, a natural gas explosion in Mexico City killed 500 people and injured 4248 people. A further 31,000 people were made homeless when the plant exploded.
- In 1984, a release of methyl isocyanate at Bhopal, India

killed 2850 people and injured 200,000 (most permanently)
- In 1979, the Great Machu II Dam in Gujarat, India failed killing 15,000 people directly
- When part of a coal spoil tip slid onto the village of Aberfan in South Wales in heavy rain in 1996, 116 children were among 147 people killed.

More than justifications, these are the righting of wrong facts. When you represent the nuclear industry as BNIF does, the research has to be extensive and comprehensive. This would enable past disasters to be put in perspective.

4

Issues and Perception Management

Public Relations practice has to don binoculars to look far afield into key issues that impact on companies. Sometimes, it takes the form of separate divisions in a corporate PR set-up, which research the possible consequences of environmental, political and other concerns on an organization and recommend steps to counter the fallout in the press in advance. Here we examine some aspects of Issues Management.

It is all about the role that Public Relations can play in going through the "What If" motions as opposed to the "What Went Wrong" cleaning up. The Issues Management departments of companies or of consultancies today have become a part of a total system of anticipative Public Relations.

A fair amount of research has to be done by the communications department to be able to track issues that could affect companies in the long run.

We would like to share the experience of the **British Nuclear Industry Forum,** which is the trade association and information and representative body for the British civil nuclear industry. It represents over 60 companies including the operators of the nuclear power stations, those engaged in decommissioning, waste management, nuclear liabilities management and all aspects of the nuclear fuel cycle, nuclear equipment suppliers, engineering and construction firms; nuclear research organizations; and legal, financial and consultancy companies.

Its Main Objectives Are:

- to influence the climate of public and political opinion in favour of nuclear energy as part of a sustainable balanced energy policy, and
- to promote the commercial performance of the UK nuclear industry by assisting and supporting member companies to develop their businesses in the UK and internationally.

BNIF seeks to promote the skills of the nuclear industry and represent its member companies by:

- providing a central point of contact for information on nuclear energy and the British nuclear industry;
- representing the industry's positions on public policy and media issues
- holding technical conferences, seminars and workshops;
- organizing inward and outward missions;
- acting as the 'umbrella' for members' participation in international events and exhibitions;
- publishing a regular newsletter;
- consulting with the Department of Trade and Industry and other organizations dealing with the British nuclear industry
- providing information on overseas markets

In fact, it was BNIF who researched the latest findings about Chernobyl. What they found and subsequently shared through the media is indicative of how issues can be managed post a disaster or a crisis. Chernobyl, long taken as a whipping boy for all disaster management discussions, is now getting out of the ill-effects psychosis to building a more positive image for itself. Through articles and discussions about the rebuilding of communities in its periphery, the setting up of schools, and showing through statistics that any disaster occurring there is minimal compared to the aftereffects of many other disasters in other situations and countries.

Other examples of the management of issues have come to us from our own Public Relations agencies in India.

Managing Local Sensitivities

The Benetton campaign

The issue, the solution and the implementation of what happened when Benetton launched their first institutional campaign in India, aimed at generating AIDS awareness is a great case study that has been shared with us by Genesis PR. Seeing the controversial nature of Benetton advertising campaigns worldwide and AIDS being a sensitive social issue in India, an effective and planned Public Relations exercise before the launch of the advertisement, led to a successful campaign and an overwhelming response from the media.

The advertisement visual was coloured condoms placed against a white background in stark graphic style. At the time that Benetton launched the campaign, the Advertising Standards Council of India was reacting strongly to companies releasing socially and morally unacceptable ads, resulting in a negative attitude being adopted by the government, media as well as the public in general.

The solution was a carefully planned and targeted Public Relations exercise before the release of the ad campaign to influence public opinion.

The first step was to append a copy to the stark visual of the ad which gave it more meaning and credibility. The copy read: "use a condom to prevent HIV and other Sexually Transmitted Diseases. Pick up your free AIDS Guide at any Benetton outlet countrywide—issued in public interest by DCM Benetton India Ltd., a joint venture with Benetton Group SpA, Italy.

Oliviero Toscani, Benetton's creative director, who is responsible for Benetton's entire communication worldwide, was invited to India to launch the campaign, revealing the visual of the ad for the first time at a press conference in Mumbai. He also made a presentation to college students at a public speaking event in one of the colleges in Mumbai, on Benetton's advertising campaigns, outlining the company's advertising history as well as the conflicting response to the advertising campaigns in various countries.

The condom campaign had already appeared in Europe, America and South Africa and was part of an ongoing project commitment on part of Benetton to communicate on the phenomenon of AIDS, since 1991 and the launch of the campaign was also to effectively integrate India with Benetton's communication strategy the world over.

The campaign was to be a long term sustained effort towards generating awareness on the illness and educating people on AIDS through institutional advertising and sponsorship of events targeted at high risk groups and young people. According to Olivier Toscani, "this campaign is part of Benetton's worldwide commitment to communicate on contemporary social and universal issues."

The AIDS campaign was selected for India because AIDS is not just a world-wide concern but recent studies of the World Health Organization indicated that India is expected to be the AIDS capital of Asia by the turn of the century with over four million AIDS cases.

This was the basic message conveyed by Toscani in his presentation at the press conference as well as at a public speaking event organized at a local Mumbai college attended by university students and the advertising community.

A number of one-to-one interviews were organized with key publications in Mumbai and the next day in New Delhi. New Delhi also witnessed a similar public speaking event.

The result is that, to date, not a single negative article has appeared on the campaign. The press conference and the public speaking events generated coverage worth Rs. 70,00,000, more than 10 times the amount spent on the campaign. There were no negative reactions to the ad from the press, government and public in general. DCM Benetton received a letter from The Directorate of Health Service, Government of Maharashtra congratulating them on their brilliant campaign regarding AIDS awareness/prevention. The company was also requested on behalf of the AIDS cell of the government of Maharashtra for a copy of each of the items including transparencies prepared for the campaign.

KFC

The entry of KFC in Bangalore was not greeted with elation. Local groups opposed it and the agency, Perfect Relations came in at this stage to avert the crisis by sharing information in a transparent manner. They advised the company to throw open their doors and invite the media and even the general public to observe at first hand the way in which KFC functioned.

Going into the workings of the strategy, it is found that the agency, following the dying down of the fracas, identified the competitors—many local fast food joints, and against this background, highlighted its international lineage. An honest stand taken by an outsider wanting to establish its reputation and foothold worked well and enhanced its image in the eyes of the target audience.

We have given only brief examples of an industry forum and the managing of local sensitivities, but there are countless other instances of the management and tracking of issues. Some of it dovetails into the management of crises—for the two do overlap. Read about some instances of Crisis Management and Crisis Communication in Chapter 2 of Book Three.

The building of the tradition of Guru-Shishya parampara

A recording inside the Sangeet Research Academy by a student of classical music

The Assam Valley School—an example of going beyond self-interest

Udita, designed for families in the higher income group.

Work of art at Udita

Chiva Som: The Promotion of Healthy Lifestyle : In Communion with the Sea

Healthy food, presented with élan

5

Information Sharing:
The Employee Paradigm

House Journals: a planned penetration of the psyche of an employee, through information, entertainment, analysis and just good in-house prattle. An evergreen form of internal communication which continues to develop and grow.

It isn't easy being a House Journal editor. He is told in no uncertain terms that all he is doing is putting together the paste-up smiles of employees. If that were so, a couple of thousand companies in India wouldn't be wasting their precious corporate resources—money and manpower—towards bringing out month after month, quarter after quarter, publications with a combined circulation of over 50 million that inform, involve and entertain employees at no cost to them.

Newspapers often look down on House Journals as being the mouthpieces of management. They regard the work of the House Journal editor as just another duty in the long list of Public Relations jobs that he does. Unfair on

both counts. House Journals certainly do have to go along with corporate policy, but then today newspapers often also have to keep in line with their owners' political and other views. And on the second count, a House Journal editor's job could be more difficult than that of the newspaper editor. The latter has a full professional team, is fed by the news services and is paid to do just that job. A House Journal editor does his job as part of a total one in corporate Public Relations, often with very little other staff, with barely any inputs, but is expected to produce a good journal that is worthy of applause from colleagues and approbation from competitors and the occasional appreciative word from the head of the corporation.

In fact, in today's over-communicative world, which is saturated with publications that cater to every possible interest group and newspapers and magazines that publish in-depth corporate stories, the status of a House Journal often becomes the subject of scrutiny by managements of companies. Why have a House Journal at all? How many people are reading it? Is it adding to the piles of junk mail being created? What purpose is it serving? Is it just providing fodder for the *kabbadiwallah*?

How about a question like the following-what is the use of a newspaper when there is television and radio, the weekly newsmagazine, and the local know-all and the next-door neighbour who keeps tabs on everything from Bosnian and Croatian relationships to the peccadilloes of the stock markets the world over.

Yet, the newspapers still forms part of a daily way of life. So, by the same token, could a company carry on its business without establishing any communication with those who are both in the vortex and on the right side of its business activities? As an integral part of an organization's communications structure, a House Journal, far from being relegated to the status of a rambunctious captive chatterbox, is, still today, the surest means of establishing a two-way traffic that is not propaganda, not persuasion. It is a planned penetration of the psyche of an employee, through information, entertainment, analysis and just good in-house prattle.

But that last bit would be doing a disservice to a House Journal. For it is a multifaceted tool that can be used to great advantage at all levels of communication, in numerous shapes, sizes, frequency and in the most creative ways. It can, apart from its reportage, also serve as a forum, on the one hand, for venting employee grievances and, on the other, for eliciting talent. Most House Journals steer clear of the first aspect, if they can help it, for stirring up a hornet's nest of controversies is not the main intention. The latter can give the House Journal a true personality.

A successful House Journal is one which remains homely enough to be an intra-company publication, but is slick enough to evoke favourable comment from an outsider. A professionally executed house magazine is somewhat like a well done office play, which, apart from the standing ovation at the annual social, gets column centimeters of praise by a drama critic in a national daily.

House Journal: Grapevine Incarnate?

A House Journal is in a sense a formalized incarnation of the grapevine. If it were to be as quick in its transmission time, it would be the most ideal form of internal communication. This is one of the key elements in the concept of a House Journal—immediacy and frequency.

To define a House Journal, it could best be called a

periodical issued by an organization in a non-commercial manner with the object of creating a forum of communication for its employees. Some people have defined it as industry's private press which is as succinct a way of putting it as any.

But of course, there isn't only one type of journal, just as there is no one single public that is the target of Public Relations activity, but a number of publics that an organization caters to. A House Journal could also be called a corporate publication, in its genre, and then again, there could be a dealer newsletter, a shareholder missive, a customer magazine or an investor journal.

Fathering the Idea

There are many ways in which a House Journal is born. An "enlightened" chief executive decides that the company needs a publication to create fellow-feeling amongst employees. Or the newly-appointed Corporate Communications director, who is dually responsible for human resources development, finds that other companies have house magazines, and why should his company miss out on bringing out one. Or a Public Relations practitioner from one company joins another company and feels compelled to start a publication because there is very little else to do in the Public Relations department. Or a dormant publication needs a new lease of life and the Public Relations man is called upon to work wonders.

What happens in most cases is that the communicator is not given much time to plan and hurtles into producing a publication which follows the formula set by hundreds before it. It ends up becoming either a mouthpiece of the management, who finds it a convenient tool for reaching employees, often in the face of a crisis which needs to be defused, or a potpourri of happenings put between glossy covers.

Advantage, Reader

Ideally the process should begin with focusing on the target audience. Somebody has to ask these very basic questions before the deed is begun. "Whom do we wish to communicate with?" "What do we want the publication to achieve?" "What do we want to say?" and "Assuming we have communicated, what is the response we want to evoke?"

Very often we have found that once some leading questions have been asked around a table and even a questionnaire circulated to senior managers, gets the predictable answer: Drop it. Or, with those who are convinced about the need to communicate, the query would be: "How cost-effective is it?"

Assuming the idea has not been dropped, then the possible answers to all these queries should form the basis of a project report. This should also include frequency, budgets, the editorial team, the designers, the printer and, very important: mailing lists. But the key to an enduring publication will be to define the character of the journal, for on that will depend the image of the company.

A simple A-B-C formula (Analyse-Budget-Create) would be worth trying in the first stages, which, simplistic though it might sound, forms a basis for take-off. And once a publication's objectives have been decided upon, they should be written out clearly, disseminated widely to all levels of management for review, discussion and acceptance. The involvement of a number of people across the board makes the project more acceptable in the long run, than for a four-colour magazine to be suddenly flung into the midst of an unsuspecting and unprepared audience.

Of, for and by the Employee

Since the bulk of House Journals are employee-oriented, we will focus on this kind of publication. But there are the dealer journals like Telco has, the customer magazines, as the banks brings out these days, or the in-house guest magazines by hotels which are more in the nature of tourist promotion glossies.

In any employee publication, the medium selects the audience and not the other way round. Which means that the approaches that are successful with a general interest or specialist magazine may not always be as effective with an employee publication. Although the general term "employee" is used, yet the audience is a diversified one, as the publication is meant to be read by everyone from the telephone operator, the typist and the bearer to the systems analyst, the R & D manager, the finance director, the marketing vice-president, and finally the big white-collared chief himself. The only thread of commonality between all these sets of employees is that they are paid by the same organization.

Content: The Core of a Journal

With this background in mind, the editor who is also an employee and not a disembodied figure, has to find the right things to communicate. Not in the simplistic manner of management to employee, for that smacks of "we" and "they", but of putting together an interesting mix of the serious company plans and policies along with individual achievements and activities of the employees themselves. It should be safely assumed that the news most likely to attract the attention and interest of an employee is what affects him or her personally, either through knowing where the company is headed or from the manner in which the rest of the information is presented.

A typical structure for a House Journal is to begin with an editorial or message from the top man. The editorial could relate what is in the rest of the journal, or comment on a current important happening in the industry, which affects the company or could be an inspirational piece. On the corporate information side, it would need to be stories of the company's performance, new products and processes, expansions and reorganizations. Safety, health and incentive schemes would form the features part of the journal. These could either be written by employees themselves, or be general features with no by-line, but the former is always preferred. In fact, wherever possible, the names of correspondents should be mentioned, or credit given to the originator of any news item, while company performance stories should also be commissioned from experts in each field. Regular performance reviews by individual departments heads are another way of involving more people to share corporate happenings and keep them interested in the success of the journal.

The news that forms the core of the journal is, of course the one that deals with promotions, transfers, recruitments, retirements, awards, marriages, births and deaths and the happenings at the various locations of a company. Contributions from employees (and their wives and children) in the form of articles and anecdotes, focusing on their special interests; poems, paintings, photographs and interviews of employees by fellow employees, make a House Journal the unique publication it is. Interspersing a journal with humour is necessary to keep it buoyant, but the humour has to be relevant and not something lifted out of digests.

How down to earth it all sounds! And yet for a person who has made it to the pages of the journal, it is a happening to be proud of, to be shared with family and peer group, and a publication to be preserved for showing to the next generation. People have been known to frame their contributions, paste them into albums, get reprints made of individual articles to send out to a wider circle of acquaintances. For many, it has been a legitimization of a talent which then launches them into a writing or a painting career. There was one person we knew who became so good at tailoring crosswords for the company magazine, that he went into it professionally after retirement. And another House Journal editor representing a company producing heavy vehicles has become a top class travel photographer simply because he started out with the necessity of showing the company's trucks in varied locations around the country for illustrating the product better.

Format: The Face of a Journal

Here, again, it might seem as if we are going into too many irrelevant details. But form can be as important because that, too, defines the character of a publication.

The most popular sizes are the ones that come in a regular magazine format, largely because of the economy of the paper sizes involved. And particularly if a journal has a mixed audience, and doubles as a publication which goes out to a company's commercial, government, overseas associates and media contacts, the A4 size is convenient and relevant.

Apart from this, layouts can be imaginatively planned and most of all, they are convenient to handle, easy to file and fit in with people's perception of what a magazine ought to be. These publications can be produced in multiples of four, eight, sixteen, thirty-two pages. The disadvantages of course is that most magazines come in this size and it could become difficult to distinguish one from another.

People have not experimented enough with a format that is half this size, somewhat like a pocket book. It could be so easy to carry around, would have the gravity and the lasting impression of being a book, and yet be a magazine. Imagine the *Reader's Digest* in any other format—it would probably have a massive drop in readership if this were ever contemplated. Similarly, the *Illustrated Weekly of India*, which has sadly been laid to rest a long time ago, could not be imagined in any other format but its tabloid size, unwieldy though it was. It is all a question of establishing an identity from the beginning and sticking to it.

The tabloid is in fact becoming increasingly popular in corporate parlance because of the immediacy it evokes. If most House Journals were fortnightly tabloids, they would never be accused of somnolence or of not reaching their target audiences.

When a company brings out a number of publications like a dealer newsletter, an employee journal and a prestigious external publication, then varied formats can be useful in distinguishing one category from another. Large corporates have publications which are multi-formatted, with qualities of paper and design differing according to the audience to be reached.

Printing Processes: The Target Group Justifies the Hardware

As with format, so also with printing processes and paper. It is the target group which justifies the hardware. Just as tabloids on art paper would look wasteful, so also would a magazine do better to have a glossy appearance. The choice also depends on a company's budgetary parameters. The rule of thumb ought to be—the more frequent the publication the less expensive need the paper quality be.

As for printing processes, it is no longer a question of letterpress versus offset, as even small runs today are done by offset process. What needs to be addressed, is the changing and growing developments in technology to make for varied, easier, sometimes cheaper, communication. Journals to link up with ever widening networks of offices through the net are also a quick and effective means of communication.

Periodicity, Language

A House Journal ceases to be one if it does not come out at regular intervals. An annual publication can certainly not earn itself the appellation of a periodical and even those published bi-annually do not quite fit the bill. For a House Journal to have any impact or use, it should be a quarterly, bi-monthly, fortnightly, weekly. A daily broadsheet is something that is not impossible to achieve, given the advances in desktop publishing. Such a daily bit of communication could revolutionize employee interaction and improve the average person's involvement in the activities and plans of a company. The publication of employee achievements within a few hours of their taking place could have no better substitute for motivation. And there is that other benefit to be had from intercepting the grapevine on people's movements within the company.

But the problems, or rather the challenges, come in the matter of the language to be used for communicating with the workforce. English continues to be widely used, but what kind of English? At different levels, the comprehension will vary. Does the editor talk down or pitch up or stay at a middle unassuming level? And when a company is multi-locational, how many languages can the communication be organized in?

Some publications get around the problem with dual languages done in simultaneous columns. Some publish one half in English and part in Hindi or in the predominant regional language of the majority of the employees. Some publish three journals, each a separate publication, freely translated.

You can't obviously please all the people all the time, but every effort is worth it to cover the gaps in communication when language could be the issue.

The Editor and the Correspondent: Who Comes First?

Without a correspondent and minus the inputs, where will an editor be? Then again, it is the editor who has to elicit information to ensure that a journal is packed with news that is of interest to an employee, views to stimulate him and contributions from him to ensure involvement.

The selection of an editor has to be done keeping in mind that the person must have a journalistic or other writing background and some knowledge of production techniques. Some organizations can afford a whole editorial team, which includes designers and even photographers. Others, which is the rule, rather than the exception, have just one person to look after maybe more than one journal. He is either part of the Public Relations department, sometimes the main PR man, or of some division of the company which interacts directly with the PR department.

In some companies, with facilities geographically scattered, there may be a number of employee publications, each autonomously edited by a local editor. The role of the Public Relations person sitting at headquarters would then be both as a facilitator and as a coordinator and one who controls the general policy information that can be used at the local editor's discretion.

It is only when a firm has just one publication and has to include the whole family of employees that it becomes essential to appoint correspondents. Often selected from personnel departments of plants or even by just picking on the most "communicative" person at a factory, the correspondent could also be picked from amongst the wives of the plant managers, or garden managers if it is a tea company. The only way to elicit valuable and creative information from such people is to give them good guidelines on what is required and, of course, their by-line. Remunerating them is not a bad ideal at all: it makes for a commitment on both sides. Payment should also be considered for contribution like articles, photographs and poetry to the House Journal.

What many companies worry about is that "news" is not generated within an organization in the same manner as the information that comes out in black and white in a newspaper. Also, that the stuff which gets into general interest magazines which are sold from newsstands can never be replicated for House Journals. Not true. A House Journal has the talented backing of a large number of employees who have numerous interests, hobbies, talents and writing ability to be able to share travelogues, hobby backgrounders, anecdotal tales, better living articles, stories on their special interests. Often freelancers are available to contribute, sometimes there are syndicated services from which to pick up articles and many times, relevant articles can be extracted from management journals or other publications and reproduced with permission, or at least with a courteous acknowledgement.

Material is never in short supply, but it is the planning and presentation of this in the most relevant manner to the House Journal for that particular company which can make it worth reading and often preserving.

A Hot Chapati Must be Eaten Hot, so Distribution is Key!

Unless the journals produced by companies reach their audiences with a reasonable period of time of their being produced, there is not much sense in producing it at all. Company distribution systems are never efficient, nor comprehensive in matters of House Journals distribution. And yet, this must be amongst the simplest of operations.

For mailing departments to pack bulk quantities as the journals come off the presses and send them out to individual locations is a matter of planning, not of expense. Some editors are savvy enough to do not only this, but they also send off faxes the moment a journal is on its way to say the current issue would be with them shortly and that they should make arrangements for distribution or put up a notice for employees to collect from a central point.

At headquarters, the distribution can be quicker. Every table should have one first thing in the morning or they should be placed at lunchtime so that something new greets a person when he returns from his break. Authors should get their copies with a complimentary note, along with a gift cheque. The rest of the mailing list should already have been planned while the copies were at the press. Which means the mailing labels should have been sorted and stuck on to envelopes, or, in the case of publications which go with sleeves, they should have been kept ready to go.

Once again, it sounds far too much like the nuts and bolts of the business, which does not merit the spelling out of such workaday details. But there's no ignoring these, for a well-distributed journal is at the heart of the real success of any magazine. With the numerous types of software for mailing lists available, updating information on recipients should become a routine matter. The only thing which is at a premium is the editor's time and he would do well to have a person spend a few hours every month reviewing names, addresses, designations and feed them into the computer. An outdated designation or a wrong address can be more detrimental to the image of company than no journal at all.

Brickbats Beget Bouquets

No editor should shrink from feedback. A few grammes of criticism could add considerable weightage in improving a publication. Unless there is a reasonable amount of response to any message, the communication should be deemed to be incomplete. One way to provide measurable response in any employee publication is to have a formalized channel for it. An important aspect of making the feedback mechanism work effectively is to make sure readers respond by having either a Letters to the Editor column which is commonplace or special questionnaires which are easy to reply to.

Everybody Reads What He Pays For

It is a strange psychology with most people, but when you pay for a magazine, you are more likely to read it from cover to cover than if it were a complimentary copy. Some magazines have debated about whether an employee should be charged a token amount for a newsletter. It could be just fifty paise, but it would mean that there is a transaction followed by the reader reading what he has consciously paid for. If a publication were to land on his desk, he may shove it aside for more pressing immediate paperwork.

So far, the logistics of the exercise have prevented his concept from working but a system could well be devised on this.

However, a House Journal is something that an employee can claim as his due and thus the matter of payment should not arise at all. Besides, the amount charged, if insignificant, could also have the connotation of cheapness, which is never the intention.

The other matter is about accepting advertisements for a publication, sometimes from a company's product division. This would result in subsiding the cost of the journal and divisions could also have a chance to air their product range. But most arguments point against this practice, as it would smack of commercialization.

Videomagazines

Give a senior manager who is not in the Public Relations department a sheet of blank paper and ask him to write a congratulatory paragraph on the latest corporate breakthrough, and he will take all day to do it. Put him in front of a video camera and he will spout forth platitudes (after the initial front of lens freeze, that is) until the cassette runs out.

Ergo, the audio-visual medium, gets people going more easily in an age when newspapers are flung aside for the satellite pleasures of garnering views from CNN, BBC and STAR TV.

So, we can hardly blame an employee of a company welcoming the Videomagazine in preference to the House

Journal. One is read in isolation, but the Videomagazine makes for a community viewing and is trying to create an increased "sense of belonging". The motivational bit is that when employees see a capsule of their own activities on screen and also the company's achievements, they view themselves as players in the totality of the corporate arena.

Does the printed word have a chance? Seeing is believing, truly. But you can still have a House Journal all to yourself to preserve for posterity. Videos are a more expensive proposition as individual keepsakes. It is considerably more costly to produce quarterly or half-yearly videos. Their reach is confined to employees, whereas a magazine goes out to a much wider audience. Videomagazines can never be a replacement, but a complementary means of communication.

Videos are also being replaced by CD Roms which makes for even greater ease of accessibility as employees just have to view it through a computer and not wait for a video presentation.

One communicator has commented that the danger lies in the "smallness of a CD" and the fact that it is tucked away by employees for a "rainy day" viewing, which may never happen. To circumvent this, formal group meetings are being structured where CDs are viewed and a discussion leader talks about the developments to these select groups.

Intranet Communication

A step even further than Videomagazines and definitely a workable option today is the communication through email. Companies like SRF are posting most of their communications on the Intranet server which is accessible throughout the organization. A more interactive platform, they say, is being developed currently, for even more effective communication.

Yet, it cannot be a substitute for the House Journal. It is like a homemade cake—freshly baked, with pure ingredients, largely for home consumption and tailored to special tastes. Numerous confectioneries may sprout all around, but the joys of making and partaking of a homemade cake are different and always cancel out commercialized offerings. House Journals should endure, likewise, as long as creative cooking at home lasts.

6

Creative PR for Enhancing Shareholder Value

The term "creative" can be a double-edged weapon. As communicators, we take it as synonymous with innovation. Our accounting counterparts would tread more carefully when using this term, as it could smack of manipulation. However, in this chapter, we will be dealing with how companies that communicate with investors in a transparent and reliable manner, and, in today's context, ingeniously, will surely be the ones to have their success noticed.

Annual Reports: The New Genre

In studying some of the Annual Reports that have made an impact on the investing community and even on those who may not have had a stake in that particular company, we found one underlying idea: transparency.

Reliance

For years, we had got used to the "bazaar" quality of the Reliance Annual Reports, born out of the necessity of the company having to communicate with its millions of

shareholders. So, when in 1997-98 Reliance came out with its Intellectual Capital Report, it gave a fresh dimension to their communication. Which aimed to "redress the imbalance between non-financial and financial data, in recognition of the belief that the value of organizations will, in times to come, increasingly reside in their intangible assets." It was also done with a view to introducing a new edge to transparency that would strengthen its corporate governance.

Described as the "aggregate intangible capability at the disposal of the organization", this intellectual capital could be derived from, the report says, investor goodwill, customer goodwill, employee expertise and organizational process. The focus shift of Reliance is described in stages thus:

"In the early years of Reliance's existence, investor goodwill was the pre-dominant growth engine—it funded aggressive asset building at a cost which made Reliance globally competitive. Realizing the capital-intensive nature of its business strategy, Reliance proactively and almost single handedly created the capital-market ethos amongst the population at large—to enable it to tap into the collective savings of the economy.

"Subsequently and almost simultaneously the focus shifted somewhat, to develop employee expertise (through training, mentoring and hiring-in of experience.) The soft skills so obtained powered huge improvements in efficiency and quality which led to profitability.

"By putting in place an efficient communication network and organization process, Reliance was able to disseminate a vast and rapidly growing reservoir of knowledge and experience to aid in effective and efficient decision-making.

"All these factors converged to produce a product service offering that was superior, thereby creating a formidable customer franchise. This further enhanced the profitability and profit potential of the organization—feeding back into investor goodwill and setting up a self-sustaining virtuous cycle."

So, there you have the complete picture of the formation of the ethos of intellectual capital. These four factors are further elaborated throughout the report, thus giving a special dimension to the workings of the corporate giant in an energized boost to its own image and in the process creating a stimulus for the recipient of the report.

Balrampur Chini

Further inspiration comes from the "Stretch" philosophy of Balrampur Chini Mills. Stretch is the philosophy of the company, their baseline and also the attitude that reflects

The era of the integrated sugar complex has arrived

everything they do, according to their Managing Director Vivek Saraogi. It is used as the title of their Annual Reports; it is also a pocket sized document that is sent out to a few thousand people encapsulating anecdotes that have been compiled with great sensitivity. These anecdotes embody the Stretch philosophy, as you would apply it to everything from uncompromising integrity to stretch as a boon, as wisdom, as an education, as invincibility. It has inspired the depressed individual as well as the corporate chief alike.

The Annual Report for the year 2000-1 gives an overview of the sugar industry and the role of Balrampur in the new scenario of progressive de-regulation, the future of the industry in the international context and then goes into the Measurement of Value, the requirements of Corporate Governance, analytical reports and a focus on Community development. The 68-page report leaves no stone unturned, giving an invaluable picture without actually doing any pictorial spreads, which seem to continue to be popular with many FMCG companies.

In an earlier year, (1999-2000) this report was sent to shareholders as a two-part document, also under the Stretch banner. One was an Intangibles Document and the other a Corporate Statement which incorporated the Annual Report.

There were two remarkable features of both reports, which should go down in corporate reportage annals. The Corporate Statement highlighted the drop in profits with a detailed letter from Meenakshi Saraogi, the Joint Managing Director. In it, the reasons and circumstances that led to the drop were discussed. But what was also brought to the fore was how the company, because of its "Stretch" commitment, had made the best of a bad situation, its recoveries had been higher than average registered by other sugar mills and the profits higher than most manufacturers in the sugar industry. Managing Director Vivek Saraogi did a detailed question-answer statement, and, in their worst year of results, brought out the positive statement: "The most inspiring performance in the history of the company is under way."

The other notable feature was of the Intangibles Document presenting "an insight into non-conventional accounting that analysts have begun to use to sift between companies that are likely to emerge as value-creators over the long-term."

This document is divided into several sections. An insight is first provided into the booming middle class in India and its consumption patterns. It then goes into the attempts to add value to the company's business, a brand valuation exercise, and an analysis of intellectual capital and EVA.

Quite apart from the research and revelations, were the sheer magnificence of presentation, with opulent photography done by a leading photographer.

Navneet Publications

The introduction to the Annual Report of Navneet is like a children's playbook, horizontal rather than the traditional vertical in format. "We are in the business of growing minds," it says, adding, "growing profits is a by-product." Navneet, which has emerged as the premier educational products and services company of India with a copyrighted archive in excess of 2700 titles in various languages, begins in its Annual Report on a missionary note. It "reflects the sober responsibility with which we continue to attract the intelligence of thousands of children and students across

India. So that they may not jut study, but become enlightened citizens. So that they may not just examine, but also explore."

The pages unfold colourfully with illustrations as in a children's GK book, peppered with Did You Knows, on the side, but in essence giving a great deal of wise information from explaining the rationale of its presence and the markets it addresses to its community development initiatives to a highly transparent guide to its financials.

The transparency does not end here. The discussion on their Forward-looking Statements is further clarified to cover themselves by cautioning readers not to place undue reliance on these and hence to be vigilant about the fact that the statements have been qualified with words such as "anticipate" "projects" "intends". Showing that at no stage is there an absolute statement, but that the reportage is tempered with vigilance.

The Ideation of Annual Reports: A Leveraging of Knowledge

The whole ideation of the Balrampur Chini report, its concept, design, research and execution has been done by Trisys, a Kolkata-based research organization. It is from their stable that we have also accessed the Reliance and Navneet reports. Their focus on Corporate Governance started, as we have mentioned in another chapter, well before it was mandatory for companies to make these detailed statements in their Annual Reports. But more than that, the study of the methodology employed in their creation of Annual Reports shows how companies can leverage Annual Reports for better funding, recruitment, brand-building. Through their benchmarking with international standards of transparency, a corporate house can be perceived in a superior light and can have a better standing in the capital market.

Although based in Kolkata, it is not a city-centric organization and in fact the clients include companies like Dr. Reddy's and Lupin Labs, the sugar companies, a clutch of IT companies like BPL Mobile, NIIT, ETV channel, Balaji Telefilms and companies like Essar Shipping—all of whom have benefited from the "leveraging of knowledge" philosophy of Trisys.

The methodology involved in enhancing shareholder value through Annual Reports is most ably demonstrated by the techniques that Trisys employs. Itself an EVA company, Trisys has as its core competence the ekeing out of total shareholder and market-interface solutions for companies—through sound analysis and the application of this research. And it offers to redefine business strategy, giving a client more than just an Annual Report. Whether it be the Repertoire Analysis done for HMV or the Segments Analysis made for BPL, it has always exceeded the clients' brief.

Key to all this is the fact that it "speaks the language of the CEOs." Trisys goes to a client, not reactively, but to say "We will improve your market capitalization." Patherya says: "We are not mercenaries, but missionaries in the business."

This point, more than any other, speaks volumes for the tomes that it produces for companies, which, apart from having been benchmarked to Form 10K (the Appendage to Annual Reports in USA), have themselves become role models for other companies to aspire to. Benchmarking to global standards of transparency, has in fact, set many of the companies apart who have gone in for the production of Intellectual Capital Reports, like the one done for Reliance.

And even more so, the one for Krebs Biochemicals, whose perception and share prices soared following the publication of an ICR.

In another case, an Ambassador Report became a sort of "handshake document" which was sent, quite apart from shareholders, to financial analysts, collaborators, students, employees and the media.

Companies have recruited people of quality on the basis of their Annual Reports and a company like Thiru Arooran Sugars, was projected in such a manner that it got better funding and could raise finance at a considerably lower cost.

What are the new trends? Intangibles reports for, say, the construction industry where the level of credibility in terms of promises made and delivered can be low. Companies in this business could well do with an Intangibles statement to their buyers which would serve as an internal driver of excellence to protect their interests in the long term and assure them of continuous transparent communication.

The worry is in the misrepresentation and overstatement. The opportunity is in the distillation, analysis and dissemination of the knowledge base about a company to give it competitive edge. The downside is in the fact that the information given out by companies is not always wholly, credible or adequate. The fine print does not match the bigger picture. People often feel that a dressed-up elaborate report hides more than it tells. This is where the challenge of reportage with credibility will make for the right convergence.

While most annual reports report only the flattering parts, the embarrassing fine print is usually edited. A couple of recent exceptions have been the Kolkata-based Linc Pens & Plastics and Saregama India Limited. Despite reporting a 49 per cent increase in its profit after tax, Linc indicated that it had under-performed on the potential presented by the industry environment. In a similar vein, Saregama India indicated that it lost at least Rs 4 crores of profits through inefficient distribution.

There are numerous other Annual Reports which project an in-depth view of the company, in an almost no-holds barred manner; some of them highly pictorial, focusing from one year to the next on something that a company would like to highlight at the time, be it R&D or People Power or Technological Excellence or Community Enhancement projects.

All of these are tools that hold out challenges for the Corporate Communications professionals in any organization, just as their recipients, the shareholders and others on the mailing list, chosen with discretion, get a weighty, attractive document that is often preserved.

The visionary company should be able to find in these new vehicles of shareholder communication, fresh opportunities to use these as instruments of leverage, of goodwill generation, of enhanced perception for better market capitalization and as credible documents of intent.

Chairmen's Speeches

And what of Chairmen's speeches? There are less and less of these being published in newspapers, possibly as a measure of saving on expensive media costs. However, some of the major policy statement speeches still continue to be published prominently and circulated liberally. These are documents of intent, state-of-the-union comments and form the basis of both a review of past performance and a presage of events to come.

These speeches are meant to be delivered at the Annual

General Meetings of companies, but more often than not, being the policy documents they have turned out to be, these are published in full and distributed. A shorter version is spoken at the AGM.

Some of the outstanding examples of Chairmen's Speeches which are looked forward to, not just by the shareholders of that company, but the public at large, are those of the heads of ITC and Hindustan Lever Limited.

We asked a cross section of Public Relations Managers whether they ghosted the speeches of their Chairmen, and the general retort was an emphatic "No". They said that their chairmen were very clear, nay, even possessive, about creating this document, which would articulate corporate policy and impact on its image vis-a -vis the powers that be. Some, who asked not to be quoted, did say that they wrote most of the speeches and one or two spelt it out more candidly. The methodology was that they were asked to draft the speeches after a series of discussions with the chairman— the word game being the purview of the communicator and the meat of it coming from the chief himself.

The Content

The address of Y.C. Deveshwar at the 90th Annual General Meeting of ITC shareholders had as its theme ITC: A Commitment Beyond the Market. Apart from talking about the role of an "Indian" enterprise Mr Deveshwar's focus this time was on the fact that ITC employees were inspired by the "vision of enlarging its contribution to the Indian economy."

To quote further: "ITC believes that its aspiration to create enduring value for the nation provides the motive force to sustain growing shareholder value. Your Company practices this philosophy by not only driving each of its businesses towards international competitiveness, but by also consciously contributing to enhancing the competitiveness of the larger value chain of which it is a part."

The Chairman went on to elaborate on four sets of value chains to do with its paperboards, tourism, its rural partnership initiatives and its swerve to branded fashion and leisure wear. In the end was a message of how the employees of the company are willing to go that extra mile to make an enduring contribution to society and to create value for shareholders.

Such messages, bordering on the philosophical, must have come out of a consensus of commitment.

But with its emphasis in the "e-choupal" initiatives in the rural areas, was it mere lip service, or are these plans to be followed up? ITC's Corporate Communications head, S.H. Venkatramani elaborates on how these initiatives are not only spelled out, but being extensively implemented. To ensure quality, productivity and global competitiveness, today's initiatives are the setting up of 235 internet kiosks, and web portals in local languages to reach 1.5 lakh farmers—aqua culturists and soya and coffee farmers. In five years, the numbers projected are 1.5 million farmers, who will represent 70% of the purchasing power among all agriculturists.

The aim: to ensure getting produce more competitively and in this endeavour ITC is something of a brand ambassador and other companies have tied up with it to reach out through their distribution network.

The reason for going into such detail is to show the involvement of the communicator in the communication that is being formulated. Not just dealing with words. But with the concepts, to be able to better convey it to key publics.

M.S. Banga's vision in his Chairman's speech ("Food Revolution—A Win Win for Farmer & Consumer") was to focus on the need to capitalize on the successes of the green and white revolutions to a Food Revolution. A revolution where HLL could see itself as a key catalyst in creating a partnership web for the mutual benefit of farmer, consumer, industry and government.

In implementing this Food Revolution, Mr Banga proposed a three-pronged action-plan encompassing (a) precision farming to improve farm productivity within the current land-holding pattern; (b) creating a structure to facilitate growth of a vibrant food processing industry and (c) identifying various enablers for the model to work.

Ever since this document has seen the light of day, what has happened to change government thinking? The public and those will surely be interested in the actioning of the models suggested.

Shareholder Meets and Visits

Pampering the shareholder takes on various guises. Statutory requirements apart, companies have, in their bid to compete for shareholder support at a grassroots level, charted out different means of communication. Some of it to do with small meetings of select shareholder groups, others to do with more than just one annual communication, and yet others based on showcasing their factories and locations to shareholders.

No matter if he holds just a share or two. Most companies have to contend with tedious rambling queries of shareholders at annual general meetings. Some of them well researched and genuinely concerned with getting to the bottom of worries with regard to financials, production, ethics and so on. Many enjoy the sound of their own voices.

As Corporate Communications people, we have had to

humour them along the way, and in fact have developed a spirit of bonhomie with those who come year after year after year to AGMs to vent their views, and to partake of goodies that companies may dispense. This gift giving has decreased over a period of time, leaving the communications department with requests for plant visits, which, once institutionalized and given in to, becomes yet another PR exercise to be gone through.

The heartening part is when you hear of companies like ITC, whose share department prides itself on the fact that last year there were zero shareholder complaints, a record of sorts.

A Word for the Student

For the students of PR and new initiates, communication with shareholders is a challenge where it requires a close working with the accounts, finance, share department and of course the top management in case of chairmen's speeches.

The areas of creative (and sometimes routine) work involve

- Research, planning and sourcing of material for the Annual Report and Interim Report as well as publication of quarterly results
- The ideation and writing of the report. Stages of interaction: accounts/finance/treasury/share departments; advertising agencies and printers for design and execution
- Preparation of FAQs for AGMs
- Assistance in writing the Chairman's speech
- Creating audio visuals for the shareholder meets
- Planning shareholder visits to plants

- Helping the share department with shareholder complaints when required
- Interacting with the press for these occasions

Annual Reports should be no longer looked upon as documents of statutory necessity, but rather as statements of intent, vision, capability. And shareholder meets present immense creative potential.

7

HRD & Public Relations: Complementary Roles

The twenty-first century is looking at certain trends, where Corporate Communication must be viewed as playing a complementary and proactive role in Human Resource Management. With each Trend we have a corollary—an Elucidation. These are subjective evaluations, and may not be taken as gospel truth. On the other hand, they may be viewed as jumping off points for further lateral thinking.

In today's integrated and interlinked world, which has wired itself up in a web through the net and e-commerce, we cannot talk of Human Resource Development as a watertight service, distinct from the other functions of management. And corporate communication, which is a strategic arm of a management function, cannot also be set apart as a mere tool to be used in times of crisis or when going through the motions of projecting image on a mundane day to day basis.

Some of the current trends will show how HR and PR have taken on cross-functional roles.

Trend 1:

Crouching corporates; brash M-brats

One of the programmes that has seized most people from the inane couch potato to the millions of others who want a piece of glitz and quiz in their lives, is Amitabh Bachhan's Kaun Banega Crorepati . There is a knowledge-hunger, no doubt, but it is combined with a thirst for the monetary rewards to be gained. The first of those who managed to win that elusive crore was a youngster. Another youngster, less of a gambler, we would say, got a plum dollar job worth a crore a year when the headhunting corporations landed at his Institute of Management and lapped him up.

Today, with the appetite, expectation and knowledge base expansion of the new MBAs and other technically qualified students, the scene is a complete sellers market. Instead of students having to polish up their image, or hone their strategies for campus interviews, it is the corporates who are on the defensive. It is they who are trying to project themselves and lure the students into their set-ups with pay, perks and miles of promises.

Sky high salaries, sky-high expectations, faster turnover, managements reaching out to trainees and potential employees. What does this bode for the Human Resource Management experts, and, in tandem for their Public Relations counterparts?

Elucidation 1:

We see a definitive role of the Human Resource Development division in conjunction with Public Relations. HR professionals have to re-engineer training of MBAs because the cleverer you get and the more systems that are integrated into their system, the more difficult it becomes to come to terms with real world problems. The challenge therefore is for HRD to do the planning of job content, of training and development, of compensation packages, but it is here that communication of a structured kind becomes an imperative.

The Public Relations person has to project the company in a correct light, for with corporates muscling one another for campus attention, it is the company that communicates its policies better that is bound to catch the more competent fish.

What has happened in the modern day world of recruitment, is the attitudes and the rankings of companies by students through the day ranking system. Which means, those companies who manage to get Day One, net in the A-One students. A survey conducted in the top 14 B schools by a portal called coolavenues .com reported that though 209 companies visited the campuses, it took only 24 companies to pick up more than half of the outgoing batch. Who is ranking whom? The world is surely turning upside down!

Which bodes negatively for companies who will find that they can no longer be complacent about their standing in the corporate world or with the student community. Their reputations have to be polished in a sustained manner. The previous year's rankings, combined with current reputations are the essentials for companies to stay afloat in a student's lexicon. Hence the combined responsibility of HR and PR to keep in sync with student parameters of excellence.

Trend 2:

Proliferation of Training & Development: Power Perk or Productive Programming?

Changes in the business environment are rapid and unrelenting. Product life cycles have shorter spans, today's trends and technologies become yesterday's inventions and established and tested management practices—both in the running of companies and governments-is being challenged. Getting short shrift in all this is the individual, or "human capital" as some observers put it.

Many organizations, instead of taking advantage of technological developments and using technology as a tool, are using it as a substitute for the human being.

To overcompensate, companies have come up with training programmes, so immense in their outward reach, that the wood is lost for the trees.

Elucidation 2:

Training and Development: every institution needs it, does it. But what about the training of the trainers? Probably this is where the HR Department and the PR Department can come together in a vital synergistic fashion. And the HR division can draw upon the creative inputs of the corporate communicator, who should participate in the totality of the training activity and not merely write a press release on the subject.

What should the communication imperatives of trainers be?

Training programmes should definitely make for greater participation, be more tangible, more capable of being applied to real life situations. Trainers have to remain current, abreast and ahead of trends in management and have to make the environment conducive to attracting, motivating and retaining people. Job satisfaction, too bland and not comprehensive any more, might have to be replaced with what has been termed by some as "life satisfaction".

Today, with executives still continuing to put in long hours, it is a reflection of their needs not only for money and achievement but also for power and social relationships. Just take mere netsurfing time and graft it onto the official working hours, to see how the information gathering from this source becomes a major factor in job gratification.

The HRD chiefs of tomorrow will have to be more than just HRD specialists. They have to be business managers with specialization in human resources. While they possess knowledge, they must also possess concern for people that extra edge derived from empathy. Redundancy could set in with the new information age. So while new concepts may be welcomed from other countries, there is a need to be relevant, local, topical. To stop any redundancy, there is a perceived need to form a nexus between HRD and PR services. The ritualizing of T& D must give way to planned management and executive development programmes.

Trend 3:

Corporate Governance

Transparency demands that Human Resource Managers cannot live in ivory towers and that communicators cannot continue to belt out management platitudes to employees and to a vast number of publics who feed on a company and make up the corporate universe.

What are the implications of Corporate Governance? Why did corporates have to be governed under the rules of CG? The background is simple: a major security scam, followed by multinationals consolidating their ownership, the case of vanishing companies and the unfair trade practices in the stock markets. These led to the importance of Corporate governance within the corporate sector, financial institutions, enlightened business associations, regulating agencies and Government. Hence as we traverse the path of globalization and a market oriented economy and with heightened competition, the new realities are high costs of failure but higher rewards of success. The pressures to dilute value systems and have more flexible ethical postures are considerable. All these require corporates to devise, develop and implement structures and systems that enable a core of values against which actions are measurable and frameworked.

Elucidation 3

The climate of trust and confidence will come about with commitment of the board all right but also with participation of stakeholders in management. It will also require HRD inputs and communication consciousness to deliver transparent and timely corporate communication with shareholders.

Here we would like to bring in a concept called the Human Capital Index developed by consultants Watson Wyatt, which highlights HR practices that have maximum positive impact on employees and shareholders. It is, most of all, carried out in the spirit of transparency, which is the key element when we have talked about Corporate Governance.

The Watson Wyatt Index looks at quantifying links between good human capital management and superior shareholder returns. Their survey, which covered more than 400 US and Canadian publicly traded companies, found that a significant improvement in 30 key HR practices was associated with a thirty percent increase in market value.

These could be grouped under five key links:

1. Recruiting excellence
2. Clear rewards and accountability
3. A collegial and flexible workplace

4. Communications integrity
5. Prudent use of resources

So while it was found that companies like GE and Microsoft are the most stressful places to work in, they are the companies which are also doing something right since they figure among the best companies to work for. Here we would like to cite the importance of Corporate Mission and Vision strategies which 'once again we stress' should emanate from the hearts of the Human Resources Development people and from the pens of the Corporate Communicator, after an initial brainstorming with the CEO. It should not be written by him/her during his early morning walk or late night insomniacal ramblings.

Trend 4:

Globalization of career development

Developing global executives is becoming more and more important in today's globalized world. For instance, large chunks of IBM's income and of Colgate's income are now generated outside the USA. And managers are being groomed to be able to tackle opportunities around the world.

Proctor and Gamble's P&G College to train mid-level managers in global issues is well known. GM has programmes to send middle managers for three months to provide them global marketing experience. Colgate established a most elaborate programme some time ago. Its global marketing programme in management lasted two years after which trainees became associate product managers in different countries.

There is now a fierce cross-border competition for talent. The financial service and economic sectors see the fastest pace of change say heads of an executive search firm—Spencer Stuart.

Also what is truly transnational today? For instance the worldwide chief operating officer of IT and strategic business consulting company Cap Gemini Ernst and Young— Paul Hermelin—talked recently about a centre set up in Mumbai to combine global knowledge and local productivity in a powerful way to ensure rapid delivery of solutions to clients worldwide. They help companies create, connect and evolve.

Elucidation 4:

What are the indicators for us in Communications? Where does that leave us? Obviously with an opportunity to do some heavy R&D for executives who are being positioned around the world, to do the homework of the cultural situations and backgrounds of countries where CEOs and other levels of executives will go in a merged or a transnational company. Being correctly advised is preferable to landing headlong in a situation and making costly mistakes for the company's image and bottomline.

Trend 5:

The Island Individual: a product of the Information Age

It can be called the TITO syndrome: Technology in, Teacher Out. Portal, vortal or mortal—all of the new technologies are in a sense making for a more inward looking individual. For although he is more wired than ever before, he is becoming a net addict, to whom the information can be culled by just clicking on google.com. Every subject will leap out at him from the computer and even if he is searching for a linked word, the thesaurus in the computer will in a trice come to his aid.

This is becoming a malaise, and while it has its numerous advantages, the responsibility of the communicator in a total corporate set up cannot be diminished.

Elucidation 5:

In India, existing wisdom defines the typical Internet user as a man 15-34 years old, either a college student or an office goer, belonging to one of the top six cities with a reported MHI of Rs. 10,000. He is most likely to access the Internet from outside his home, say office or college or from an Internet server.

Things are also projected as changing with home usage more than doubling this year, more women coming online. Thus detailed mappings have begun, which could make the HR person sit up and take notice of how to track this type of employee and how to steer him or her to more productive areas, without wasting valuable office hours—stolen hours to be precise.

Trend 6:

Shrinking Companies and the WAP-enabled Workplace

Some HRD experts refer to the seamless offices of today as the Anytime Anywhere Workplace. Another terminology would be the Virtual workplace, which we have covered in Book One, Chapter 8.

With corporates demerging and merging, consolidating, going through the re-engineering process, the trend that is grabbing the imagination of the new age employer and the individual employee, therefore, is the actual, physical workplace. There seems to be a tendency to do one of several things—

a) have flexible working hours
b) have no fixed place of work, and use the laptop and PC and WAP technology to work from home
c) to be wired from any place in the world, so that elaborate offices do not have to be set up in distant lands and a multinational company could end up employing far less people for far more effective solutions

Elucidation 6:

In this new scenario, we have a worry on our hands. Will we see a shrinking of the Personnel function? Of the Human Resource Manager who has become a business centre head of sorts? Of the Corporate Communications expert who is integrating the internal and external communication needs of companies?

We see it not as a threat, or as a lessening of the importance of the HR and PR functions. The prospects are in fact more challenging, the creativity more demanding of solutions.

From a reality perspective, we have to move towards a virtual viewpoint. One where the comfort cocoons of the workplace have to be kept up in a manner where the employee still feels he belongs. These functions will become more and more advisory, but not disintegrated. There will be an objective "from the outside" role where the training and development programmes will achieve a quicker focus.

There will have to be reinventions of hiring processes, of communication strategies. The ultimate responsibility of managing and developing people will be that of the line managers—the functional and divisional heads who are expecting results with the assistance of people under them.

Line managers therefore will have to equip themselves

with the art of developing people, motivating them and managing their performance.

Issue management will be a major thrust, and IR-HR-PR expertise will have to be stretched to evaluate changes in environment and evolve appropriate business strategies. And HR people, even more than trying to assist the Nowhere, No-place manager to readjust and acquire new skills, will have to prop him up to live in a continual state of readiness to change and modify, in keeping with the dictum: Change is the only constant thing in this world.

The ultimate lesson is that as long as human beings and not robots people an organization, the manager of this body of human resource has to lurk somewhere in the picture. As does the communication expert.

8

The Lobbyist as Communicator

---

*The lobbyist is more than just a fixer. Whether it is in the corridors
of power in the government, or as an advocate for citizens' rights or
for a specific cause, the function is a critical one, which comes under
the purview of Corporate Affairs in many companies.*

Even in the wake of a grave human crisis, PR battles are fought
to the bitter end. Thus, in the wake of the Massacre of
Manhattan, as we marvelled at the shifting bases of influence,
Pakistan's image vis-a-vis Washington got a huge lift up by
its ubiquitous and well-oiled PR machine. Within days of the
collapse of the twin towers, senators, columnists and eminent
America watchers were talking about the "bold and fearless
decision" of Pakistan and its "commitment to peace" and
calling the country, where some of the terrorists might have
had their early lessons, the "old and reliable friend".

In contrast, the Indian counterparts continued to dish
out clichés and suffered a defeat close on the heels of the
loss of face gleaned from the Agra summit.

The question that comes to mind is, should India not step up its PR efforts in Washington? In terms of both money spent and a heightened aggressive, proactive stance? A report published in India Watch by Krishan Khanna talks about how Indian's Public Relations spending in the USA should be increased substantially. The author sees India's PR expenditure in relation to other countries as grossly inadequate.

According to his estimates, which he bases on discussions with NRIs in USA and other parts of the world, Pakistan spends about US$ 10 million on lobbying; Israel's spend is US$100 million, the same as that of China, while India spends only a million dollars.

In order to lobby with various senators, advisors, in Washington, Think Tanks, Universities, NGOs and the American media, for the size and complexity of a country like India, the spend should be 25 times more at least. Khanna expands on what NRIs in USA say about the advantages of appropriate PR spend. NRI Republicans have, he claims, mentioned that since they are on President George Bush's council of CEOs, it may be possible to push through a thought process, that India, the largest democracy in the world, should get grants of US$10 billion per year, say for 4 years! For this, a proper PR plan and PR budget has to be allocated. "Our PR should be tilted towards the Economy, Trade, Tourism, Heritage of India, Disaster Management, Spirituality of India and Military and Defence of India. In that order," he emphasizes. Adding that, by following the example of Chinese NRC's, India could tap in some generous funding from its own NRIs into investing for India's growth.

What is the picture as perceived by well known correspondent Chidanand Rajghatta, writing for *The Times of India* from Washington? Writing on this scene in USA, in the *Sunday Times of India*,(26 August 2001) he gives us a candid view of Washington and the World of Lobbying as he sees it today. He says:

"In New Delhi they are called fixers. Washington has a much more respectable term for them lobbyists. But quite unlike the safari-clad sleaze bags in India mouthing off and making out in front of hidden cameras, America's lobbyists are an impressive lot.

Genuinely well-connected, they are among the capital's movers and shakers. Typically, lobbyists are engaged by various "interest groups" representing businesses, a profession, and even labour unions and foreign countries and organizations. Last year, various such entities spent more than $1.5 billion on lobbying in Washington. Lobbying itself is a fairly well regulated activity, although there have been frequent murmurs of disapproval about the clout lobbyists wield and the purpose they use it for.

Lobbyists provide access to decision-makers, monitor and influence important legislation, provide knowledge, expertise and analysis, and generally lubricate the wheels of government to the advantage of their clients. Of course, lobbyists are neither saints nor scientists. But the fact that they are part of a recognized profession (there is even an American League of Lobbyists: ALL which lobbies on behalf of the lobbyists), gives it some respect and legitimacy."

He traces the formal act of hiring a lobbying firm for India to 1993. We recollect, too, how in that year, Siddhartha Shankar Ray was our ambassador in Washington, and we were extremely surprised at the engaging of the services of the firm of Springer, Rafaelli, Speer and Smith for US$ 46,000 a month. At the time, we did not realize the implications or the importance of such firms. Today, we are told, the firm of

Verner Liipfert, one of the top firms in Washington, has been contracted to the job. And apparently the days of India being bit players in Washington are gone. He sees the role of smaller intermediaries, additionally, representing Indian entities from software sultans to steel makers and basmati growers who may "want to get the hang of Washington."

There are also new sets of people representing industry associations like the CII in Washington, who will be able to project a sane, business-like picture of India, and get the credibility that industrialists and business-people from India deserve.

Somewhere, the ugly, cigar-chomping lobbyist, who wines and dines the nations' lawmakers and fattens their purses (as Jeffrey Birnbaum puts it in his book on Lobbying) is increasingly giving way to the ones with more "potent skill"—the economists, lawyers, direct-mail and telephone salespeople, Public Relations experts, pollsters, economists and even accountants. These are the people who "bend the political process on behalf of the richest business interests in the country."

We are also concerned, not just about lobbying, in Washington, and in New Delhi, something which a few Perception Management agencies, and liaison experts— individuals specially appointed for the purpose—are tackling, but also about lobbying by special interest groups. On the one hand, there are individual crusaders, campaigning against the creation of new dams, and on the other are powerful groups representing big business who have made their voice heard over issues, but are still in the reckoning to change governmental legislations.

There are the single voice campaigners carrying lonely causes; or causes that have a limited following (People for Animals); or environmental crusaders (Narmada Bachao) or large corporations seeking to minimize huge duties, creating an awareness of the impact of their products on the larger growth of the nation or companies coming into the country and seeking understanding from government. Can lobbying reverse cabinet decisions?

BOOK FOUR:

A la Carte:
Case Studies

1

Rural Rehabilitation: Making the Village Voice Heard Louder

Most companies have done yeoman work in their plant-peripheral areas. Focussing on rural development has been a priority with many corporates. We have taken the liberty of quoting the example of the Tata Steel Rural Development Society, because it is a structured model and has worked for two decades. The example of Usha Beltron's Krishi Gram Vikas Kendra is another laudable one. Both have one feature in common—the involvement of employees in the projects just as much as they have involved the villagers themselves and given back the initiative to them.

Tata Steel Rural Development Society

Whenever it becomes incumbent on you to do something it takes the whole zip out of the effort. If Government guidelines were not present for compulsory reportage of rural development projects in their Annual Reports, companies would probably put a lot more effort into getting out into their sylvan surroundings to scatter the seeds of their largesse.

Our findings in fact show that companies have made their rural presence felt for many decades now. But they do not publicize their involvement as much as they do their urban events in art, sport, music, dance, theatre, seminars and civic spruce-ups.

Some of the work that is done rurally is often inward looking, which benefits the community of workers in factories that are in backward locations. Other companies extend this to embrace the plant-peripheral community to villagers. Often, this could be because of a particular industry generating pollutants around; hence the need to look after the surroundings, to turn guilt into greening the environment and the souls of those at the receiving end.

A lot of time, though, companies feel the need to get into underdeveloped areas and give the village yokel a chance to become more market-conscious. We could question this frenzy of companies to help villagers, who may be quite content, thank you, to carry on peaceably. But companies which have well-developed rural programmes see the need, not only to give a man a fishing rod and teach him how to fish, but also how to sell the fish profitably.

While recognizing the need for and the possible benefits of such an ideal symbiotic relationship between industry and the community at large, you are still left wondering how the citified management expert can bring his learning to bear on an alien, rural situation.

What, for instance, did a company like Tata Steel have to offer to its rural audience when it started out the Tata Steel Rural Development Society? The company said, "Just as large industries have been involved in the setting up of ancillary and small-scale industries in their neighbourhood, could they not go out a little further and use their knowledge and expertise in selected rural areas for providing greater employment opportunities to the working population and help them carve out a better life for themselves?"

Granted that participation from the corporate sector could be in many form—land, labour, lucre. And enrichment of village life could be a major unselfish consideration.

Does does this really benefit villagers, who could be quite content with their ongoing systems of working? Does it not sometimes muddy up the tranquil waters of a rural situation when a corporation goes in with money and the verve (and nerve, some say!), to plant what they feel are the seeds of progress. How much involvement is there actually by a company in the work they undertake? Those fishing rods they hand over to the villagers could get brittle with time unless the corporation which has doled them out has sat and angled with the recipient and seen both the downside and the benefits of their rural plans.

A classic example of a deliberate attempt to assist in the promotion and growth of the rural economy is the setting up of the Tata Steel Rural Development Society (TSRDS). Their originators believed that no rural development could be meaningful unless the inputs provided by an outside agency could create a permanent village asset and inspired villagers to become self-reliant. This could only be achieved through the active participation of the villagers in the developmental process.

Perhaps this what we could be looking for—the participative angle and the idea of letting the rural folk continue the good work after the initial corporate impetus.

The basic intention of the Tata initiative was to improve the overall socio-economic condition of the rural populace. Fundamentally, this was through two or three routes. Instituting a replicable model of village development, establishing a self-sustaining process of integrated rural development and having a catalytic role in mobilizing the resources of governmental and other agencies.

TSRDS set about getting a community profile to catalogue information on their cultural, sociological, political and economic structures. These findings then formed the basis of a course of action which sought to establish and promote cottage industries, impart technical training to village youth and see the formation of allied vocational training centres, such as dairy, pisciculture, piggery, poultry, and community forestry. Making soft loans available to enterprising youth and womenfolk of the village for a variety of self-employment schemes also fell within the purview of the scheme, as did agriculture and crop extension.

Their publications make fascinating reading. The highlights of the achievements of each unit are published separately. A typical publication lists the activities under such heads as Agricultural Extension, Animal Husbandry, Drinking Water, Educational Programmes, Forestry, Health and Hygiene, Irrigation, Link Road, Sports and Cultural Activities, Women's Development Programme. For instance, you can find out how many goats were distributed to how many farmers, how many kitchen gardens planted, the number of children immunized or the length of roads constructed and how many villages are covered under these heads. And then, the names of the collaborative agencies and what they have provided is also made available.

The reason for us to focus on this aspect is to show that a scheme of this sort requires verbalizing and dissemination. Such companies, after a point of time, are not trying to shine individually, but are happy to share their experience and modules for others to take on. The gainer is a community of people who needed the initial boost to get them to a level from where is no way to go but forward.

Today, two decades later, TSRDS efforts impact approximately 650 villages in and around their business locations in Jamadoba, West Bokaro and Noamundi, in Jharkhand and Sukinda, Bamnipal, Joda and Gopalpur in Orissa. A cross-functional team of 195 full-time professionals and trained social workers and 11 full time doctors depute by Tata Steel implement the three interventions—Empowerment, Income Generation and Health and Hygiene. The network span of TSRDS is at a national, international and government level and the awards have been highly prestigious ones.

Most of all, as Shakti Sharma, of Tata Steel, one time part of the Public Relations set-up and now totally involved with the Rural Development Society says, "The project has gained its own momentum and has its inbuilt motivations, whether it be the skill development aspects, the freedom from hunger or the better healthcare practices and the new attitudes of self-reliance that have percolated to rural communities. Tata Steel has been a facilitator. But we continue to be involved, emotionally, with funding, with commitment because we have to give back something to the very fields and rural habitations that sustain us."

The Krishi Gram Vikas Kendra

When Usha Beltron decided to launch its Krishi Gram Vikas Kendra (KGVK) in 1977, it could not have foreseen that its work would touch 9 villages and 8000 families, apart from involving a team of 70 experts in the fields of agriculture, horticulture, social forestry, soil conservation, livestock management, medicine and veterinary management. Farm practices in the region addressed have dramatically improved, as have incomes.

The Community Development Reports are assiduously published by the Company every year. The documenting of their effort is an exercise in projecting their efforts within a cloak of modesty, and yet with a pride in the model farms, animal husbandry units, health sub-centres, cottage industry initiatives, social forestry programmes, primary and vocational education that they have evolved.

The Managing Director, who is the president of the Krishi Gram Vikas Kendra, humbly declares in the document "What we are doing in Bihar is a drop in a vast ocean. To that extent the work does not deserve this document. On the other hand, we recognize that there are a number of companies, NGOs, governmental agencies and individuals who have the capacity to do more than we have. Let this document serve to inspire, albeit in a modest way, so that we can all join hands and become partners in progress and help the state regain its rightful place in the national community. And, in turn, help India regain her rightful place in the international parliament of communities."

The work is not overstated, but the push and the inspiration for others to come into the fray is exemplary. The raising of living standards, the helping of people to evolve and adopt integrated and indigenous processes by which they can assume responsibilities to manage their own resources, comes through as the essence of the community investment initiative of this company.

Communicating this in a highly attractive, readable form, with a deep insight and human angles to it, gives such documents credibility and marketability, and that is why we picked it as an example. Both of how to communicate creatively and correctly and also as an instance of how individual inspirational acts of development has affected the quality of life. And how the motivation levels of villagers have undergone dramatic changes.

2

Banking on Goodwill

Are Banks consciously embarking on a policy of giving back to a community from which they secure their business? Being socially conscious has its benefits as much as its responsibilities and problems and the less ad hoc it is the better for the giver in the long term. There can be no substitute for planned altruism, as the examples here show.

The friendly neighbourhood Bank offering personalized service for small depositors is no longer there merely to mop up small savings. It is busy mopping up your front door instead, for you, the customer, have become part of a larger scheme of things. The Bank is not merely taking your money from you, but is now keen on putting money into sponsoring art exhibitions, music conferences, horse racing, golf, and many other areas, which weave its image in with the fabric of the community.

This was never so. The Bank provided a host of financial services, interacting with an individual or a corporation in direct proportion to his stake in the game. Today, there is

no let-up in the regular Banking activity of resource mobilization. In fact, for the small depositor, there are new schemes every day that we come across on hoardings, through direct mail along with Bank statements, on stand-up billboards on the Bank premises, in newspaper and magazine advertisements.

But additionally, people are beginning to see the names of their Banks emblazoned on traffic dividers and traffic islands and garbage bins, latched on to scholarships, and appended to city events never associated with financial institutions before.

What has changed, and how has it all changed for Banks? Have they suddenly realized that they need to garner new goodwill from the community and hence, with a slick signature of a cheque, are ready to buy it? Or is the involvement a more planned one?

Are Banks consciously embarking on a policy of giving back to a community from which they secure their business? There is no direct transaction involved as would be the case at a Bank counter. A Banker is better able to put down in terms of figures the return on investment he would expect from participating in a community relations programme or a sponsored event, which it would have a lien on.

Hence, although the events that Banks undertake can sometimes be one-off affairs done for reasons emanating from the top, by and large, most Banks are now pledging their names and money to longer term commitments.

The questions that will be asked (by those who always question motivations behind good deeds) are whether Banks are going into events for the immediate benefits they offer or are they meant for more recognition? We must stress that no corporate body, and particularly not a body in the service sector, gives away its money for the sake of pure philanthropy.

Rather, these are events to get coverage, to become known, as a celebration of a Bank's other face. For a sponsored event is by its very nature, something done to elicit comment and spur on the image of the body putting its generosity on the line. It is, to that extent, not a donation, nor an endowment. It devolves on the Public Relations department to put up, not only the proposal in monetary terms, but also the returns expected, through press coverage, a pat on the back by local government, approving nods from the principals overseas and good cheer amongst those benefiting from the tournament.

CitiBank

When we queried CitiBank about their schemes, we found a well-focussed programme of community support launched in June 1997 to focus on micro credit organizations working to empower under-privileged urban women through income generation.

The programme is based on the philosophy of self-reliance. It works, not in isolation by the Bank, but with five identified partners who are not-for-profit organizations:

- Society for the Promotion of Area Resource Centres (SPARC) in Mumbai. SPARC works in alliance with the National Slum Dwellers Federation (NSDF) which has a membership of 3.5 lakhs households in 32 cities and towns spread over 6 states and 1 union territory in India.
- Friends of Women's World Banking (FWWB) in Ahmedabad. FWWB India is an apex organization providing loan and capacity building support to NGOs

providing financial services to women in low income households.

- Working Women's Forum (WWF) in Chennai, a nationally and internationally renowned union of women workers in the informal sector, the Working Women's forum (WWF) is a mass movement of over 3,50,000 poor women today

- Sasha in Kolkata Since it's beginning in 1978, Sasha, a craft making organization, perceived it's objective as supporting women's income generation through microcredit. Today Sasha works with 15 craft groups in 15 communities in Bengal. Nearly $250,000 has been given to 55 craft groups

- Sharan in New Delhi. Sharan (Society For Serving The Urban Poor), was established in 1979. With 22 years experience in the development sector, it is a progressive organisation working in the slums and resettlement colonies of New Delhi.

All these partners extend microcredit to low-income women in urban areas. They have successfully organised women's collectives and channelled financial resources to those women who are otherwise left out of the purview of the Banking sector.

This Community Support Program stands out in the financial services industry in India as highly effective and sustaining, combining active employee participation and cause related advocacy. The idea is to provide CitiBank employees with a vehicle to volunteer their time and skills should they choose to do so. Based on the concept of volunteerism, the employees have grouped themselves into teams in response to need areas identified by the NGOs.

The various teams are Marketing Advisory, Advocacy,

Employee Communication, Housing Advisory, Cause-related marketing, Technology, Financial Advisory and Regulatory Advisory.

The key aspects of the program are: Funding, Volunteerism, Cause-related Marketing, the last-named involving customers.

One of the unique successes has been the effort of the Housing Advisory team. Working with SPARC in Mumbai, they have structured a cross- border financial partnership for Community Housing. This loan forms part of the Bank's strategy to support low cost housing in the Community Support Program. The main borrower in this transaction is SPARC (Society for Promotion of Area Resource Centres), which is one of CitiBank's partners in its Community initiatives.

Given the focus by the government on low cost housing, this transaction represents a real effort on the part of CitiBank to work on this agenda of the government. This transaction is an effort to create a template for financing developmental organizations in order that they may raise funds from financial institutions through a structure that is saleable.

The project is structured as a project finance transaction against a lien on sales proceeds from the saleable area of the project, and partly against cash collateral. Of the loan amount Homeless International (a UK based NGO) will provide a part guarantee (about 20%) to CitiBank in India. On the strength of this guarantee, and based on the due diligence and processes set up here with SPARC, CitiBank will advance a loan to SPARC/Rajiv Indira Society to help them develop this project.

CitiBank stresses that it is not a handout scheme that it has devised, but a hands-up.

HSBC

Our main aim was to know if Banks are institutionalizing their community support and philanthropic activities or merely scattering their fire through sporadic help. The good news is that HSBC aims to concentrate at least 75% of its funding on the areas of education and the environment, in support of communities around the world.

In their efforts, the other plus point to note is that the Bank is keen to involve its experienced and supportive staff in building and developing mentoring programmes and offering career guidance and job internships for talented young people.

In its support of environmental initiatives, the Bank feels that today's society should not be fulfilled at the expense of future generations and that sustainability is paramount. They are one of the founding signatories to the United Nations Environment Programme on which their own environmental policy is based.

The Bank is sensitive to the cultural and historical traditions of the markets in which it operates. The work at a local level with established partners and those with new ideas, in delivering the programmes that are best for the community.

Some of their community initiatives in Kolkata, Mumbai and Sri Lanka have as their target underprivileged children and imparting teaching and training at various levels. For instance, the Future Hope programme cares for 50 homeless street children of Kolkata and the HSBC staff volunteer their time to help with additional fund raising, particularly for the gifted boys to compete in international school rugby tournaments.

In Mumbai, the Prem Dan opportunity centre has given hope to thousands of children over the past 20 years. The

Bank supports the founder, Sister Felicity and her staff who currently teach vocational skills to more than 800 abused children in the centre's three purpose-built schools and provides a home for them. Also in Mumbai, the Happy School and Home for the Blind takes in children as young as two, teaching, feeding and clothing them. The project seeks to offer practical vocational training for their future.

In Sri Lanka, HSBC funds salaries of 20 specially trained teachers who coach nearly 200 deaf children at St Jóseph's Deaf School, lessons that help children expand their vocabulary and communication skills.

State Bank

The State Bank of India must be amongst the most talked about because of its sheer size. It still rests on its laurels of having got into the Guinness Book of Records for its over 6,000 offices that form the largest network of any commercial Bank in the world. The SBI is divided into "circles". A dozen of them exist, each with a few hundred branches under its purview. Each of these circles has a Public Relations Manager and a whole department under him. They coordinate their work in conjunction with the Bank's policy guidelines and with those received from a centralized PR department.

Its Public Relations activities are mentioned in this chapter because it is not only by its sheer size that it has made an impact with its publicity activities which are multi-media and multi-lingual, but it has also been philanthropic in a planned way. Apart from publicizing its own services in an extensive manner, it has used its muscle to support large sporting events. A few years ago, a coffee-table book on Kolkata was published by the Bank. Unlike other Banks, which merely printed their names on fat glossies costing thousands of rupees to select customers, this book was put together by the Bank as an original work. This was an excellent way of showing its involvement with the community.

The New Communication from Public Sector Banks

It is a new wind blowing through the corridors of some public sector Banks which are now getting more transparent and more committed in their communication. The Corporation Bank Chairman's speech for instance, this year shared its long-range plan, a Vision 2006. Among other things, its social concerns were highlighted.

Rehabilitation relief was of course top of their agenda, for the Gujarat earthquake victims, but since we are dealing with the identified areas of concern, mention must be made of some special initiatives, like the series of students meets in select cities to motivate the younger generation, on the one hand and bringing out a bulletin for senior citizens on the other to help them voice their concerns and an Economic Development Foundation responsible for giving out large scale grants for infrastructure development to schools.

Communicating the Negatives

The period of the "scam" or the securities market scandal was a harrowing one for the Banks that were accused of an involvement in the process. Standard Chartered was one which came in for the largest slice of adverse publicity and there was no way in which it could keep the press wolves away from its doors. Seeing that reportage in newspapers and magazines could hardly be suppressed, it took the next best step.

It issued an eight-page statement as a direct mailer to

its numerous customers all over the country, in a document titled "A Commitment to India." The contents were in a question-answer format, one with the Stanchart CEO on short and long-term strategies for India, and another with the Bank's Special Representative for India, explaining how the Bank was defrauded and giving the measures being taken to prevent further occurrence. There was also an article by a well-known financial journalist on the Bank's emphasis on growth to give the document a measure of objectivity.

It was a kind of two-in-one brochure, part of it a corporate projection and some of it clearing the air of all the accusations. First published in Euromoney, it was subsequently reprinted and sent out in India, with a covering letter from the heads of each of its centres in the country. This is possibly the best way that the Bank could acquit itself of its seeming guilt in the eyes of its customers and showed some fine planning in the creation of the document where every aspect of doubt was answered.

Saying No

Just when or where does this largesse stop? When Banks initiate their own projects or find their own pet areas to prop up, there is no problem. It all starts when you open the floodgates to requests from the community, when social service groups come with the most "viable" projects which would make a good loan application look like a schoolboy's workbook. Whom do you yes to and which ones get a refusal?

The very act of starting to give out donations should be a matter of planning by the Public Relations department or, if such a department does not exist, then by the customer-services people. Some may be employee-driven, others could be commitments to customers, and yet others could be for causes that stand on their own merit, but which do not get funding from other sources. Each Bank should be governed by its own compulsions. And at the point when philanthropy has to be stoppered, the way to say no would be by suggesting alternatives rather than turning the hopeful a way.

Being socially conscious has its benefits as much as its responsibilities and problems and the less ad hoc it is the better for the giver in the long term. There can be no substitute for planned altruism, for reactive Public Relations activity can only be waste of resources. Planning for philanthropy is as important as a stratplan for crisis management. A service organization like a Bank with its inbuilt advantages of customer interaction should come up with a long-term game plan for its extra-curricular bounty, sharing something that benefits community causes first and its own self-interest thereafter.

3

The Media and the Media-user—and the Public Better not be Damned

---

Truth, transparency, credible information. The Public Relations practitioner and those on the other side in the Media, need to trade in this all the time. We look at the new, non-adversarial roles. Also at how the Media is reaching out to serve the community beyond providing news and views

---

When both the corporate communicator and the newspaper reporter are dispensers of stories, shouldn't they have an empathy towards each other's approaches or problems? Ideally, yes. Why, then, do companies continue to churn out unusable press releases and concomitantly, newsmen persist in publishing semi-informed stories about companies?

Our question is—do they really? Is the scene as amateurish as this? Look at the sophistication and the advancement in the way Media views the progress of corporations and, in reverse, the more reverential way in

which Public Relations people dialogue with the Media. It is hardly what you would call adversarial.

And yet, some grey areas remain. So, we have to continue to talk about the responsibilities of the Media towards business and also the devolvement on the Public Relations industry to speak the truth. When it comes down to a question of writer versus writer, the publication of a short statement or an in-depth story on a company is dependent largely on veracity from the PR person's side and the will to interpret from the other side.

If this sounds ponderous and convoluted, the heart of the problem, for a problem does exist, is the truthfulness factor. In this chapter, we seek to re-examine the "correct" means of putting it across to the Media and also look at how the Media can and should be more constructive in its approach to business information.

We hark back to the days of Ivy Lee, and the move away from pure press agentry. This scenario comes to us from turn-of-the-century America. Lee, a young reporter writing in the shadow of Wall Street, in the era of muckraking, decides he has had a raw deal, monetarily, and moves over to the other side of the fence. He sees the world of business as not only providing him more succour financially, but also as a world, which needs articulation by professionals. He has already viewed it from the other side but now seeks to believe that corporations have to come out of their veil of secrecy and communicate honestly with newspapers to "get their case directly to the people."

He makes his famous Declaration of Principles to the press: "This is not a secret press bureau. All our work is done in the open... Any editor will be assisted most cheerfully in verifying directly any statement of fact."

Ivy Lee saw press agentry as being contrary to the public interest even if it did get across the client's message, which did not always reveal the whole truth. Most textbooks quote some of his work for clients as being trailblazers in that time. The case of the anthracite coal strike is one where reporters were given free access to information, although in a well-controlled manner where they didn't actually come to the meetings on the strike, but were able to get the equivalent of today's press release.

He was also ahead of his time in issue management when he went to work for the Rockefellers. They were being heavily criticized in the press because of a massacre during a strike in the Colorado coalfields, which they part-owned. Lee's role in getting Rockefeller to come face to face with the facts succeeded greatly in erasing the petty, conniving rich-guy image to one of benevolence. The press began to view Rockefeller as someone contributing constructively to the US economy and their attitudes changed significantly towards him. In their book, *Effective Public Relations,* Scott Cutlip and Allen Centre maintain that Ivy Lee was "among the first to realize the fallacy of publicity unsupported by good works and to determine that performance determines the kind of publicity a "client gets." He changed the concept of what he did from "pure agency" to "a brains trust for the businesses we work with."

What Ivy Lee did in 1914 is something we saw happen in a surprisingly similar manner, several decades later. This is the story of tractor giants, Escorts Limited, who were suddenly faced with spectre of a takeover by a non-resident Indian, Swraj Paul. We get the story best from the then PR manager of Escorts, Murad Baig. He maintains that it must have been one of the biggest corporate battles ever to hit the business scene in the eighties. When things got really steamy and the corporate raider made a lot of allegations, they were sought to be countered in a dignified way. The "way" was to have the Escorts Chairman, H.P. Nanda, meet groups of key financial journalists so that they could see in person the man who had created the company with blood, sweat and tears. This is much in the manner of the Rockefeller interaction with the press.

There is a great difference in the way in which the companies communicate with the press when they have good fortune stories to convey and the communication during critical times of a strike, a crash, a takeover, a closure, an uncomfortable revelation, the hiring and de-hiring of key personnel. A company which has a heady story to tell goes all out to do so with press conferences and with separate, exclusive interviews granted by the heads of companies or of the division concerned. The press gets a readymade story which can credibly fill the business columns. It is hunky dory for both sides.

In fact, with the closer relationships having developed between chief executives and newspaper representatives, they periodically and mutually keep in touch. It is not unusual for a CEO to pick up the phone and talk to a reporter or a correspondent he has been vibing with to give him a piece of news about the company. The reporter's sense of involvement increases and although he may not be held to writing something immediately, he either files away the information for the appropriate moment or uses it right then if the occasion warrants it. Journalists are no longer one-time news reporters. They follow stories through and keep up a continuity if interest in the fortunes of companies, provided of course, the cooperation from the other side is enthusiastic and informed.

Business papers today are getting into detailed, developmental and analytical writing. They need as much information as they can lay their hands on to do X-rays of share issues that are forthcoming, or analyse the effects of a merger or ponder over the prospects of new companies making global issues or of corporations going into diversified fields. The more information a Public Relations practitioner can cull and pass on, the more credible will be the end output.

The real problems that a PR spokesperson can encounter are during a crisis, when sanity takes a back seat. That is when companies, from being lavish in their sharing of information and lunches with the press, suddenly turn tight-lipped, dodging direct interaction and giving out the party line.

That is when the true mettle of a practitioner becomes apparent. A guilty company will have its guilt further endorsed if it doesn't speak. The responsibility on the PR person is at its peak in dealing with such a situation. In theory, the way to deal with communications in a crisis situation is to keep in mind a few basic steps. Being fully informed about the facts of the case is at the heart of it.

Additionally, there is a need to anticipate what journalists will ask and be prepared with arrangements for the right people to answer them, particularly the CEO, who should be available to talk and clarify matters. Nothing is worse than a CEO in hiding. What do you hide? If a situation is being reported falsely, there is a superb opportunity to give the real facts. If the matter has just been blown out of proportion, but there is an element of truth in the allegations, there is also need to communicate. And if the fingers pointing at the company are completely justified in doing so, then the need to plead guilty does become necessary. But explanations on why or how events happened and what the company is doing to take corrective measures, become vital. If expensive action needs to be taken by companies, as for instance with contaminated food products being withdrawn from shelves, the damage control exercise would more than justify the cost.

Unfortunately, a lot of time, the relationship with the Media is crisis-oriented, where it ought to be planned, without deceit, and with the idea of conveying information candidly. So it is always going to be old techniques surfacing, and new ones being tried out. Always, at the core, will be the message, in The Bard's words that "truth will out."

Can a press representative be bought? Why should purchase and barter enter the agenda anyway? Buying the odd lunch or dinner for a Media person is perfectly permissible, but anything more durable than that, and seen to be more lavish, could only mean that there is something which requires either a cover-up or an inflated splash. Journalists are getting better at our own game than we think. They are also more sophisticated, responsible, receptive. One pressman recently even refused packets of biscuits given out at a press conference I was involved with. Another, a news editor, wouldn't dream of lunching with clients, or even drinking, but yet was available to come and talk when his friend, the local Air-India chief in Bahrain, called him over to the house to meet me. This newspaperman even had the courtesy to drop me back to my hotel, en route giving me a total run-down on the Bahraini economy.

My other friends in the press are people who give us information, urbane guys and gals who play golf, entertain rather than be entertained and are ready to give a sympathetic ear to a new development with a client without being the perpetual adversary.

The point is that both the image and the needs of the newsman have changed. It is a change from the notebook-in-hand nosey newshound to a more self-contained journalist, who gives you as much information as he gets. Who is less a cadger, more a counsellor.

The Media Moguls

What has also changed is what Media houses are doing themselves for the promotion of culture. Newspapers have gone into cities where they had no presence at all to establishing local bureaus and the numerous city-centric colour supplements are a testimony to their brave new efforts at carving out special niches for themselves.

In this milieu, they are seeking, not just advertising revenue share, but are now trying for the mindshare of their potential readers through sponsorship of events related to sport and intellectual pastimes, contests, and numerous other interactivity.

One area of new focus has been the Awards instituted by the various newspaper groups.

No small-time, one-off awards, these, but major events in a corporate and social calendar. Their aspirational levels are high, the Media hype huge and the reader interest and involvement immense.

The Ananda Bazar Group: Awards Galore

Talking to Aveek Sarkar, scion of the Sarkar family who have made a major dent in the Media scene with the multi-publicationed mega Ananda Bazar Patrika group, the significant fact that comes to the fore is "bonding with the community." Sarkar, who is Chief Editor of one of the youngest English language dailies in the country, The Telegraph, acknowledged as the best presented paper in the country, feels that you "cannot divorce Media from its environment." Hence, when we were trying to find out why large newspaper groups like his have gone all out to support art, music, education, sport, entertainment, we found a large clutch of awards instituted by the group. These have become a significant landmark in a citizen's calendar of events that are sought out competitively.

The Telegraph Schools Awards started out small, under the aegis of the Telegraph Education Foundation. Sarkar does not sit in on it, but his Editor, Editorial Pages does. It gets a strong internal support, with reporters and editorial staff eager to garner stories from the awardees who span a huge cross-section of schools, some of them underprivileged, so that the stories become human interest ones, serving as a beacon to others.

The Awards have become larger than lifesize, moving to the Science City Auditorium in Kolkata with the Chief Minister giving away the awards and a large number of corporates wanting to get involved. "It has got a life of its own" now says Sarkar. He is of the opinion that you do not have to spend huge sums of money on such initiatives. If you have a great idea, you build it up as your "property", but it can only be good and grow if it touches the heart somewhere. The Telegraph Chess championship is another solid achievement, which is less glamorous than the Schools event, but definitely more niche. Niche, but reaching deep into the psyche of a specialized chess community.

Its other awards are related to films, numerous other merchants cup sports, fanning out to districts, and of course its special Ananda Puraskar.

Another important initiative which the group can be proud of is the Centre of International Modern Art, (CIMA), which is a world class property, a centre which presents professionally curated works of select painters and produces topflight catalogues and art books to give connoisseurs and artists a forum for display, debate, discussion and development.

Where does all this place the newspaper group? There is no direct measurable benefit; rather a relationship building with readers and the community at large.

The Economic Times Awards for Corporate Excellence

A similar line of thinking can be seen with the awards that other groups have institutionalized. The Economic Times Awards for Corporate Excellence have come to be regarded by corporate bigwigs as a recognition of companies and individuals as the crème de la crème of the corporate world. In terms of measurables like market capitalization, revenues, profitability, return on net worth and a whole lot of other financial parameters, judged for a period of three years.

The awards for Company of the Year, Emerging Company of the Year, Business Person of the Year, as well as for Lifetime Achievement and even a Corporate Citizen award have given a benchmarking chance for corporate India to show their best face. Other factors that are taken into account are the softer issues, such as quality of management, corporate governance, the competitive situation, and the fundamental difference a person or a company has made to industry and society. The idea of combining database-driven sharply focused numbers and ratios and ranks with a broader, relatively more subjective and perception based exercise is to ensure a well-rounded selection process that weighs all the pros and cons before arriving at a considered and balanced decision.

There is a distinguished jury to judge people and companies of this caliber, with corporate chiefs bigheartedly pushing the case of their business rivals. The Economic Times said:

"Picking the best of the best is not an easy task. So, to decide the winners of The Economic Times Awards for Corporate Excellence 2000-01, we put together an extremely eminent jury comprising S.M. Krishna, chief minister of Karnataka, Arun Jaitley, Union Minister for Law, Justice and Company Affairs, Deepak Parekh, chairman of HDFC, also chairman of the jury, Narayana Murthy, chairman of Infosys, Kumar Mangalam Birla, chairman of the AV Birla Group, M.S. Banga, Chairman of Hindustan Lever, Nanoo Pamnani, chief executive of Citibank and Ranjit Pandit, chief of McKinsey and Company in India.

"At the core of the ET Awards is our abiding philosophy to recognize achievement, not just in terms of mere numbers, but on a much broader canvas. The awards seek to honour those who have

- Dared to dream big, lived life on the edge and influenced the way we think and work;
- Challenged established paradigms, thought laterally, broken new ground and made a fundamental difference to the way business is done;
- Created benchmarks in excellence, ethical standards, transparency and corporate governance;
- Achieved global standards in quality and competitiveness;
- Made dramatic turnarounds in the face of enormous odds;
- Built depth of management, instituted best practices

and developed sustainable performance models; created and distributed wealth, benefited stakeholders and ultimately, made a significant contribution to society at large."

What was interesting was the fact that since three of the jury members were on the shortlist of nominees, some rules of fairness and transparency had to be laid out,.

While 350 of India's top CEOs attend the glittering function, the award-giving and the philosophy behind it is spreading a larger message to the corporate world in general to rev up standards of excellence.

And to show how the Media not only cares, but proactively pushes for the recognition of benchmarks.

The Statesman Awards for Rural Reporting

The Statesman, perceived as an elitist English language daily with a 100-year heritage, came out of this mindset, to create, over 20 years ago, a special slot—The Statesman Awards for Rural Reporting. It was a new and revolutionary concept, an English daily accessing contributions in other languages and acknowledging the most excellent ones by awarding them publicly.

It required a special infrastructure to find, read, sift and judge the best reportage. The whole exercise was made further attractive for the community through the institutionalising of the awards ceremony. The attraction became, not just the awards, which can have limited interest amongst those who are not involved, but in the panel discussion that went with the awards. Top luminaries from all fields of society—politicians, writers, social activists, are invited every year to debate on a current topic of hot interest. This is followed by the awards. The reportage following this is one where the awardees get a lot of publicity for their contribution.

It is an event that has become an essential part of the social calendar of events in the city.

Srijon Samman

The same spirit of encouraging work in regional languages has impelled Pratidin, a Bengali newspaper which is only a few years old, to start a series of awards for excellence in language advertising. The beginning was made just a year ago, and already the response by the agencies to the entries and by the public to a glitzy ceremony of entertainment and rewards, has made it an event that should encourage more work in this area.

4

Niche Public Relations

---

*These are projects that could have remained local in their reach.
Their global marketing efforts have paid off in the way the world
has responded to what started out as a country initiative.*

Sun City

One fine day, Sun City appeared out of the wilderness in
South Africa's Bophuthatswana homeland. We were
travelling in South Africa partly to watch the Indian
cricketers battle it out with a rejuvenated South African
team on their home wickets and also to tour what had been
forbidden territory to Indians. The places of tourist interest
on our itinerary were Cape Town, Port Elizabeth, driving
along the garden route which connects up these towns,
Durban and Pretoria and Johannesburg and trying to sight
the Big Five at Kruger National Park.

When people started telling us about The Palace of the
Lost City at Sun City, we had no clue about what or where
the place was. But soon enough the hype started. Weren't

we interested in seeing a fabulous resort that had grown right out of the desert—something that was Las Vegas and Monte Carlo combined, but with flora, fauna, grandeur and a whole accommodation in The R350 million ($ 1 = Rand 2.80 in the early nineties) custom-made Palace, getting tickets organized for the Miss World Pageant, putting together our casuals for the Million Dollar golf. All because Sun City and its promoters had worked towards pushing the concept before we had even seen a single brochure.

And then, it all came. Everyone talked of its cost—the Rand 800 million (or Rs. 800 crores) African fantasy theme resort. And everyone was given stories about the hovels to highflying hotels success of Sol Kerzner, hailed as a legend in southern Africa. We were told about Kerzner as the chairmen of Sun International, a self-made, multi-millionaire hotelier who had "singlehandedly transformed the region's tourist industry." And we were told even by those who had no stake in promoting this piece of exotica that what we would witness was the Eighth Wonder of the World. A tribute to man's imagination, they said, a homage to art and architecture from past centuries in Africa.

In fact, when we asked for information on Sun City, instead of a tourist leaflet, what we received was enough to fill my overnighter. I have personally never seen so many press releases done on one subject. Executed exquisitely on tinted handmade paper to make it look like sandstone, each set of information notes covered a different aspect. There must have been at least thirty of those, some going into 20 pages. Subjects covered were about Kerzner himself, the concept of the Palace, the "legend" of the search for the Lost City, a focus on the artists who designed the murals and on the mould makers, on the food and entertainment, on thee first time the Miss World pageant was being staged in Africa.

Even before our 90-minute ride to Sun City from Johannesburg, we could almost picture the mysterious landscape with lush tropical gardens and rain forests, cascades, waterfalls, a simulated beach with waves and of course the legendary palace.

But the actual place defied all imagination. The opening night with an extravaganza by the world-famous Jean-Michel Jarre showed how the Lost City was found and the subsequent days saw an unfolding before us of what has been described since in the most prolific terms in the prestigious *People* magazine by James Carry, a principal of Wilson and Associates, an international interior architectural design firm which was selected to design this African fantasy. When he said that "everywhere we have used architectural elements to shock, astound and awe", that was but a small part of the blitzkrieg of this monumental creation.

The 8-page splash in this magazine, which has a select clientele and sent only to people who have made it, is a testimony not just to the incredible project, but also to the fact that detailed information had been made available by Sun International. There were two features, one on Sol Kerzner, focusing on the rapid recouping of his investments and the other on the Lost City, written with commitment and hyperbole of a person who had actually been part of designing it. No amount of advertising could have ever created the excitement and come hitherness that these articles.

It was always in the most exclusive places that these articles appeared. In fact, before The Palace of the Lost City opened in 1993, the *Penthouse*, December 1992 edition, had carried a cover story on Sol Kerzner, complete with a nubile blonde by his side.

There has never been any dearth of information. When I requested one of the directors of Sun International, Joe Pamensky, to let me have some background material, it was with me in a matter of hours. If you were an architectural expert, there was enough to give the person an idea of how to build a similar complex, detailing as it did the amount of earth moved and concrete poured, the quantity of rock blasted, the length of piping installed, the number of workmen accommodated, the huge quantities of LPG gas used for special effects, lighting and so on. For the interior designer, the fact sheets talked of Palladian Terrazzo flooring, Axminster carpets, ceilings painted Sistine Chapel style, handcarved walls. The nature study buff could get lost in the descriptions of the designer-jungles spread over 25 hectares with 1,600,000 plants, trees, shrubs, orchids, transplanted baobabs and a computer-operated irrigation system. Golf 18-hole, par 72 golf course designed by Gary Player with live crocodiles in the water hazard at hole 13 and could well reconstruct courses themselves with the details of earth moved, grass laid and pumping stations. For the gourmet, the finer points of cuisine and dining were tantalizingly presented.

All literature had names and phone numbers of the person to seek out for more details. And the contactable person was contactable.

If just the literature about the place could be so thorough, what about the other promotional gimmicks? In the space of a year, with the beaming of the Miss World contest on major networks, and with the packages that have been promoted through the airlines, Sun City has suddenly become a destination that people, not just in South Africa or that continent, but from all over the world, have placed prominently on their itineraries. It has appealed to people's aspirational and adventurous levels, through its glitz, and more than that, through the tremendous accessibility of information and continuous projection.

One of the chief attractions of Sun City was the casino, immense and fabulous in scope. But today, there is fresh competition from many other casino-centric places and Sun City seems to be losing some of its glitter. But having institutionalized the concept of the Miss World contest, (something we have been stressing on when we talk of companies pinpointing specific projects and "owning" them), it may continue to draw crowds and media attention.

Chiva Som, Haven of Life

Turn to another part of the world. Another country. Thailand. A tourist's paradise, which attracted people so far for its sun, sea, shopping, and also sex. In this milieu, a resort presented itself in an entirely new vein— a health spa in an idyllic setting that would give you mental relaxation, emotional stability, physical invigoration, creative cuisine—in short a total overhaul of sense and sensibility. Named Chiva Som, the Haven of Life, this resort is today ranked number one among health spas in the world.

How did it happen? Sampling the health—giving benefits of Chiva Som first hand was more than what I had set out to do. I wanted to find out how they had made the place tick, what went into their marketing efforts and what got them the publicity and the people. Our initial exposure had been with the visit of their then director of sales and marketing, Pamela Balce, who had done a soft-sell presentation to a select, invited group over lunch at The Conclave, an exclusive business club in Kolkata. It was basically a short video show, lots of very finely produced literature about the place for everyone present, and a few gimmicks with lucky draws that fetched people prizes ranging from leisure wear to free stays at Chiva Som.

The press loved the slides and the well-packaged spiel, the audience had their appetite whetted and what was achieved was the targeting of a niche up-end set of potential users.

The strategy remains pretty much the same for this 7-acre beachside resort, not too far from the King's summer palace at Hua Hin, a three-hour drive from the airport. The brainchild of Thailand's former Deputy Prime Minister, Boonchu Rojanastien, who heads a small consortium of Thai business people, investing between them US$ 26 million to build Asia's first health resort. It was originally meant for Thai residents. But today it is a true international resort, complete with a large number of memberships, PR representatives in UK, Germany, USA and 35% repeat guests—an extremely high figure for a specialized place of this sort.

Talking to the assistant director of sales, a charming, vocal woman from the Philippines, Cora Tagunicar, it was possible to get a complete picture of the marketing and Public Relations efforts and also being able to get a spelt out philosophy of the spa. For although I was physically there, taking in the benefits of the "positive aspects of health prevention, rather than cure, innovation rather than accepted practice, the application of wisdom rather than the passive acceptance of aging", it was a revelation to find the well-crafted philosophy of selling.

To quote Tagunicar: "In order to retain its classy image, there is no aggressive selling. The costs have to be perforce pitched high, but having said that, we do have a special "Essential Luxuries Package" for India as an initial promotional effort." She sums it up succinctly: "You don't go into everybody's faces." You don't overstate, or oversell. In fact, it is the representatives stationed in key areas around the world, the visits by their own marketing people to places like India and the huge snowball effect of world of mouth publicity generated by the visitors and converts to the unique spa that have made Chiva Som a popular, yet discrete resort.

Coming away from it and feeling like a million dollars, I have concluded that soft-sell (and of course the amazing well-being from the effects of the spa) can give a place an amazing edge over others. Which says, come to us, but remember, the costs are high, the lifestyle focused on fitness, and we are not just any other resort. Brash is unbeautiful here. Footfalls are soft, people speak in low tones, sugar and salt are minimal, but the end-effects are unbeatable.

The same goes for the selling and Public Relations techniques. It is not a heavy come on, and yet the tempo is kept up of telling the Chiva Som story through well-structured Public Relations presentations and in giving guests enough take home stuff to make it easier for them to share the experience with their friends and indirectly get the marketing benefits.

There are two aspects to sharing this case with readers. One is of course the fact that marketing a product such as a holistic health spa is 80% word of mouth through the experience-sharing by guests; 20% through the structured representations in different parts of the world, backed up by up-to-date publications and a flexible approach to meeting targets. The other part is the reality and quality behind the product itself, which exceeds expectations of guests, with its 250 staff catering to the needs of 57 rooms.

In its international resource persons giving classes on·all aspects of physical and mental well-being. And in the original clutch of members who have a financial stake in it to continue to use and promote the place further.

On a personal note, I found the Public Relations efforts were not confined to select individuals like the sales director, but trickled down to every medical representative, front office person, room service personnel, and even those who drove you around in motorized caddies through the verdant expanses. If you have a great product, it needs to be backed up by personal belief which runs through the fabric of this world-starred spa. Niche PR needs a deep involvement and individual commitment—a lesson to be gleaned from Chiva Som's tailored communicative efforts.

5

Communication Snowball:
The Impact Story

Corporate initiative to reach out to the masses with philanthropic projects could remain static and company-centric. Unless initiatives like the Impact Foundation's Lifeline Express involving several corporates, state governments and volunteers down the line can be conceived. The publicity potential is enormous. So are the benefits to the end user.

How much time and money should a company spend on social projects where the primary motive is not direct publicity but the actual development of cultural activity, sporting initiatives, civic amenities and medical facilities for a build-up of corporate goodwill?

My cynical friends in the media dismiss these as tax write-off moves. Imagine—hours of precious executive time and involvement and crores of corporate money being blown on sheer gimmickry and attention-getting!

If only they would stop to think for a moment, they would see a corporate body as being amongst the most misunderstood of all institutions. They're on the firing line from all angles: taxation imperatives, increased demands from shareholders for more dividends, rising employee expectations, better deals to be thought up for competing dealers and the continuous anticipation of the general public about what the corporation can do for them.

The worst of it all is that companies can no longer voluntarily be do-gooders. Government expects them to put in money for ventures which should be funded from State budgets anyway. The reason, among others, is the perfection and commitment with which a private organization executes these, so that they are not able to buy themselves out of this newly-imposed faith in their purse-string and organizational capabilities. The time will probably come when every meadow, grove and stream, every street and building and park will be tagged and brassplated with names of companies which came forward to build and maintain what was the responsibility of the municipality. Every little amenity will have been bought into. Could companies then hold the complete whip hand and call the shots?

Unfortunately not.

That's the reality of it.

The reality also is that companies are not megalomaniacs wanting to hog a particular project for themselves. They believe that they could start something and let others take up from were they leave off.

One such thought was a hospital-train known as Lifeline Express, which sought to reach out to millions of villagers living in remote areas of the country. The brain behind the project turned out to be Zelma Lazarus, who, apart from giving a major boost to the Public Relations efforts of Voltas, as its Corporate General Manager , also wore several other hats, one being that of the Impact Foundation which she heads in India as Chief Executive Officer.

When the project started, people asked: How could one company –Voltas—just whip out a couple of crores and put it into refurbishing railway coaches? Coaches that were complete with surgical and medical facilities which would be hitched on to a train that would travel the length and breath of the country and become a walk-in hospital? A train that would be periodically shunted about to 7,000 sidings? And serve 70 million disabled in need of attention and treatment?

The idea was done not by the company, but under another banner, Impact India, to which Lazarus had been generously seconded for a number of years to parallelly give her PR expertise to a charitable UN institution which takes initiatives against "avoidable disablement". Impact India's successful programme has hinged primarily on its vaccination and polio prevention programmes, eradicates guinea worm and has travelled far afield under its "Cure on Wheels" programme.

When it came to Lifeline Express, the target audience was a large mass of illiterate, hedonistic individuals, lost in the smog of superstition. They were ignorant of the powers of modern medicine. Into this scene chugs in a mysterious train, with strangers clad in white, speaking in hushed tones and ready to treat patients with varied ailments. At no cost to them. There had to be a catch somewhere.

Impact realized this phenomenon and started planning the most appropriate modes of communication to meet the following objectives:

(a) Communicating with governmental and non-governmental agencies to get adequate resources;

    (b) Dealing with government to get sanctions and support and

    (c) Approaching prospective beneficiaries to create a demand.

The project—to launch Lifeline Express—a daring move which sought to bring medical relief to scores of villages living in remote areas of the country.

The idea of railway coaches, refurbished with medical and surgical facilities, hitched onto a train and travelling around the country as a walk-in hospital found instant favour. This thought was mentioned to the then Railway Minister, George Fernandes, who mulled over it for just one day before giving his go-ahead for three coaches. The main hurdle, that of finding a crore and a half of rupees, was crossed in less than three months.

"And then," says Lazarus, "those magnificent railwaymen went to work to transform the ramshackle coaches into a hi-tech mini hospital."

Painted a dazzling white, with flowers and a rainbow to get away from a staid hospital image, the first of the coaches has an operation theatre with three adjustable operation tables, a sterilization room, a diagnostic centre and a lying-inward with twelve beds, train style, one atop the other. The second and third coaches serve as the living quarters of surgeons, medical and paramedical staff who are housed on the train. The fourth is a training coach for upto 50 medical persons.

The beauty of it is that there is no regular staff but at each of the carefully chosen destinations, separate companies, in this participative programme, get involved in providing infrastructural facilities, nurses and doctors, housing and food for patients and also generate publicity of the train amongst villagers. They have to register the droves of patients who come from distances as far as 300 kilometres, often several months in advance of the arrival of the train.

A typical camp lasts 35 days, the first ten devoted to the treatment of polio patients, the next ten days for cataract cases and the next seven for the treatment of the deaf and the last for correction of clefts. But the Impact initiative does not end here. There is an arrangement with its collaborator-run hospitals for the follow-ups to ensure post-operative care and periodic evaluation.

On the 16th of July, the Lifeline Express has completed 10 years treating over 3,00,000 persons in 16 states in India.

Today, exactly a decade after its dramatic start, according to National Coordinator Neelam Kshirsagar,the Lifeline Express is "racing ahead at full speed in its mission of avoidable disablement. Recent projects have been at the invitation of the Governments of Gujarat and Chattisgarh States. We have just completed two back-to-back projects in Chattisgarh, one each at Durg and at Pendra Road, surpassing all previous records in terms of number of operations performed. Over 6000 disabled were treated, more than 2000 surgeries performed and 900 cleft operations erased facial disfigurement. About 15,000 people who were registered had to be turned away. The response at Chattisgarh State with Chief Minister Mr. Ajit Jogi taking a personal interest, is unprecedented. Impact has been invited to hold more projects there." The chain effect will continue throughout this year and the next, involving at various stages of its journey, companies and state governments, Rotary and Lions Clubs.

Impact's Malaria Control Project is gaining new ground with its emphasis on Malaria Prevention, involving college students doing door-to-door counselling, and through posters, jingles and street plays. It is also involved in the reduction of Disability initiatives.

One of its Fund-raising Projects is through the Gandhi Book. Each book is a collector's item printed on long-life parchment paper bound in hand-spun hand-woven silk and presented in a silk—lined box. It is available in German, Spanish, Italian, French and English languages. Containing the sayings of the Mahatma, one of its excellent corporate gimmicks, which we subscribed to years ago, was in offering companies a chance to buy these book as corporate gifts and having their name superscribed, almost as if they had taken the original initiative. For every copy of the book bought, you could immunize 50 children from polio, 20 against all childhood diseases or 6 persons could have their sight restored through cataract surgeries on the Lifeline Express.

But while Lifeline Express cannot solve more than a tiny part of India's health problems, it is impossible to deny that the programme may provide a thought provoking prototype for improving access to basic medical facilities rurally. Its lesson for communicators is the great multiplier effect that can be a powerful Public Relations tool. This involves the cooperation of volunteers, the local populace, social welfare organizations, the support of government, the participative efforts of enlightened sponsors.

The coverage in prominent newspapers and magazines for this programme was due largely to the communication efforts of the Impact team. Whoever had not heard of the train by word of mouth found features in magazines that were splashed across in colour spreads. Because it made such a good story, these were correspondents who actually contacted the company and wanted to get to where the train was to do a piece that lent itself to empathy and drama.

According to Simone St. Anne, who wrote a whole research paper on Impact India as a case study in health development, it is "an effective and exciting alternative to the management of economic and social development." By further analysing the Impact initiative, the researcher found that the driving force behind its performance lay in the character of its leadership.

To quote St Anne, "As catalyst, it is playing the role of social animator, but it also provides the technology and methods required for the programme. It activates empowerment and also uses the power of the elite, be it government, the private sector, or institutions and individuals, for purposes of sanctions, resource collection, and delivery of services. It uses a mixed-media strategy with an emphasis on interpersonal communication."

This is at the heart of the multiplier effect we mentioned at the beginning. One vital message comes out of all this effort: that a project done in isolation can give you the immediate kudos, but one that involves corporations in a kind of strung-along effect, could benefit not just the giver, but the needier recipient. It is a communication snowball, both for the work itself, and also for the response generated. The success of the Lifeline Express has inspired its replication in China, Zimbabwe and more recently in the form of a hospital riverboat—*Jibon Tori*, in Bangladesh.

Lazarus continues to emphasize it in very simple terms: "All our work is PR. It boils down to getting things done. It is wide-ranging PR, doing it at the highest elevated level of the United Nations, right down to the poorest woman whom we communicate with at the grassroots level." This communication, incidentally came to me from the laptop of Lazarus, as she was sitting under a tree in Chattisgarh, surrounded by grateful villagers.

6

Job & Executive:
The Perfect fit—the Tata Steel Way

The terminology has changed, as has the way companies look at fitting employees into correct slots, downsizing with the minimum amount of heartburn, and communicating frequently to strengthen links and build confidence.

When we talked in an earlier chapter of the interlinking of Human Resource Development, we were discussing a number of trends and giving our recommendations. One actual case stands out in this intertwining of disciplines. That of the Performance Ethic Programme (PEP) that was carried out at Tata Steel, an initiative that was as much the responsibility of HRD as it was for Corporate Communications to take to the people concerned. The first part was structured by the experts in HRD and the monitoring of the communications by the latter, to ensure that a difficult transition in organizational redesign went through smoothly.

The communication at each stage was addressed by the Managing Director himself and the MD's office held itself responsible for overall coordination of the programme. At each juncture, various people of responsibility made available for people to come and get their queries answered, to have counselling, to go through assessments, talent reviews, compensation concerns, and a huge number of Frequently Asked Questions were circulated.

As Sanjay Singh, who flew in from Jamshedpur to Kolkata just to keep an appointment with us to explain all queries, said: "You don't have an option but to communicate."

Asked how he had so much leeway to function with the media, and with sharing information in the way he did for this book, he said that "the ability to communicate by the Director of PR is directly proportionate to the trust placed in him." Conversely, all PR managers should remember that they have to wrest this trust from managements, by involving themselves as deeply as possible. Singh is able to attend all key meetings of every department, thus keeping himself abreast of all developments, so that the interface with the press becomes easy, credible and a responsibility that managements can safely put on his shoulders.

To establish the credibility of PEP: the CEO had to have all communication emanating from him and all people involved had to have communication skills of the highest order to be able to tackle the delicate issues.

As the Managing Director in one of his communications said:

"On the 1st May, Tata Steel made the transition to the new organization and took the first bold step in implementing the Performance Ethic Programme. Implementing a change programme of such magnitude calls for resolve and courage, and the entire organization has passed muster admirably. Several of you have demonstrated great fortitude. I want to congratulate you all on having realized the importance of this transition and of making it well."

Quite apart from this communication from the top, certain key personnel who were both knowledgeable in PEP and empowered to speak, were chosen as "listening posts". These people were available to lend an empathetic ear to problems that individuals faced.

There is a competitive nature to the change programme which the CEO has taken great pains to explain to employees through regular, periodic, well-researched, transparent communication. This whole business of downsizing, dehiring, voluntary retirement, retrenchment, and in Tata Steel's terminology—Rightsizing—can be agonizing.

The tackling of this transitional period of anxiety, without compromising quality, is what brings out the grand master plan that was devised in conceiving and executing the Performance Ethic Programme.

Fears allayed. Aspirations acceded to. Performers rewarded.

First, they conveyed the overall objectives of the Performance Ethic Programme and also articulated the importance of the initiatives on organization redesign and strengthening of the human resource management system. The Managing Director said: "As per our overall plan, we are now in the process of assessing officers for the one hundred jobs that have maximum impact on the company's performance." He went on to assure employees that because of the underlying concerns in their minds about the details of the programme, they had compiled a number of FAQs and tried to answer them to the best of their ability.

In the process of their change from being functionally organized to becoming an organization with Strategic Business Units, the questions that were anticipated and the replies set out to them ranged from the broader ones about impactiveness of changes on the company to the more immediate personal concerns of employees. Are we cutting jobs and positions? In case I am not staffed with my job, will I be asked to leave? How have the top 100 positions been selected? What was the process involved in identifying candidates to these positions?

These FAQs then went into further details, which again went in the form of a detailed letter, where the Managing Director congratulated colleagues in taking the Performance Ethic Programme forward. In that, there was also talk of tightening belts, and in an inspirational will to win message to beat the odds.

Another initiative which facilitated the process and was a remarkable move on the part of the company, was the involvement of wives. Hundreds of wives attended two sessions in the Tata auditorium where husbands were not present. This made for a frank and open set of discussions and answers to all queries and worries.

Today, several progress reports, assessments and communication initiatives later, the PEP is well on its way to being implemented.

Corporate Communications has played a stellar role in this process, something that in any company would not have traditionally been tackled by Public Relations people at all. While the research of the concerns of VRS employees like marriage, medical benefits, education of children, housing, getting monetary compensations were studied by the Human Resource Development department who were the main implementing agency, the Corporate Communications department acted as internal consultants to complete the picture of assessing and abetting employees in transiting through this life change.

7

Patronage as Development of Cultural Heritage: The SRA prescription

---

There are types and types of glamorized patronage. Some take the form of high-profile events to raise funds where the giver puts in his largesse and creates hype about his contribution. There are other corporates who set aside generous amounts to support causes. Here we have taken up just one instance, from amongst a host of others in the country, where an institution has accorded its patronage, institutionalized it, and built upon it to reach out to larger audiences.

Altruism for its own sake can become self-defeating, rather than self-perpetuating. The gamut of corporate philanthropic activity, from the building of specialized hospitals, setting up of new-age schools, formation of fabulous art centres to mega events connected with sport and music has made a significant mark on the cultural, medical and social face of our country.

But considering the enormous sums spent, and the planning and energy expended on these, the returns have, on some occasions, left something to be desired. Which is, that many of these events are one-off; many areas of philanthropy done with the univision of the chief executive of the moment. This is not a criticism, but an observation of how some of these activities could leave a more permanent mark, if structured for the long term. And institutionalized.

Also, in the creation of institutions of learning, the danger of stagnation and becoming too static needs to be avoided. This is why we chose ITC's unique initiative of cultural philanthropy, the creation and institutionalization of ITC's Sangeet Research Academy. ITC-SRA is the only modern Gurukul of its kind in the world, an unparalleled modern institution embodying, in face, epitomising the traditional Indian system of learning through a Guru-Shishysa-Parampara. ITC-SRA is today an institution which has moved from point A to point M, by dint of its keeping up with the times, and the paradigm shift in its focus, using the latest technology to move forward and outward.

It is one thing to sponsor individual musical events, which also require some injection of Vitamin M to carry on performing, but to create and sustain an institution on the lines of the royal patronage of ancient times is commendable. In fact, the raison d'etre of ITC-SRA was that Hindustani Classical Music was beginning to wilt with the gradual whittling down of benefaction. The Academy has now etched itself firmly in the cultural landscape of India. The image rub-off on the company is indisputable.

When the ITC Sangeet Research Academy (ITC-SRA) was created more than two decades ago, its stated objective was to preserve and promote Indian Classical Music. Adding to the charm and romance of such an institution of learning, which promised to carry on the guru-shishya parampara, was the building itself in which the SRA is housed. Aldeen—a 200-year-old wooden-shuttered bungalow which originally belonged to an heir of Tipu Sultan, became the abode of musical learning. A natural ambience to facilitate and enable close teacher-student interaction to disseminate the knowledge of Hindustani Classical Music.

All this is known by the students who have passed through its portals, the noted musicians who have taught here and the cognoscenti who have enjoyed the classical recitals in its munificent ambience.

The progress which we extol is that the cultural lineage has been extended beyond the shores of the country to embrace into its fold an ever-increasing band of followers of Indian Classical Music through the creation of a magnificent musical portal. So elegant in its concept, so clever in its interactivity, that it has become a portal to be possessed like a whole music system, complete with a huge library of music and information, available at the click of a mouse.

To rewind to its beginnings, ITC-SRA started out with three basic objectives:

- To create a system of effective training in Indian Classical Music
- To buttress the oral tradition of Indian Classical Music with modern research methods and technology
- To promote and propagate Indian Classical Music, beginning with Hindustani Classical Music

That they have achieved this in excellent measure is evident from the galaxy of legendary names in Indian Classical Music who are attached to the Academy as Gurus. The numerous famous maestros and ustads produced by the Academy also bear telling testimony to the efficacy of its teaching method. More than 100 students or "shishyas" have been initiated into the wonderland of Hindustani Classical music in this two-decade span.

The weightage that the Academy gets and the solid reputation that it has acquired comes from its deep knowledge back-up. Its Expert Committees periodically assess scholars. Through regular weekly sessions, where a discerning audience closely critiques new talent and offers detailed suggestions to hone musical prowess, and scholars are moulded as performers. The Academy's training is backed up by deep research and formal documentation.

While its Central Library and Archives have a comprehensive range of books and manuscripts on music, and a sophisticated recording studio, the Scientific Research Department, which has received governmental recognition, has studied all elements that have an impact on sound and music and a state of the art acoustics lab and acoustically treated studio.

The real progress, though, and this is what we applaud, when we talk of corporate philanthropy and creativity exceeding its brief, is the virtual realm that it has entered through the creation of the landmark website that could surely change the way in which the average person with access to a computer can see, hear and imbibe a hugely-researched repertoire of music and information. Sitting at your computer you can listen to some very rare recordings, familiarize yourselves with various *ragas* and *gharanas* through text and audio, learn about India's priceless *guru-shishya-parampara* and watch video clips of concert performances.

It is monitored and updated regularly for quality, content and expansion. At any given time of day, logging into itcSRA.org will give a person an experience that is immeasurable. The raga of the time of day will play and an explanation will float across the screen to help even a layman appreciate what is being relayed.

The company itself succinctly acknowledges, "For music lovers, the ITC-SRA is an institution. For ITC, it is a corporate tribute to the great tradition of Indian Classical Music."

What could have remained cocooned into a city-based initiative, with limited access for musicians who are able to make the grade, has now been given a wider berth and a global reach through the innovative step of using today's technology for keeping up and furthering musical tradition and enjoyment beyond Indian shores.

8

Reputation Garnered but not sought: The Udita Route

This case study is one with a straightforward message. That when the product is good, and the past reputation sound, the goodwill generated far outstrips any formal Public Relations efforts.

Being a builder in a market where demand far outstrips supply, will always give you the popularity edge. But there can be many more aspects to the building of homes— issues of credibility, cost-consciousness, class. To be able to meld all of these into one and reach out is one part of the projection. The subsequent gains of mileage and the snowball effect of replication of these concepts make it an appropriate PR story.

Bengal Ambuja Housing Development Limited is perhaps one of the first joint venture projects in the country where the state government and the private sector have collaborated to augment the supply of housing, particularly in the urban areas, and have added to the government's efforts to provide affordable housing to the masses. Their core business focus is to create affordable and fair-priced homes with allied facilities and infrastructure for all sections of society.

This three-tier set-up was itself a revolutionary project—how could several income groups live in the same colony? It was conceived by Harshavardhan Neotia with a simple vision: "Housing for all". The business model was simple as well. " Make quality homes, charge reasonable prices and provide the customer with a product that is value for money, " is the straight-from-the-heart philosophy of Neotia.

He roped in world-renowned architect-visionary, Balkrishna Doshi, to conceive the entire complex, christened Udayan—The Condoville, itself a creative name for a new-age condominium. Doshi's ideas further added value to the quality and design of every single home along with its environment friendly surroundings. The architect was so keen on maintaining the quality of open spaces that, even at the cost of sacrificing valuable building area, about 65% was left open to sky to create the feeling of space and the perfect ambience for living in harmony.

The project is more than an edifice for living. Hailed as a concept ahead of its time. With built in promises of the likes that no one had conceived before. The most amazing being the self-imposed penalties for delays in deliveries of the flats beyond the scheduled delivery time. Which consist of pledges to pay back amounts proportionate to the loss in interest for the investors. Such a step is unique in the real estate market in India.

Even before the first part was over, Bengal Ambuja was hailed as a model project, much visited by ministers and dignitaries from other states, and the President of India himself. Requests galore came in for replications of similar projects outside West Bengal. The quality and imagination invested has brought Bengal Ambuja many other laurels. Neotia was conferred the Padmashreee by the Government of India for leveraging such a significant and socially relevant scheme.

Going back to the beginnings of the project, Neotia explains: "We were able to create a housing colony with a difference: high quality, aesthetic planning and affordable in price.

We did not ever have to convince people to participate. Also this triple-tier concept of lower, middle and high-income group housing almost cheek by jowl is something where I would like to share the Indian philosophy with you. We believe India lives heterogeneously. To make it more palatable to all sections, we have limited segmentation of activities and yet a pluralistic ambience. This whole process makes the township more sustainable."

Other unique features were a cross-subsidy maxim by pricing the low-income group at below cost, the middle income group at only the cost of construction (without including the land and overheads) while the high income group ended up providing the subsidy for the LIG and MIG housing schemes. By this method, they were able to create a neighbourhood of people from different walks of life and varied income groups with limited segregation and yet within close proximity of each other.

Another aspect which brought in media attention was the Lower Income Group and Middle Income Group housing, which were subsidized, and were embarked on before the HIG launch—in spite of the fact the company was bound to lose some money initially.

The subsidized housing was handed over well within

schedule and this generated considerable goodwill amongst customers who felt they had got a quality product at a great affordable price. Naturally, when the HIGs were launched, with a pricing that was market-driven, selling the product was a cakewalk. And this, at a time when the country was witnessing the worst real estate downfall post-independence.

From the point of view of the company's interaction with buyers, with the media, and with other sections of society who were observers to this whole process, the Public Relations exercise was one which saw enormous amounts of publicity generated with a minimum degree of effort. All the issues were heavily oversubscribed and allotment of apartments had to be done through a public lottery. The first of these involved Mother Teresa, whose presence drew a huge press. The Missionaries of Charity were, as a special gesture, given two apartments for their use. The whole purpose of these lotteries was to prove to the thousands of subscribers how the company could be transparent, caring and share the whole process in an open forum.

There is never a week when the press does not contact the Ambuja office to get a story. It could be about where the company has progressed with regard to the requests from other states, or when dignitaries come visiting to see the place or how some of the sculptures were done with scrap material to beautify spots at the housing complex. The concept begat stories, the methodology got coverage likewise, as did the architectural advancements, the additions to ambience, and the interest generated by progressive states like Andhra Pradesh, whose Chief

Minister took a personal interest in the project and wanted the concept and execution to be taken on by this company.

It is a combination of class, creativity and conceptualization that made this a project that became sought out by the media, and a talking point for the citizens of Kolkata. In conversations about the positive happenings in the city, this was one which featured as a can-do effort, saying that there are companies who deliver quality and who keep their promises.

9

Globalized Approaches

Thinking local, acting global. This has become a cliché. What is still import reasing networked and globalized world is to keep current with new trends and techniques and adapt it to specific corporate needs.

The companies which want to appear even a step further than this talk of thinking local and acting global, do it in the belief that this one-upmanship will show how theirs is a corporation which, after making the world its oyster, has expanded its corporate philosophy to embrace universal management approaches.

Either way, this is the trend. Not just in India, but around the world. It is a sign of the times, which, today, is showing once again, in politics, music and in corporate life, the return to power of councils, rather than all-powerful individuals. Isn't this what would explain how the three surviving members of the Beatles are once again echoing the words of one of their ageless numbers—*Come Together*—by doing a joint recording. Isn't a similar trend also

apparent in the internal structure of corporations, where a singleminded president or managing director is not sound enough policy any more and the managing committee makes the mare go?

And, in the context of the globalization of business, isn't the trend now to look for synergies and restructuring, strategic alliances, mutually agreeable mergers and equitable joint ventures? This new expansionism probably shows that this is the era when companies would prefer not to go it alone. It is the age of networking. Could this mean that corporate capabilities are wearing thin and risks and costs are being looked at to be farmed out with profits coming as a smaller slice of a bigger cake?

Whatever be the motivations, for the world of communications, networking is a working, current trend in terms of actual fibre-optics and "virtual realities".

What does it mean for the people who are the core of communication for corporations? For Public Relations firms who have to respond to this globalization, the instant accessibility is something that they have to be outfitted to do if they do not want to go into obsolescence or be left behind in the rat race.

Only a few of the top Public Relations firms actually have offices worldwide, and that, too, in select cities. The majority of consultants have tuned themselves into the networking system by which they can claim to their clients that their reach is as good in Kolkata as it is in Copenhagen, which is only a fax message or E-Mail away.

At one time, and this is probably the most traditional way of approaching geographical spread, Public Relations companies used to expand by actually setting up shop in places of their choosing. Not only were inputs in terms of costs great, but the business of working in places they could not relate to in terms of local strategy, could be a difficult one. Then came the era of acquisitions, which saw companies like Shandwick buying up the assets of smaller firms, thus acquiring not only a presence, a readymade set-up, but also a chunk of goodwill for all its alien intrusion.

But for the rest, it is the network that works, whether it be owner-operated firms getting together in a loose arrangement or in associations formed where every member is handpicked and who then pay into a pool.

Total independence has its share of hazards. Because, from personal experience, it has been found that when you have a loose networking arrangement when there are no monetary transactions involved, the following scenario takes place.

Consultant in Hong Kong on an urgent summons by phone to consultant in Kolkata: "Hi Rita, my clients in France are trying to establish a presence in India. Can you give me costings and a time frame for media interaction and also let me know how soon we could do a market survey for gauging the competitors' capabilities? Let me have your quote for the work by return fax, please."

And so the quote is sent. But there is no comeback for another two weeks. At the end of it, the answer is: "We have to wait." Meantime, the Kolkata consultant's time and effort in getting the information and costings to do the work has cost her money, annoyance, interruption in current work. And heartburn.

It has happened more than once. When we raised this nettlesome question at a conference, consultants said that this is part of the game of winning some and losing some. They commit to a big client that they can deliver the goods in any part of the world, then quickly fax their contacts in that country and then quote for the whole package that may not materialize.

But, largely, the Indian scene is looking professional, with many of the big players from the west doing link-ups either with advertising agencies or with the new firms on the block in the Public Relations field.

This should augur well for the new breed of Indian multinationals who are setting up joint ventures or even acquiring companies outside the shores of this country or reaching franchising agreements with the known names amongst consumer giants.

Several reasons are advanced for Indian companies setting up outside India. There is of course the need to access foreign markets. Although this could just as well be done by exporting and getting the resultant benefits, in balance, companies are finding that the costs of actually being there far outweigh the export earnings. There is the more localized response time to both consumer preferences and the securing of on-the-spot orders. Then the numerous restrictions from quotas and customs duties can be avoided.

But that is not all. The bottomline of increased profits is a major consideration. When these companies decide to enter new countries and new markets, the savvier ones will realize how they have to get updated information about these markets, and set about building in these new countries a brand new image which they had so long taken for granted in their own climes.

These are the areas of opportunity for Public Relations. The sooner we get out of our day-to-day responsiveness to problems of companies and start accessing the information needs of the expanding companies, the better it will be for the advancement of the profession as business counsellors.

Teleconferencing

Technology has simplified the networking concept to such an extent that the concept of video conferencing no longer holds any devils for users. At one time, it was seen to be the preserve for large-scale global events, with political leaders from across the world talking to one another. People still have not forgotten the first time when Rajiv Gandhi communicated with Swedish Premier Olaf Palme on a video link.

But today, video conferencing has become a business necessity. Close to home, the Chief Minister of West Bengal, Buddhadev Bhattacharya, can now link up with districts through teleconferencing, an unprecedented move for a communist government.

A Public Relations firm need not have offices or affiliates or contacts worldwide to be able to serve the wider communication needs of its clients.

Business Television

If you thought video conferencing was one way of ensuring that you had networked and arrived, there's still business television to contend with. It has been hailed as the shining star in the internal communications arena.

Business television is the use of TV by industry and commerce to broadcast direct to audiences who can, in theory, be anywhere. It could well be the tool that could cut out the expensive roadshows that are being used to promote the Euro Issues of companies, thus saving on the valuable time of top corporate bosses.

Nobody is totally certain about what business television actually does. A lot of people feel it is just an extension of the corporate video into a somewhat larger audience framework. And even for those who have been exposed to this concept, their queries are to do with the cost-effectiveness of the exercise.

We came across success stories of some of the largest names in the business using this particular idea. There are two ways in which they have done it. One is the one-off launch of products or the sharing of Annual General Meetings or sales conferences, where a live broadcast is made from one location to a multiplicity of centres, or from those centres to yet others. The other way is to have permanent networks, by which companies broadcast regular, live or pre-recorded programmes to employees.

It's the latter initiative which can be attractive for a company willing to spend its big bucks for the bigger reach. BMW's is a strong case in point. They could be numbered among the pioneers in this form of communication. The difference between what we have been viewing so far and what, say, BMW went into doing, was that they aimed it at their own staff. A highly professional, captive communication effort that went out to 140 dealerships around the UK.

The methodology goes thus. Every week a 20 to 30-minute capsule brings details about sales and marketing, including how competitors are faring in comparison with BMW, focus on new models and even instructions on correction errors if product defects were to crop up.

A lot of this material is produced beforehand and recorded, say, on a Monday, but there have been live segments which would enable an employee to phone in while the programme was going on and ask pointed questions of the executives present. This particular "product" is made by a company called Visage, whose work one had a chance to know about on a trip to the Middle East where they were looking at new markets.

The beauty of this system is that only BMW decoders can pick up the signal, thus ensuring exclusively and confidentiality. Apparently, the company was so enthusiastic about the equipment that it made it compulsory for all dealers to install receiving equipment and pay for it themselves. This consists of a satellite dish, decoder, television screen and a video recorder.

The benefits are seen as immediacy and the fact that although, in the long run, they could end up saving on elaborate conferences and travel, the need was to grab the moment and respond to today's technology.

Another equally effective programme was when this production company did the Levi's launch of a brand new "Originals" commercials. This is said to be one of the "most ambitious private satellite broadcasts ever staged in Europe." When it broke, 45,000 people in 10 countries from Sweden to Israel, from the UK to Spain, participated in a live celebration of the launch of the new commercials. Presenters in each location hosted the event, co-ordinated the links and drew immediate feedback on the new commercials from the audience in each location. Ultimately, staff, friends and suppliers were able to get a preview of the new advertising before it broke publicly. This was a great employee and supplier morale booster.

On-Line Information Databases

The more advanced you get in your communications systems, the more outmoded you tend to feel. But the world is shrinking, businesses expanding and there is a constant need to be up-to-date. How do you do this without expending huge amounts of in-house time?

Timely information is what drives companies today to respond quickly to any situation. Writing about this trend in the Public Relations Journal, John Masterton, a freelance writer based in Manhattan, said: "Using a variety of on-line information databases, Public Relations practitioners can do everything from monitoring breaking news and client press coverage to researching key issues and social trends, Research topics are diverse, ranging from product recalls to recycling to employee communications. Databases also help firms craft new business pitches."

This is a brave new area—that of using databases to prospect new businesses. You can monitor what the competition is doing; you can also keep tabs on your own industry. The well-known packages are the **Dow Jones News/Retrieval** which accesses more than 1,300 national and international sources, including newspapers, magazines, newswires, Public Relations wire services, company and industry information and quotes, statistics and other business commentary. **Investext** is like the one mentioned by us earlier, **Data Times** and **Dialog** and **Burrelle's Broadcast Database** and **Nexis** are some other computer databases, Burelles being devoted exclusively to programmes aired on television and radio. It contains full-text, word-for-word transcripts within 24 hours after the programmes are aired.

What Next?

The easy and interesting part is to read about the new technologies and feel updated. The hard part is to use them, to assimilate them into your system. One practitioner said: "Telling me I have access to any technology is akin to telling me I have access to the space shuttle. I'm glad I've got it, but I have no idea what to do with it."

That's true. But the practitioner who will win in the end is the one who can arm himself with a mixture of the right technologies, their timely applications and a client-mix whom they can persuade to use it for better business prospects.

If used properly, this kind of development could be turned into a gold mine of opportunity, rather than be just another costly experiment. The producers of such programmes in fact feel that there is an element of motivation and inspiration in the whole process, of encouragement and feedback, obtained instantly. The floodgates can open up for more open discussion, and, during a crisis, there can be no substitute for this kind of communication link.

Today, there are specialist satellite services, which broadcast not just to a single but to a whole sector. Racing takes this very well and this system has been in place in betting shops for a number of years. Apart from Racenet, there is something called Medical Television Network, through which many of Britain's teaching hospitals and post-graduate medical centres can avail of updates on medicine and briefings at frequent intervals.

But Yet Again, Back to Basics-Nearly

These new technologies are drawing companies and their clients and key audiences closer by sheer dint of the satellite. But easier and faster does not necessarily mean better.

Sometimes, in wanting to become globally responsive, we could well be losing sight of the meat of the message. Anyone can hire video conferencing equipment, or even buy it and then put together a worldwide launch or share the immediacy of an Annual General Meeting with shareholders in other locations.

But as true Public Relations strategists, we cannot ignore the importance of integrated communications. While not undermining the use of these satellite tools to better the communications impact, we have to believe in the value of melding, advertising, marketing and Public Relations strategies to make a global campaign more credible.

A number of cases of such integrated strategies have come to light from USA, compiled by Deborah Hauss, who runs an appropriately named agency-In-Hauss Strategies-in New Jersey. She put together the findings of the approaches of five different companies with varying backgrounds on their integrated campaigns which had worldwide impact.

The companies discussed these cases with the Public Relations Journal of the USA and the conclusion was that international Public Relations efforts gel best when there are no boundaries for "integration teams" that work hand-in-hand to share ideas, media information and strategies.

What could, then, be common between a leading American airline, a razor blade manufacturer, a freight forwarder, a bank and a car manufacturer, when it came to achieving their objectives on a global scale?

Each had a different objective. The approaches were also varied. The commonality came from the cutting across of disciplines and having a totality of approach.

Thus it was that Gillette managed to reach more than 27 million people in three days with simultaneous announcements about its product in 19 countries. At the heart of the multi-million-dollar campaign was a well researched and meticulously worked on Guidelines Manual. This served as a strategic framework which communicated Gillette's overall business goals and provided country-by-country guidelines for the new product launch. Masterminding this was a Public Relations agency whose consumer marketing division served as a central contact point and who coordinated with Group company and with its Public Relations partners in Europe and Canada on a daily basis.

They orchestrated the announcements so that the impact of the North American announcement would not be pre-empted by reports leaking back from European wire services. The way they did it was to embargo announcements in Europe until the US releases were done.

In their efforts they really thought global and acted local, as we mentioned elsewhere in this chapter. Thus, Public Relations firms locally developed material to suit the language, customs, retail outlets and price points in their areas in coordination with Gillette's marketing team.

With American Airlines, it was the use of Public Relations to influence negotiations on air and landing rights between the US and UK governments. But their move was not just a one-off exercise in Public Relations strategy. They actually structured a client service organization which integrate Public Relations, advertising and marketing. While policy and operating strategies were dictated by a planning committee, in a communications issue, the Public Relations team was drawn into it.

The Bank of America approach was to use integrated communications to announce a merger involving two mega banks, something that affected 3,000 employees and 30 facilities in Pacific markets. The main hazards the communicators had to avoid were employee, customer and market uncertainty in the countries involved, with imponderables like downsizing of units, clients accounts moving, layoffs and so on. They also had to be alert about media tracking the changes and speculating on the next sale. In the end, by avoiding individual responses to the various components of the merger events, they came forward with a total candid picture and the coordinated announcements broke without a hitch.

The Public Relations role in the positioning of a product came into play with the introduction of the Nissan Infiniti J30, a personal luxury car. Designed in America, it was engineered and manufactured in Japan and marketed in Japan, USA and Canada. Their Public Relations Manager said that every discipline—including marketing, Public Relations and advertising—had a "legitimate role and voice in determining the positioning of the vehicle."

These three, of the five instances cited, had varying strategies, but all with one common thread. That each of the disciplines had complementary roles to get a global reach for their message or project, but that there was a community of approach.

10

The Cricket World Cup 2003—where communication is a daily imperative

One of the world events in sport that will bring international media and tourist attention to focus on South Africa is the Cricket World Cup 2003. In November 2001, 15 months prior to the actual event taking place, a major Public Relations exercise to showcase the plan took place that dazzled the elite spectators and international media alike. The meticulously planned communication exercise is what we are detailing here.

Africa to the rest of the world was always the dark continent—and darker was the mysterious little corner tucked away in the deep south known as South Africa, where even the traditional colour of the continent was anathema, where white was might and something the world looked on with disdain. Suddenly in the spring of 1991, the Republic reached out to the rest of humanity as Nelson Mandela emerged from his Robben Island confinement and a new multi-racial cricket association known as the **United Cricket Board**, of South Africa was born. Soon the untouchable would become the incomparable as first the entry to the 1992 World Cup was cleared and later the hosting of the World Cup itself.

A nation that has been speaking in louder and more vocal tones to reach out to the world is now on a different communication high to attain credibility at home, through empowerment and development and kudos outside, through a mega image building exercise for cricket and country-alike.

As we participated as a select, invited audience in the unfolding of die World Cup 2003 logo in zebra stripes, held significantly in once-shunned black township of Soweto, the dreaded ghetto of racial repression, lines of distinction between black and white and of racial prejudice began to blur. And a larger emancipated canvas emerged which was all about a sporting event that would unite a nation, enhance international image and serve as an implement of

developmental activity. Specifically as a Public Relations exercise, it could not have been more spectacularly streamlined, an exercise that began at the grassroots level, embraced the disadvantaged people and reached out with a flourish to the international media.

Significant, too, is the fact, that South Africa, once the pariah of world cricket, because of its apartheid policies, has now become the patriarch of a world event that will dazzle the country and draw international credibility When Dr Ali Bacher, executive director of the World Cup 2003 organizing committee, and former chief of the United Cricket Board of South Africa, spoke at a Wisden Dinner in London a score of years ago, promising that South Africa would survive its international isolation and that "out of Africa will come something new. It will be dazzling, it will be strong, it will be good." He could hardly have foreseen then the magnitude or the integrated approach of this world-class event. On that historic launch at the Soweto Cricket Oval, we saw the word "dazzle" acquire a new brand equity.

Having just finished a stint at a game reserve, where we had seen a pride of lions and a herd of elephants, we had pondered on the plural for zebras, which we had seen in droves at the Pilanesberg sanctuary. As the World Cup logo and mascot became a reality through dramatic acrobatics, the black and white zebra striped emblem became newly significant. The collective noun for zebras is a "dazzle" and the World Cup mascot—a zebra in 12 cricket poses—will be known as Dazzler The logo, designed by TBWA Gavin Reddy was explained by Nathan Reddy of the agency as representing the fusion of black and white peoples and the cultural diversity of South Africa

Adding to this was the reaffirmation of a World Cup

Mission by Dr Bacher, which promised to enhance the lives of South Africans in all walks of life through the event. Germane to the whole exercise was the transparent communication, the easy accessibility of the top organizers, on the one hand, and the reaching out, not just to the media, but also to people who would matter through a direct interactive exercise, that made the event acquire a special dimension.

A few days before the launch of the ICC Cricket World Cup, we were to take in an India-Kenya fixture at the picturesque Paarl ground, which is in the heart of a beautiful wine district. Well before the match was to begin, Bacher addressed a large group of local councillors who were key opinion makers of the region, to drum up their support for the forthcoming world event where they could voice their opinions, and were also given the carrot of how their own ground would be funded to make it of international standards. It was not a media event, but a closed door one for the legislators to give them a sense of importance and belonging.

This was the same message that came through as we entered the Soweto Oval later in the week, to the lusty cheering and flag waving of black and white children, who lined the way for all invitees. One had a brief spell of celebrity-dom as they clamoured to shake hands, crowded to take pictures with us and cheered us on into the bowels of where the launch was to take place.

In a subtle manner, which was not stated, but which became clear once the programme unfolded, was the mix of key people of all colours in the presentation of the programme—black, white, coloured and Indian, showing a more unified than ever before South Africa as the world media watched. Where the Olympic Games span a fortnight, this will run for 44 days with 54 matches to be played for the most part in South Africa, with Zimbabwe hosting six and Kenya two. 14 teams will compete— Australia, Pakistan, India,, England, Zimbabwe, Netherlands, Namibia, South Africa, Sri Lanka, New Zealand, West Indies, Bangladesh, Kenya and Canada. 8-lakh ticket holders are expected, a media contingent of some 2000 and the viewership—a 1.2 billion television audience.

Standing to benefit from ail this are the "previously disadvantaged" (black) communities who will inherit 50 new turf cricket ovals. The country will be able to showcase itself to the world, where quite apart from the tens of thousands of tourists expected, before each match, short inserts of all the major tourists attractions will be aired on TV Partnerships have been forged with government, the Mint and the Post Office So that coins used for the toss before each match will be an ounce of pure gold, one for each game with the face of South African President Thabo Mbeki on one side and the logo on the other, along with the date and venue of the match and names of competing teams. While we were at the launch, a commemorative stamp was released, more of which will be in circulation.

So, in many respects, the tournament goes far beyond cricket. Ensuring the sport's continued viability in the country is a major goal of course, but the empowerment element is writ large. In its broader communicative aspects, the 2003 Cricket World Cup is also about developing people, spreading ownership of the World Cup, the transfer of skills, broadening the cricket market (black, youth, women and girls), facilitating a mentoring process for black South Africans, which includes black cricket writers. And on a wider scale, to ensure a great commercial return on global sponsors and local suppliers' investment.

South Africa has, through the hosting of this World Cup, ensured a return on investment of its capabilities to wrest for itself a long-lasting credibility in the eyes of the world, some of it still clouded over with memories of a darker era once described as "an affront to human dignity."

The era of the rebel tours during which the lure of the gold and diamond-backed Kruegerrand had attracted mercenary cricketers to the Republic in defiance of boycotts, was now a page in cricket's multi-hued history. South Africa was now part of the mainstream league of cricketing nations. We were privileged to see in Calcutta in 1991 the transformation, first hand, when a 737 load of South African cricket supporters, journalists and officials landed in India, and we saw the beginnings of the change in attitude and the melting away of apartheid laws.

From the unpardonable to the unputdownable—the change has come about through a process of attitude transformation that has seen a large element of structured, deliberate communication. During this Cricket World Cup, there will even be a unique volunteer system, where at least a thousand will come forward from all walks of life to man information kiosks and act as guides and ushers When this was announced, a well-established member of our Indian press immediately volunteered Such was the build up of the commitment sought and given.

Afterword

QR: Surely what communication is all about!

QR is not what you think it is, for these lists are not what we are talking about in a Communications book. QR is Quick Response. **You write, I reply. I ask, you answer.** Not: I write, remind, request, plead, cajole. And finally give up. This is what happened to me when I started the process of restructuring this book. In all good faith, I wrote special, individual, personal letters to CEOs, to my fellow PR professionals, to Advertising and Public Relations Agencies, to my many contacts in the Corporate Communications field around the world.

Considering we live in a wonderfully wired world, where you no longer have to wait a week for a letter to arrive, where, in a flash, an email can speak volumes, or a phone call can ask for time to reply to queries. But no. Our CEOs are too busy, too stressed out to heed letters written by communicators where we have an interest, not in a handout from them, but in a brief utterance from their Holinesses about themselves and their own organizations which they are at pains to project.

Sadly, one must give poor marks to the Indian corporate leader. Okay, so he's busy. So am I. Does he not possess a competent executive assistant, or a secretary? Does he not scrutinize his mail? Does he never dictate replies? And most of all, does he not have an able Public Relations manager to whom he can re-direct queries?

For those handful of CEOs who took the trouble to reply, I owe a special note of gratitude; they find place in this book for posterity. For the rest, it is a drab commentary on the efficiency, the credibility and the simple courtesy of CEOs that they do not find it necessary to respond to communication directed at them.

In contrast, the response from outside the country is so starkly, strikingly different. One agency wrote that it was a privilege for him to be asked to comment and be included in the book and another apologized profusely that he could not comment as he would be away for a long stretch and would not be able to do justice to my queries.

Some of the PR agencies were fabulously forthcoming, and the ones which do not find inclusion, just did not speak, write, phone, fax, email.

They are all supposed to be business communicators.

We decry red tape so glibly, but there seems to be a red gag around the mouths of those in the business of communication, and worse, the mouths of those leaders who must show us the way. If one of the large newspaper groups which institutes awards for excellence were to have a special slot for Most Communicative CEO, the whole ball game might just change.

I've come across a delightful little piece in Time Magazine (10 September 2001), which I would like to share:

"After an American tourist named Mike O' Shea enjoyed a sightseeing tour of China, he decided to send a thank you note straight to the top. Manners pay: O'Shea received a reply from Chinese President Jiang Zemin thanking him for his good wishes, conceding that China's tourism department needs steady improvement and musing on Indo Chinese relations." The President is even said to have asked after O'Shea's wife and daughter.

Cheers, Comrade Jiang. Alas our CEO's do not believe in replying to lesser mortals, even when we are:

a) not asking for sponsorship or advertisements
b) not accusing them of having laptop secretaries
c) not threatening them with unexpurgated biographies

I have been sustained by the corporate world for years, but am in a happily independent position to blow off steam.And offer this comment for those who will heed it.

to situate particular cases, such... just to part of, and
... ... on high Chinese officials? The President is well
said to have asked him.? The experts will denounce...
Great Comrade Jiang Abe our CIA with individuals
men plans to fasten itself upon a... we...

a) not asking for Ayatollahship, or at very least;
b) not accusing them of having broken ventures;
stand threatening them... with disrepute, and
biographies

I have been granted by the corporate world for years
but am in a largely independent position to blow its
alarm. And offer this comment for those who will heed it

BOOK FIVE:

A Subjective Abecedary

A Subjective Abecedary of Usage, Abusage, Misusage of Public Relations, Marketing, Printing, Net-related, General Communication and even some Accounting Terms that a Communicator ought to know

A.A.A.I.

One way of ensuring that you are always first on any list or agenda. You have to call the Advertising Agencies Association of India The Three A's of I, for to pronounce it in staccatoed initials would make you sound inebriated, which agency personnel are often accused of, although they claim that the days of languorous lunches are a thing of the past. The Three A's of I don't monitor this aspect, but do try to keep agencies on the straight and narrow with their set of ethical advertising standards. Debarment is a stigma an agency could do without. (see also NRSC)

A.A.A. Rating

The highest safety rating given to an investment opportunity by CRISIL, indicating maximum security of repayment of both principal and interest. See CRISIL.

A.B.C.

The Audit Bureau of Circulation. Another regulatory body, founded in 1931. To certify a net per issue sale figure of newspapers and magazines averaging over six months. Its members are clients or advertisers, advertising agencies and publishers. The body audits and certifies circulation figures of publications twice a year, so that they don't arbitrarily fudge figures by just printing and dumping. For the space buyer, it is a way of assessing the worth of the publication by the rates it charges for Advertising and also for the reach it wishes to have.

A.B.C.I.

The Association of Business Communicators of India. A body of house journal editors which, from being the erstwhile Indian Association of Industrial Editors founded by Victor Paranjpe (who was as much at home with music as with the Musica typeface) took this new name. This happened sometime in the seventies, when the scope of activities of corporate house journal editors expanded to include the electronic media. It has over 1,400 members. But there is a large overlap between the membership of the Public Relations Society of India and the ABCI. There was once a move for a merger of two similar organizations internationally, but it was rejected on the plea that they were as different as apples and oranges. Which was which, we were not told.

The ABCI's Magazine of the Year awards have become a coveted thing over the years. Even if some companies have been known to gear their magazines to winning these awards, it is probably a good thing in the interests of better-produced magazines for the corporate world which have a fight on their hands in the magazine boom scenario of today.

Advertising Club

And one more body to add to your membership list. The Ad Clubs awards are greatly sought after, with judging, stretching over several days and judges coming from a cross-section of the communications industry and from the corporate world. The hyped up Ad Club Awards Nites in the big metros have become a particularly big time event in advertising circles, the planning of which gives the already harried agency personnel further sleepless nights and probably adds to client costs at the end of the day. The Ad Club quizzes, lectures by top professionals, training programmes, the Hall of Fame conferments, have received their due attention and mileàge. Everything they do, they do it for you, but then the business of selling your business is their business.

Advertising

Advertising is the hawking of your product. Contrast it with its subtler cousin, Public Relations, which is to make people gawk at your image. There is a formal definition that says "Advertising presents the most persuasive possible selling message to the right prospects for the product or service at the lowest possible cost." In that case, there must be a zero investment in Public Relations if we are to accept the cynics' view of Public Relations being unpaid advertising. For a formal definition of Public Relations, read on until you come to P. By which time you will realize the heavy bias in favour of Public Relations and understand that P plus R or Performance plus Recognition is at the heart of this corporate communication management function.

Advertising Agency vs. Public Relations Consultancy

As different as durian and jackfruit. Both are from the same family, but the former, which has its origin in Southeast Asia, gives out a peculiar odour, though if, when eaten, it can be quite pleasant.

Without going into the merits of one versus the other, we need to briefly differentiate the workings of Advertising and Public Relations.

Advertising Agencies are agents of the media—commission agents who rake in the revenue on the media space or the TV or radio time they buy for their clients. They operate on an agency commission of 15% of the gross amount, which is equivalent to 17.65% of the net cost. The media owners grant them this and fortunately their clients can't get it even if they were to go to the media direct. To that extent ad agencies hold the key. They may even get an "accreditation" for this purpose, a kind of empowerment to act on behalf of newspaper and television barons, but while the money can be good on large advertising budgets, the guillotine is sharp, too, for they are responsible for defaulting clients. The latter have the money, so do the media, but an agency's assets are its people, who, unfortunately, keep moving from agency to agency to enhance their marketability or whenever they feel tired of working on the same brands and need the excitement of something new.

In its most basic form, though, an advertising agency creates and executes Advertising campaigns for its clients—a reactive sort of process.

Compare this with Public Relations consultancy—the word Public Relations agency can be a misnomer as Public Relations consultants are not agents. They are like doctors and lawyers, professionals who diagnose a problem and dispense their skills and expertise on a time cost basis. They charge by the hour or monthly retainership and all projects or events are then billed at cost or on a total turnkey basis. A Public Relations consultant is a more proactive animal than his Advertising counterpart—anticipating, rather than acting upon briefs or problems of clients.

Since this whole book is about Public Relations, we will not go into any further details at this point.

But for those interested in further delving into the commission angle, go to "Commission" for a few extra interpretations.

Advertorial

A sly way of garnering revenue for a publication. It is a *quid pro quo* route for getting advertisers to pay for advertising space. A sort of sugar-coated leeway to write about themselves in articles, rather than in advertising phrases.

Account Executive

Advertising Agencies are in the business of confusing the creativity out of you by using terminology like accounts and billing which don't mean what they were originally meant for. An Account Executive, (Account Representative/ Account Service person) for instance, is the term for the overworked executives sandwiched between facing clients and taking flak from their Account Directors. They are expected to possess the ability to interface with clients, but also to be the general dogsbody, doubling as copywriter and visualizer at the nth hour and the people who have to do all the dirty paperwork. They are seldom given the status that a media expert or a creative chief gets. They could be the being more sinned against than sinning, they remain in the perpetual line of fire, Eastwood style. "Ashes to ashes, dust to dust... what no one else does, the Account Executive must."

In the rapidly changing scenario that is advertising, the Account Management/Servicing profession is also expected to re-invent itself. Globally, client organizations expect Account Servicing persons from their advertising agencies to involve themselves in all aspects of Marketing the client's brand. This explains the new fangled craze for 'Account Planners' whose responsibilities include supervision of consumer research and advertising research, working on brand names and packaging, field testing in addition to the traditional functions of managing the conceptualization and execution of advertising campaigns. Other terms that are conferred on A.E.s today is Brand Services Manager, which encompasses a few more responsibilities and makes for more meaningful terminology.

Air Brush

Part of an art department's armoury, an air brush helps in glossing over blemishes, although the art director maintains it is strictly for retouching and special effects with a spraying technique.

Alphanumeric Characters

A mix of alphabetic and numeric characters, commonly used in the context of computerized data. Punctuation and special marks are often, loosely, included in alphanumeric characters.

Annual Reports

Annual Reports have been called a company's most significant and expensive written contact with its shareholders and the financial community. From a mere statutory document, the annual report has grown in size and style to being the annual creative statement of a company's financial performance coupled with a display of its prowess in other areas.

Although its production and handling has been initially the preserve of the Secretarial Department of the company, and, in some cases, of the finance department, from where it has all originated, today much of the Public Relations department's time is spent on re-writing of the Director's Report and the conception and production of the whole document as an art form. This department is left to face the final hectic stages of printing, to meet the required 21 plus 2 clear days for mailing it to shareholders, prior to the Annual General Meeting.

The latter love a well-produced report, but question anything too glossy, grousing that some of this expenditure could be better spent on dividends to themselves.

Content wise, the practice of publishing the salaries of personnel earning more than a certain amount annually was initially a prestige thing with those who figure in the "list". But it has lost its charm and is now considered an invasion of privacy. Other requirements in India for disclosure of energy consumed, R & D expenditure and rural projects done continue to make for further unnecessary paperwork. Environmental audits are another marking matter for companies who could come unscrubbed if they don't disclose what they are doing to purify what emits from their industry. The new thing is the disclosures under Corporate Governance, which has become a statutory requirement for publication in Annual Reports of companies.

A.G.M

The Annual General Meeting of a company is a forum where shareholders get a chance to have a face-to-face, and often a head-on confrontation with the management. It is an occasion which the small shareholder prepares for, armed as he comes with a long harangue and occasional compliments for the company he has put his money into. On the other side, the management has to prepare for months in advance as well, for what the chairman will say, how the shareholders will be checked in, what the press might investigate, how the event will be presented, and detailed answers drawn up to every possible financial and other query that the shareholder might have. For the Public Relations department too, this is a major exercise in communication and organization particularly the press angle with AGM's getting noisy or contentious issues are to be discussed.

Some AGMs show video films and have product displays, some are held in corporate offices, but the large majority are in hotels with a good infrastructure or in auditoriums or even in the open air with massive "shamianas". Serving refreshments of some sort is necessary, but can be a headache. A worse headache is the doling out of gifts for which there is usually a stampede and special planning of this aspect also becomes a necessity.

Video conferencing an AGM has been tried selectively by companies.

A.V.

Audio-visual devices reflect the growing illiteracy amongst the communications fraternity and the increasing need for people to see and hear pre-fab information. These include the production of videos with slides, sound and special effects that now take the form of multi-screen and multi-projector extravaganzas and cinematic films. Techniques having advanced, costs have concomitantly come down, so that videos are produced with the regularity and ease of an instamatic camera. Everything from AGMs to histories of companies are recorded on video, which is fine except that we advocate a greater use for them and better initial research to know if they are absolutely necessary.

Artwork

The final stage of an advertisement or a publication, just prior to making a positive for printing. Not to be confused with initial pencilled layouts, or even paste-ups, nor with the inspired handiwork of a child. This is the stage where the client makes the maximum changes, resulting in hiked costs, more time wasted, deadlines gone haywire and plenty of heartburn for the agency. Surely an area where client education is essential. A good ruse is to take a colour photocopy of the artwork or do four-colour printouts from the computer. All client billable, of course.

Above-the-line Advertising

Terrible misnomer, on the face of it. Nothing to do with being above board, or otherwise. Mainly means the use of press, radio, television, outdoor advertising such as hoardings and cinema. Its counterpart, likewise, does not deserve denigration, but merely gets the distinction because it includes such things which come under the purview of the Marketing guys—merchandising, point of sale, direct mail. Also exhibitions and sponsorships which have to go often under the Public Relations function.

Amylum

To amylum a company's image is to starch it. Pity this word is never used in this context. Here's a start.

Audience

The failure of a message is usually when this factor is not looked at scientifically, especially when, in blindly following Marshal McLuhan, the medium becomes the message.

Banner

Advertisements painted, or printed, on cloth or other fabric, which are then displayed outdoors or indoors as required. These are inexpensive and convenient, but have a short life.

Banner ads

Not to be confused with banners (see above), these are advertisements in the form of horizontal strips incorporated into websites, usually at the top. Some are static, others animated. By clicking on the banner ad with the mouse, the visitor to the site is automatically connected to the advertiser's website. Often make visitors to the site see red, as the banner occupies part of the screen and may take ages to download, especially those with cute animations. See Click Thru' and Visitor.

Billboard

A billboard is also a hoarding, just as a pavement is also a footpath. The former is undeniably American, although the British use it to mean the little stand-up signs which have cinema posters or other announcements plastered on them. A great and cost-effective advertising medium as long as trees are not felled and buildings are not defaced by their use.

But having said that, the prettying up of the hole-in-the-wall cigarette and pan vendor's shop with illuminated frontages advertising a branded product, help slicken broken down establishments and give the advertiser luminous mileage.

The side games of hoardings are sandwiches and lollipops, the former being effective when repeatedly done in rows on lighting poles on a major road artery, while the latter are ideal for pictorial images with corporate names discreetly painted in. Outdoor advertising today is more than a hoarding, what with digital printing advancements and their use by the very people who own them to do public service advertising.

Bleed

When the printer asks you if you want the pages of a publication to bleed, don't head for the nearest first-aid box. He merely wishes to know whether a particular illustration or any other element in the page should extend to edge of the page, leaving no margin after trimming.

Block

While you could have a writing block, generally an excuse to procrastinate, the one referred to here is usually a metal sheet engraved with a reversed image of the matter for letterpress printing. Rapidly going out of use due to advances in printing technology giving rise to better methods of printing that do not require blocks and give superior results, faster and sometimes at less cost.

Brandvertising

Coined by god, a.k.a. Alyque Padamsee, who looked ahead at integrated communication strategies to include a multitude of communication options, beyond Advertising, to grow brands with more economic leverage than ever before.

Broadsheet

This is the size that most newspapers come in, unless they indulge in yellow journalism and then need to be in those infamous tabloid sizes. Therefore, see tabloid.

Broadside

The commonest expression using this word is the phrase: Delivering a broadside, when the strongest, abusive terms are flung at a person. It probably originates from the shipping term, where it means all the guns that can be fired from one side of a ship.

In printing, it means a large sheet of paper printed on one side with a political or promotional message.

Brief

Brevity has never been the strong suit of any communications expert. (see K.I.S.S.). But a brief consists of all the pertinent facts a client gives an agency before launching a campaign. In military usage it is used for the important information given before a planned operation. Legal briefs are common parlance.

The key to a successful brief is to get the client to encapsulate his points in writing without wasting your billable time. Perhaps a VAT (value-added time-freeze) could be imposed on the garrulous client. Sam Black talks about a brief being the starting point for designing an exhibition stand.

Bog

This means B.O.G. and not the other stuff that is part of frequent usage. It is this old Marketing gimmick of Buy One, Get-one-free. Works for everything from leaner products which have not been moving to those that are bogged down to airline offers like British Airways' when they gave one ticket free for one purchased.

Booklet, Pamphlet, Folder, Monograph, Brochure, Catalogue, Book

A *booklet* or *pamphlet* is larger than a broadside, smaller than brochure. It is usually a publication in six or more pages, with a cover for the title and stapled. It can be printed by letterpress or Xerox offset or regular offset, but is generally in a single colour.

A *folder* is not only a printed four-pager, it is also a stand-alone jacket (usually with a pocket) for inserting other printed material. The jacket may be printed or otherwise.

A *monograph* is generally on a single theme and comes in the form of a book, an article or paper written on a subject requiring considerable research.

A *brochure* is an extended booklet, often multi-coloured, and going into many more pages than a booklet, but not as weighty as a book. Corporate brochures range from product promotional publications and catalogues and employee handbooks to elaborate glossy creations that blow the corporate trumpet.

A *book* separates itself in length, form and intent from all these other publications. Books also tend to have a longer shelf life than their less weighty counterparts.

Bowdlerization

Talking of books, particularly corporate literature, hopefully, bowdlerization would not be required, for presumably there would not be offensive passages to be thrown out, or bowdlerized.

Boomerang

When you send out a signal to a select audience group and they react in a manner which is quite the opposite of what you expected.

Bromide

We tend to use these bits of sensitized paper all the time, before printing. Hence many of us lose the import of the slang which refers to a bromide as a person who says trite things. Thus a bromide remark could well land you with acid on your face!

By-line

An author's name appended to a report in a newspaper or magazine, which is not easy to come by.

Cognitive Consistency, Cognitive Dissonance

The reason we have to grapple with these terms is because in a Marketing man's basket of terminology, these behavioural inconsistencies have to be tackled for reaching the correct target audiences. The first believes that, to be persuasive, the material in a message must be consistent both with the recipient's own beliefs and with itself. With the latter, it is a question of understanding double negatives. To quote an authoritative source: Relating to the consumer world, cognitive dissonance arises after a choice decision has been made and the consumer is committed to a particular choice from a product field, leading the consumer to dissonance reduction behaviour .

The theory was developed by Leon Festinger.

Collage

Not to be confused with montage. Lazy agencies, when at their wits end, usually serve up a collage of pictures to make for an artier or offbeat look. More appropriate for school goers' workbooks.

Colophon

All books have them at the beginning of the publication showing the name of the author, publisher, printer, copyright details and so on, but this does not include the more arbitrary dedication section which can run from the cryptic line to a whole essay.

Column Centimetre

That by which many clients expect to measure the capability of the Public Relations Consultant's ability to reach their message following a press release or a press conference.

In just mathematical terms, it is width x depth of a column of type, usually in a newspaper. Advertisers are charged by column centimetre, but payments made to writers in this manner may not be so lucrative.

Caption

The legend to a picture, which describes and unfortunately often confuses, what is going on in it. Should ideally be pithy. Editors of corporate publications are warned never to state the obvious, for the reader is not an idiot. Captioning is a fine art, which should be done in conjunction with a story, not as an afterthought. There is evidence that captions increase the time spent by readers looking at a picture, especially if the picture is incorporated into an advertisement.

Centrespread

The most sought-after and coveted place in any publication as readers of many a "sensational" magazine would amply vouch for. Whether a centrespread or a cover girl position is more attention getting is a subjective matter.

As for other positions in publications, the *inside covers* and *back cover*, in terms of mileage to the advertiser are immense, as are the rates. In books and in corporate literature, these are the wasteful areas, which either have an overabundance of pictorial techniques, or that messages covers. In these publications, a *frontispiece* is a good affectation, as is a *gatefold* or *pullout*.

Circulation

There's a difference between circulation and readership. The former means the number of distributed copies of each issue of a publication, whereas the latter was earlier based on assumption and claim. At present the readership surveys take the guesswork out of calculating readership. Rivals often talk of fudged figures, but the Audit Bureau of Circulation does exist to monitor such claims. There's a third element: print order, which probably means the number of copies you can afford to give away. See IRS and NRS.

Click Thru'

The process of clicking with the mouse on a banner advertisement or a hyperlink on a website, thereby connecting to the advertiser's website. An easy and convenient way to travel from site to website. See Banner Ad, Hyperlink and Website.

Colour

When in doubt, clients plead colour-blindness. Must be told that the primary printing colours are yellow, magenta and cyan with black being the fourth colour. A well-known paint company in India has the monopoly on the slogan on colour, but most CEOs have a monopoly on seeing red when deliveries are untimely, or on using a blue pencil when what they read is what they don't think is passable. And, although red-tapism is frowned upon, it has its merits when you think of the failsafe methods involved in the extensive notations which leave nothing to chance on a government file.

Commercial

A commercial is an ad film made with big budgets for a small time-span. Commercial breaks come in between your attention span in a television or radio programme and have become so much the order of the day, that the conditioned reflex seeks these interruptions. Great for the advertiser, who can place his message, depending on his budget, in the appropriate and premium times when viewership is at its maximum.

Commercialization

In normal parlance, the profit motive dominates any talk of commercialization. But for those in communication, it should have another angle in the context of the businesses they interact with. And that is the phase in the development of a new product or process when it is ready to go commercial or be launched in the market. Then the whole vicious cycle starts. Beginning with installation of capacity, there is then the production and building up of inventories, the maintenance of adequate supplies, the ensuring of distribution, the creation of markets which will receive the product.

Commercial Artist

Once again, it is not someone with just a profit motive, but an artist who works with advertising agencies and business houses to do industry-related work. It is still creative in nature and the only distinction between this kind of artist and the ones who paint for pleasure—and ultimately for profit—is that the latter has to often motivate himself, while the commercial artist can be client-driven.

Commission

The bread and butter of an agency. Discussed briefly under advertising agency in this glossary. There we touched on the methodology. Now we talk about the other side—the fact that while this 15% exists, it does not really make room for the creative aspects. Thus, there are separate costs for production, creative work and other jobs related to the making of an advertisement or the conception of a project. These are billed to clients on actuals, or built in with turnkey costs. It has been suggested that agencies could work on a service fee rather than on commission. But that would involve an understanding to be reached between an individual organization and an agency.

Commission rebating is another issue which is never clearly spelt out, although it basically means a system of price discounting or invoice discounting for media rates which is then passed on to the client, so that its commission is eroded in proportion. Not permitted under the regulations governing the business of advertising, but unofficially reported to have become fairly common practice.

The marking new developments are in respect of commission on television billings. Clients have suddenly found the golden road to direct buying of time, which could leave ad agencies hopelessly in the lurch and leave them out of the picture in the negotiations for advertisement placement. The advertisers see the agencies continuing to do the creative work, but feel that the saving of the commission on their massive budgets could well be put to better use on buying better programmes and enhanced research to help them focus their advertising better. Which really doesn't help the agencies' bottom line, who should be able to come up with solutions to such developments with their creative brainpower.

Another new development, is the business of getting out of the old 15%, and a more business-approach deal of a percentage on sales achieved.

Composition

Not the term commonly used to mean the essay, which in itself is a dying species today. When you set or compose matter you are finally setting the typewritten manuscript in one of a variety of printing types, an essential pre-requisite to printing. With rapid changes in printing technology, computerized typesetting has replaced the older methods like monotype and linotype machines.

Copy

To imitate is to admire. But to copy is to plagiarize! Or is it? Copy can be the hard copy that is the written material for newspapers, or the ad copy that forms the text of the advertisement, or the disembodied "copy" that the printer works from to translate into metal types. The copywriter is a highly creative individual in an agency, who is constantly put on the spot for brilliant one-liners when he would rather be writing theses. Or would he?

Contact Report

Made generally by agencies to pass the buck. Also called Service Report, Contact Meeting Report etc. Once you've documented who is responsible for what action, and you bombard the client with bunches of reports, some of which he may not read, you could win out in the long term. After all, there is still nothing like putting it all down on paper. But such documentation of action could backfire too. See Boomerang.

Corporate Identity, Corporate Image, Corporate Culture

Corporate identity is the style, quality, character and personality of an organization.

Corporate image is the way others see the company.

Corporate culture is the way a company behaves, often largely the result of the strong personality of the CEO.

A separate chapter deals with this, for that is what Public Relations grapples with a lot of time. Putting a face to a product. A personality to a face. Saving face. Et al.

Client

The consultee, cash cow, the one who calls the shots. You scratch his back and you will be rewarded with a back scratcher. The more successful you are at it, the better will be the billings. The client is the consultant's bread and butter. Bad servicing should not stale the infinite variety that the former has to offer.

Consultant, Consultancy

Public Relations companies are both consultants and agents. Public Relations consultancies can either be full service ones when they offer the full range of consulting and agency services across the different specialities within Public Relations like media relations, employee communications, international affairs, government liaison and so on. But there are also specialist agencies which do everything from financial Public Relations to special events management.

While appointing a consultant, the client would do well to go by the let-the-buyer-beware dictum.

Conflict of Interest

The ball is in the consultant's court to ensure that two rivals in the same trade are not being serviced at the same time. But having said that, there is no rule which says that a consultant cannot represent competing interests. The thing to do is to be clear with both parties. Sometimes in a large consultancy set-up, it is possible to have different teams work on rival clients.

"Don't double-deal" is the message.

Confidentiality of Information

Stems from the above, really. You definitely are not supposed to disclose information given in confidence by a client or an employer *for personal gain*. It is so wildly tempting, for instance, to play the market when you know the corporate results in advance and the company's possible decisions on dividends and bonus issues. But that is what amounts to insider trading. Naturally the phrase points more to those running the company, than to the image-setters.

Code of Athens

Surprise! Surprise! In case you were wondering whether there are any rules or ethics at all in the codes of conduct of Public Relations people, a code was adopted by the International Public Relations General Assembly, Athens, on 12 May 1965 and modified at Teheran on 17 April 1968. In May 1961, an IPRA Code of conduct was adopted in Venice, which is set out here.

IPRA Code of Conduct

A. Personal and Professional Integrity

By personal integrity is meant the maintenance of both high moral standards and a sound reputation. By professional integrity is meant observance of the Constitution rules and, particularly, the Code as adopted by IPRA.

B. Conduct towards Clients and Employees

1. A member has a general duty of fair dealing towards his clients and employees, past and present.
2. A member shall not represent conflicting or competing interest without the express consent of those concerned.
3. A member shall safeguard the confidences of both present and former clients or employers.
4. A member shall not employ methods tending to be derogatory of another member's client or employer.
5. In performing services for a client or employer a member shall not accept fees, commission or any other valuable consideration in connection with those services from anyone other than his client or employer without the express consent of his client or employer, given after a full disclosure of the facts.
6. A member shall not propose to a prospective client or employer that his fee or other compensation be

contingent on the achievement of certain results; nor shall he enter into any fee agreement to the same effect.

C. *Conduct towards the Public and the Media*

1. A member shall conduct his professional activities with respect to the public interest and for the dignity of the individual.
2. A member shall not engage in practice which tends to corrupt the integrity of channels of public communication.
3. A member shall not intentionally disseminate false or misleading information.
4. A member shall at all times seek to give a faithful representation of the organization which he serves.
5. A member shall not create any organization to serve some announced cause but actually to serve an undisclosed special or private interest of a member or his client or his employer, nor shall he make use of it or any such existing organization.

D. *Conduct towards Colleagues*

1. A member shall not intentionally injure the professional reputation or practice of another member. However, if a member has evidence that another member has been guilty of unethical, illegal or unfair practices, including practices in violation of this code, he should present the information to the Council of IPRA.
2. A member shall not seek to supplant another member with his employer or client.
3. A member shall cooperate with fellow members in upholding and enforcing this Code.

Crisis Communication

It is not just a matter of dousing fires. Read all about this in Book Three.

Consumerism

The champion of them all is Ralph Nader. He is particularly well known for his criticism of the defective welding of the Chevrolet Corvair, which General Motors abandoned after its sales plummeted. Consumer rights have become a big issue in India but the limited reach of the Consumer Action Forum or PUBLIC (People United for Better Living in Kolkata) or the aborted consumer magazine "Which?" show that much more needs to be done. Public Relations has a catalytic role in this.

Cannibalization

In Marketing terms, any new activity undertaken by an organization which adversely affects existing business is said to cannibalize it. The launch of a new product into a market in which the organization already has an existing product will, almost inevitably, have some adverse effect on the existing brand. Actually, it is a good way to sideline that flagging product for a new one—all of which are in the family, anyway. As they say in Marketing, it is infinitely better to shift customers from existing products to your new ones, than see them shift to competitors' products.

CRISIL

The Credit Rating and Information Services of India Limited is the first agency of its kind in India and has been functioning since 1987. It was set up by ICICI, UTI, HDFC, LIC and other insurance companies. To be rated by it—the highest being a triple A—means a validation for a company of its financial and all-round soundness. The Public Relations people feel that if the profile of a company can be presented innovatively enough, then value-addition to the bottom line from CRISIL's viewpoint could make a one A point difference. This is not to advocate that they can be fooled about a badly performing company, but simply to stress the merits of better presentation.

CRISIL doesn't just rate, but gives out invaluable data through a number of publications like *Rating Scan, Crisilcard* and so on.

The age of competition has ensured that other rating agencies are now in the fray—ICRA and CARE. The Investment Information and Credit Rating Agency of India (ICRA) has been founded by the Industrial Finance Corporation of India, while CARE—Credit Analysis and Research Limited—is under the aegis of the Industrial Development Bank of India. The fourth rating agency is the relatively new Fitch Ratings India, formed when Fitch International took over the operations of Duff & Phelps. Do corporations stand to gain?

Consultancy Fees, Costs

Varies widely from one country to another and from client to client. Fees can be one-off for a particular project. Or they can be negotiated annually with clients, which would take into account the volume of work and the time cost. Some pay in equal instalments. Then there is the fabled retainer fee, which makes it incumbent on both client and agency to regularly interact, for fees' sake anyway. But it is the best way of ensuring that a PR consultant keeps his involvement with the industry on a regular basis, replacing the need for a full-time PR person within the company, yet giving sound advice and good service.

There are different rates for the head of the consultancy firm and other ones for his juniors and the client is billed by the rates that different individuals can command. A better way is to charge a uniform team time, based on an average of the combined time of consultant, executive and secretary.

More on consultants in Book One.

DTP

Desktop publishing has made life easier and cheaper and the printed word more devalued than ever before. But composing on the computer with its attendant graphics, and the megabytes of software available like Adobe PageMaker, Corel Draw, Macromedia Freehand, Microsoft Office, Quark Express and many others are giving more elbow to instant publication, but appear to be making artists redundant and creating a new generation of computer buffs who turn editor at the click of a mouse.

PR companies equipped to do this can save a client time and money and enhance credibility because of the quick response it generates.

De-Massification

This originated with Alvin Toffler to describe a move away from network TV to narrow casting with special programmes for certain viewing groups along with a multiplicity of separate delivery systems.

Today, the concepts of Business Television, which are described in Book Four of this publication, show how this segmented broadcasting is making waves with companies with elaborate dealer networks. It requires money, research and someone to produce imaginative programmes.

Digital Camera

A camera that takes photographs without using conventional film, and stores the images as electronic information. See digital photography.

Digital Photography

"Fast to shoot, quick to see"—does not use conventional film to record images. The photograph is stored as a digital or electronic image that can be displayed, edited and manipulated by a computer. Eliminates film processing, can be used directly for preparation of printing material or for use in a computer document.

Digital Printing

A method of printing in which the deposition of printing ink on to the substrate is controlled by a computer rather than by mechanical means. Expensive, but produces superior, uniform printing. Commonly used for producing illuminated billboards, hoardings, displays and shop signage.

Direct Marketing

Sometimes its denigrators call it dirty tricks Marketing because through direct mail, catalogues, the telephone, pullouts in newspapers and magazines, you reach customers direct but in the process litter up their letterboxes with junk mail. Public Relations people have been known to get into the act, but it is much more of a Marketing function. Direct selling has become another narking intrusion into people's lives when they are plagued by salespersons pushing everything from vacuum cleaners to computers and soft luggage.

Documentary

A documentary is an extended commercial, produced, also with large budgets, but of longer duration. It is an informational film produced by companies or countries or individuals. Some documentaries are made with such an artistic bent, that they could be feature films and some well-made feature films are grouted in historical fact as was the case with the award-winning *Schindler's List*.

Dotcom companies

The Millennium has seen the rise and fall of dotcom companies—set up with large doses of enthusiasm accompanied by immense amounts of hope and hype. Alas, little attention was given to sources of revenue, leading to a crash from the stratosphere to below sea level! Hence the popular view "dot come, dot gone". The game is now largely back to brick and mortar.

Drop Letter

In the good old days, really old that is, way back in the time of Gutenberg, it was called an illumination. This oversize capital letter occupies the depth of two or more lines and is used at the beginning of an article or paragraph, sometimes with embellishments added to the letter. Computers are making life easier for those making formats with drop letters.

Dummy

A great cutout. From dummy runs of presentations, which ensure that snags can be detected before the final act, to dummies for publications, which show the first steps in the plan of the magazine, the use of a dummy makes for less heartache and expense at the end.

Duotone

When you get a two-tone effect from a single photograph, by using two halftone plates.

Ear Panels

Advertisers who persist with putting their messages on the ears of the newspaper, get long-term mileage from the seemingly pedestrian position. And yet, sitting there, on either side of the masthead, these advertising messages could be used to great effect.

E-commerce

Business or commercial transactions that take place using the facilities of the Internet, including payment for goods and services. If payment is not made over the Internet, then it is, strictly speaking, not e-commerce. Order fulfilment usually happens in the real or 'bricks and mortar' world.

Economies of Scale

When the client asks you to print 50 copies of an item like a booklet or poster or whatever, throw economies of scale at him, for reduction in average unit cost results from increased productive capacity.

E-mail

Nothing to do with black or green mail. The former has been well defined forever since we can remember. Green mail is a comparatively newer happening—a result of the spate of mergers and acquisitions. It essence, the invadee pays the invader to keep off his territory.

With E-mail, either you're on the bandwagon or not. For those who are, you can hook up to a total system and correspond on your own computer screens and not have any cumbersome deliveries by messenger. It is instantaneous and inexpensive, with almost 100% guarantee of delivery. But it cannot reach those who are not part of the system— those who do not have an e-mail address. And, you cannot despatch anything physical. No chocolates... no red roses... no champagne, either.

Em

In printing and production, you've got to watch your 'em's and 'en's as much as you want your p's and q's. An em can be a lethal weapon in the vocabulary of the conscientious scrabble player, harbouring no connection with the dative, third person plural of the middle English word hem or "em". In printing jargon, the em was formerly the letter "M" in any given font of type. Now it is a unit of measure, as of column pica being equal to about 1/6th of an inch. An "em" dash is not a hyphen but a dash between phrases.

Employee

The target group of both the Human Resource Development and the Public Relations specialist. The word sits in a curious position in a thesaurus. It comes under a broad category of "Volition", which means the power of free will, and therefore puts an employee in a wonderfully elevated position of a free thinker with initiative. So, this "public" should be addressed with greater maturity of thought.

Editor

The editor of a newspaper or a magazine is the non-management head honcho who directs the news content and the newsworthiness of a paper. Newspapers which are owned by business houses often have a compromise on their hands with editors having to play the managerial tune.

An independent editor is the one who gets the most kudos, receives the greatest brickbats and has the power to bring down governments and erring people in high places, but if he's dethroned himself, there's always room at the top at the next paper.

Public Relations people have to interact with editors, assistant editors, feature editors, financial editors, news editors and often they are editors themselves of house journals so it's a double-edged sword.

Exclusive

When your client gives someone an "exclusive" story, make sure that it is not given to ten publications simultaneously. Credibility rather than the circulation of the story is at stake if this happens.

Exployee

When an employee ceases to be employed by an organization, which has, due to various constraints, had to downsize. Or "rightsize" as some companies have done. Part of the "de-hiring" process. This coinage is our own!

Face

The part of the anatomy of a corporation which, when well presented to the public, can gain it support for its market borrowings, bring it better employees, give it stature with those in power in the governance of the country.

For a printer, it is the top of the type used for printing and means the various typefaces in his armoury that have made printed work so varied and exciting to deal with.

FAQs

Factious, flippant, asinine queries. But more specifically— Frequently Asked Questions. Advertising Agencies have to prepare lists of FAQs for clients to answer, from which a detailed brief or approach paper may be prepared. Websites usually have FAQs worked out for first timers to their site. A new site agencyfaqs.com has become popular among those wanting to get an update on advertising agencies, clients, profiles and a whole lot of other Advertising related information.

Financial Public Relations

Financial Public Relations is understood by most corporations to mean the part of the Public Relations department's job that deals with the production of annual reports and interim reports, the arrangements of shareholder visits, the handling of statutory financial announcements, financial press briefings, giving exclusives to journalists from business papers, putting together conferences connected with share issues and road shows.

In India, specialized agencies handle such press and broker conferences and Euro Issues, but some recent guidelines imposed by the Securities and Exchange Board of India (SEBI) have put somewhat of a damper on creativity prior to a share issue to build up corporate profile. Their argument: misrepresentation.

Feedback

What most otherwise well-conceived Advertising, Public Relations and sales promotion projects suffer from at the end of the day. Tail end research and reaction-gathering are invaluable to gauging the success of the programme or activity.

Flush

A term used very often by modern-day interior decorators while putting in doors that do not bang. Also much in vogue for illustrations which have to extend up to the edges of page. Often used interchangeably with "bleed", but while both result in the same, or similar effect, the two represent something of the optimist-pessimist enigma of a half-full half-empty glass.

Foreword

A foreword is so often misspelt foreward or even forward, that it is better to give it the appellation "preface". Yet the word has great clarity—signifying the beginning or the introductory statement.

In speech, you preface your remarks, you don't foreword them. To that extent, the former can be used in books as the preliminary remarks about the contents or author before a speech.

Some books contain both, one a pat on the back by someone other than the author, and the other, a pat on one's back by oneself.

In musical terms, a preface is really a prelude. A foreword is the andante cantabile.

Fundraising

Strictly not a Public Relations actionable item. Not to be confused with sponsorships.

Four-colour Printing

Usually, companies expect five to six-colour results from four-colour printing. Just to set the record straight, the technicalities are set down here. In order to print a full colour picture on paper, a printer requires a transparency, a slide of the subject. This is then processed electronically to the required size to split down the picture to its basic colour components. This part of the process is called "scanning and colour separation". Once the colours are separated, four separate film positives of the subject are obtained in the primary printing colours of cyan, yellow, magenta and black. These are subsequently printed over the same surface to create the impression of a full colour picture.

Fax

A quick solution for the procrastinating letter writer. Truly a great invention for saving time, but there are some backfired negatives—the generation of more paper, and sometimes the receipt of junk mail on fax. Many people of the "old school" prefer a fax to an email, which they claim is not seen physically staring you in the face, and waits for the recipient to open it at his whim.

Goodwill

Unmeasurable. But the Sword of Damocles that is brandished over Public Relations practitioners' heads for them to generate. In business terms, goodwill is that non-quantifiable term which is tagged on to an institution and becomes quantifiable when a valuation or sale of that organization takes place.

Gatefold

One of the most intriguing items in an editor's bag of tricks to assist him in catching audience attention. It is essentially a format where a page opens out double outward and makes an impact like the centrespread. Often used for corporate publications or annual reports or by magazines which want advertisers to pay enormously high sums of money for unusual formats.

Gallup

Synonymous with opinion polling. Originating in the USA, you find Gallup in a large number of countries worldwide, engaged in market research. Gallups' services include "Advertising and communication, publishing periodicals and media research, omnibus research, social-ethical and religious studies, computer analysis"

In India, with the establishment of IMRB, Indica, ORG—MARG and Sofrés Mode, to name a few, the whole process of market surveying and opinion research has reached fine-tuned heights and psephologists like Prannoy Roy have become a *de rigeur* part of the political process before an election.

Grapevine

Communicators are hired by companies to formalize on paper what is more effective and quick fire when passed on from person to person. Still, the best way of conveying news of promotions, transfers, deaths, takeovers, even if there is a bit of rumour mongering attached to it.

Hard Copy

A copy of a document printed on paper. See Soft Copy.

Hardware

Any piece of machinery, but commonly used to indicate the pieces of equipment that make up a computer—the processor, storage devices, keyboard, mouse, monitor etc. Stuff that can be seen and felt. See Software.

Headline

That which a Public Relations person is supposed to seek eagerly for his company when things are going well and try to shun when the red marks appear in the balance sheet.

Hidden Persuaders

Advertising Agencies are supposed to be this and Public Relations people are meant to emulate and achieve this through means other than four-colour statements in newspapers. Vance Packard was the originator of this phrase and his book is among those that continue to be read for its insights into the advertising profession.

Histogram

Just a bar chart. Presentations using bars and pies can be put through Windows programmes to get accurate and innovative methods of quantification.

Hoarding

(See Billboard)

Homepage

On the Internet or World Wide Web, an initial page presenting information (text, visuals, animations, graphics, audio) about an individual or an organization. Details are usually incorporated on separate web pages, hyperlinked to the home page. The complete set of web pages is often called the website.

House Style

Makes for standardization. The western nations are adept at producing full scale manuals which set out the correct typography, size, colour and methods of using the logo and symbol of the company on the tiniest things like pencils, to their use on vans and buildings.

House Journals

A name change surely required here. A corporate periodical would sound infinitely better. A whole chapter has been devoted to this because it is a vital communication tool which some companies use as a me-too effort, others because it has always been done and still others to provide jobs to the Public Relations department to keep them out of productive mischief. The video magazine is a close rival but cannot oust the printed word in a hurry. (See the detailed chapter on House Journals in Book Three)

Hyperlink

The address or location of a website incorporated into a computer document and programmed so that by clicking with a mouse on the hyperlink, the user is automatically connected to the website. Sometimes shortened to 'link'. See Mouse and Website.

ICE

Information, Communication, Entertainment. This is the new chillout mantra.

ICS

Integrated Communication Strategies.

A Public Relations tool for presenting multifaceted approaches to the formulation of a non-Advertising based set of communications.

Integrated Marketing Communications

Defined by one Advertising CEO as "an orchestration of communications vehicles with the 'brand idea' (not the ad idea) as the central focus."

INS

The Indian Newspapers Society is made up of representatives of newspapers and periodicals in India and controls the standards and rules governing Advertising Agencies, their accreditation and payment norms. Through its various committees, it administers the conduct of newspapers and agencies on a number of aspects. The committees cover Advertising, Newsprint, Periodicals, Research & Development, Industrial Relations & Legal Affairs, Press Freedom. There are also committees looking after building-finance and staff and a negotiating committee for Advertising matters.

The *INS Press Handbook* is a manual that no advertising agency should be without. Advertisers need to have it around, as well. Its reference ambit covers details of newspapers and periodicals on their circulation; ad rates; personnel; ad agencies and their clients, a list of press organizations in India and abroad and accredited press correspondents, and a set of guidelines for allocation of newsprint.

The advertising ethics and medical standards are poorly subbed and need an update on what constitutes morality, considering what condom advertisements are getting away with these days.

INFA

The INFA Press and Advertisers Year Book is another publication that an agency or an advertiser or a newspaper ad department should not be without. Its various sections provide different types of information relevant to a number of target groups. The section on press in general has accredited press correspondents, news and feature agencies, printing and machinery, newsprint dealers and trade and professional associations listed and also gives laws that are relevant to newspaper publishing and advertising.

Other sections list information services of the government, Who's Who in the Indian press and in Advertising and Public Relations, and there are large sections dealing with media planning and rates and data for advertising in every kind of publication.

In-film Advertising

As, for instance, when your heroine is playing tennis and the camera focuses on her Nike skirt and carry bag, Reebok shoes and Head racquet and she picks up a Pepsi when she sits down between sets. For small budget feature films, this has been known to be one way of raising revenue.

I.R.S.

The Indian Readership Survey, similar to the National Readership Survey. A joint effort of media user organizations and industry associations. Like N.R.S. it provides audited data about the readership of various publications, viewership of television channels and cinema and listnership of radio, thus helping media planning for advertising purposes. While a lot of the data are similar to N.R.S, fine tuning a media plan requires in-depth knowledge of the differences. See N.R.S.

Journalists

A vital "public" of Public Relations practice. The past decade has shown an increasingly refreshing trend away from the adversarial role to a more developmental and constructive one.

Jingle

A jingle is to a commercial what a doggerel is to a poem. Both give zip to the subjects they mingle in, but both are made fun of in the main. And yet, today, a well-made jingle can make or break a product, can become a song on everyone's lips and get top slots in music charts. Remember "dip...dip...dip..."? It is largely a question of how much you want to spend on what could establish a brand for all times.

Junket

It is so pejorative that a media person who is the target would hate to accept it. But junkets exist because corporate bodies have to show off a new plant or a happening at one of their locations or need to do a hype job on the launch of a product, or an airline gets a new route it needs to promote. And they dole it out to newspaper people who are then meant to write about the flight or happening in fairly complimentary terms. Many papers shun these, but they are a part of the system and should not be junked.

Junk mail

Unsolicited mail—conventional or electronic—that is sent in hundreds or thousands by organizations usually wishing to sell a product or service. These commonly incorporate 'hard to resist' offers in an effort to get the addressees to agree to buy. Generally considered a nuisance by addressees, deleted or discarded without being read in most cases.

Job Description

That which Public Relations departments ought to help HRD in, if only to make some job specs more palatable and give the company the right image for people to flock to.

Keyboard

The collection of keys covering alphabetic, numeric and punctuation marks along with special functions that is used to input data into a computer.

Keynote Address

The main speech at a conference or seminar, that sets the tone. Delivered by, who else, the Keynote Speaker.

K.I.S.S.

We are cross-referencing this with Brief. Keep It Simple, Stupid is more talked about than implemented, as rare is the person who does not like the sound of his own voice on a podium or who can write précis instead of thesis.

Kodak, Fridge, Hoover, Xerox

What do they have in common? Their generic nature. A challenge to an Advertising professional to create terminology which can go into brand building books. Can you ever forget the lines of jingles like "Have you Cheery Blossomed your shoes today?" Or, for the oldies: "Have you Macleaned your teeth today?"

Laptop

A portable computer that is commonly used by placing it on one's lap, especially by high flying executives, though there are innumerable cases of the lap being occupied by other, more interesting species, especially in the privacy of the office!

Launches

The Millennium is witnessing mega launches of a book, a product, a whole company with agencies who have specialized divisions for this purpose waiting to put the whole act together. Public Relations departments and consultancies are specializing in launch conferences with huge budgets and plenty of glitz.

Lunches

In the new millennium, wet lunches are passé. The phrase "There is no such thing as a Free Lunch" will always remain as long as there are strings to be attached.

Lobbying

Barracking with a sameness of purpose; making formal forays or representations for special interest groups via legislators; stalking the corridors of power with a one-ness of purpose, influence aplenty. (see chapter on Lobbying)

Marketing

Just as there is no single definition of Public Relations, for the Marketing function, there are also the honest ones and the convoluted explanations. A few are given here:

1   "Marketing is the process of determining consumer demand for a product or service, motivating its sale and distributing it into ultimate consumption at a profit."
2   "Marketing is selling goods which don't come back to people who do".
3   "Marketing is not only much broader than selling, it is not a specialized activity at all. It encompasses the entire business. It is the whole business seen from the point of view of its final result, that is from the customer's point of view. Concern and responsibility for Marketing must therefore

permeate all areas of the enterprise."—Peter Drucker, *The Practice of Management*.

Marketing Mix

No two theorists agree on the Marketing mix menu. The shortest of them all by McCarthy talk of product, price, place and promotion. These days there is talk of factors such as packaging, people, physical evidence and processes, in addition to the earlier four.

The Marketing mix, says one authority, is the apportionment of effort, the combination, the design, and the integration of the elements of Marketing into a programme or mix which, on the basis of appraisal of the market forces, will best achieve the objectives of an enterprise at a given time.

As for MIS, basically, that requires the organization of all data in connection with Marketing so that there can be an ongoing system of information availability.

The interactive process of Public Relations and Marketing cannot be undermined and one of the key areas would be in PR overseeing the whole business of corporate identity during a product planning stage and also Public Relations serving as an antenna of public interest.

Machine Proof

The printer looks at it quite differently from the production in-charge of an agency, or a corporate PR department person or the head of the company. Considering that it is the stage when the printed matter has to be actually seen on the printing machine and approved, it is a practice that is not done correctly. Companies want to see it in their offices, which holds up machine time and defeats the whole purpose. On the other hand, it is a great failsafe, for the possibility of minor colour correction still exists, and there is always that lurking printers' devil, which, if caught even at the final stages, can save ultimate embarrassment and costs, and perhaps possibility of legal hassles.

Make ready

A term which has seen a transition in meaning with the advancement of printing technology. It is essentially a term used to describe the undertaking of a process or series of processes by which the evenness and quality of printing is to be ensured after the form to be printed is placed on the machine.

Manuscript

Although commonly abbreviated as MS, in itself, the manuscript has generally nothing to do with gender, marriage or feminism. In editorial jargon the manuscript or MS is simply the sum total of matter to be ultimately printed, inclusive of both text and illustrations.

Masthead

A bone of considerable contention between students and certain practitioners of Public Relations in the USA and the rest of the world. In India, we tend to follow the popular understanding of the term that refers to the top of page one of any newspaper or publication that gives such details as its name, volume number and date of publication. Others, particularly Americans, who always like to do things differently including simplified spellings, maintain that this is a misrepresentation of the term. The masthead, according to them, refers to that position in a newspaper of publication that gives details of the publishers, owners and editors, the location of the business, advertising and editorial offices.

Media

That vehicle through which messages can be transmitted, whether it be visual, written, audio or a combination. While we generally think of it in terms of newspapers, magazines, radio and television, media (the plural of medium) is really anything which could be, at one end, posters and handbills and stickers and, at the other end of the spectrum, art and artefacts and music and dance.

But while media planning and media selection are largely the preserve of Advertising and Marketing disciplines, the other "media", which is a broad term for journalists, both in the written and in the audio-visual medium, is "dealt with" by Public Relations personnel.

Media Buying

The process of negotiating rates for advertisement space and time, carried out on behalf of advertisers by advertising agencies or specialist 'Media Independents'. The process is based on the fact that media owners willingly reduce prices compared to the published rates, for bulk annual purchases committed in advance. While most of the reductions are in the form of lower rates, other concessions are also possible, such as prominent positions being obtained without attracting premium rates.

Memory

Humans and computers both have memory. While humans need memory to pass examinations and remember others' faces or names, computers use memory both to manipulate data and store information on a permanent basis. Computer memory is of two types. Random Access Memory (RAM) is used for working and is lost when the machine is switched off while information that is required to be stored permanently (unless deleted deliberately) is stored on floppy disks, hard disks and CDs. The third type is Read Only Memory (ROM), not accessible to the user, which the computer uses to start up.

McLuhan, Marshall

There are few who are untouched by the "medium is the message" theory. Medium sometimes overpowers the message, though.

Merchandising

Although largely a Marketing term, merchandising is a concept in an area which needs Public Relations expertise— the ensuring of wide acceptability and visibility of this "message".

Merchandising covers activities and items from dressing up show windows, shop frontages and counters to wearing T-shirts and caps emblazoned with logos at promotions and events.

Merchant Banking

What do merchant banks really do? In recent years, merchant bankers have been handling capital issues, and playing a key role in institutional finance. It is the new proactive arm of banking and Public Relations people interact with them today because they are increasingly being involved in the process of corporate image building for competing in the market to gain investor confidence.

Merger

When a company is not acquired, it is merged. Which means, no predator involved, but a marriage of two, reasonably equal, synergistic companies to take on the world with their combined larger strengths. But sometimes, disparate corporations also merge, thus giving the new entity added strengths.

A large role for the Public Relations professional when the whole process takes place.

Mexican Statement

During one of its international conferences in Mexico in 1978, the International Public Relations Association focused on social accountability. A definition emerged then: "Public Relations is the art and social science of analysing trends, predicting their consequences, counselling organization leaders and implementing planned programmes of action which will serve both the organization's and the public interest." A somewhat more committed definition than the standard one which says: "Public Relations is the deliberate, planned and sustained effort to establish and maintain mutual understanding and goodwill between the organization and its publics."

Publics, note the word. In which case, the term should be Publics Relations. Unfortunately, this does not gloss off the tongue easily and lisps, somewhat. So Public Relations it is, and actions ultimately will speak louder than words.

Modem

Modulator-demodulator. An electronic circuit that converts digital signals (which your computer works with) to analogue (signals that telephone systems can handle) and vice versa, permitting a computer to transmit and receive information over a telephone cable. Essential for sending e-mail and surfing the World Wide Web using an ordinary telephone line. Modems are also used in fax machines. See e-mail and World Wide Web.

Mouse

A convenient method of providing instructions to a computer. For those who are not computer savvy, a source of worry: does this mouse bite?

Multi Media

The method of combining several communication elements such as moving images, static slides, text, voice over commentary, music and special effects. Terrific for corporate profiles, advertising presentations, product communications... even business cards with a difference. One thing to watch out for: let not flashy video techniques and special effects take the place of substance. In other words, there has to be both the steak and the sizzle.

Murdoch

Before Rupert Murdoch came Iris Murdoch whom pulp fiction readers could identify with. Anna Murdoch, Rupert's wife, wrote a nippy work of fiction, without using him as a platform to launch herself. Murdoch the media baron cannot be ignored today as he has leaped around several continents acquiring print and visual media and India is the current honey pot for Murdoch Jr.

Networking

Usually, the word brings up images of TV networks. In the world of Public Relations consultancy, networking involves the means of accessibility of PR service in different parts of the world, usually through a formal agreement between those in a networking group, when fees are paid into a central pool. Often, there is a loose networking arrangement by which a consultant could call upon a counterpart in a country where his client wants access and the payments could be direct to the person doing the work in the other country. Consultants, thus, can pass on business to one another on the principle of one good turn deserving another.

One way or another, the old boy network will never cease to be effective.

Newsprint

Not all the news that's fit to print, as one newspaper has as its slogan, but the paper on which news is printed. Still at a premium in India and quotas are strictly controlled. Coated newsprint is great stuff to print on, when available.

When the previous book on PR was written, the Government of India had a Newsprint Allocation Policy. Newsprint, under it, was allocated by the Registrar of Newspapers for India to such newspapers as were registered with the RNI in accordance with the relevant provisions of the Press and Registration of Books Act, 1867. To be eligible, a newspaper had to have a regularity of 90 percent in the case of a daily and 66 percent in case of other periodicity. Since then it is under OGL.

NRS

Started in 1972 to provide reliable data about publications. It provides the basic data for media planning and evaluation, indicating the efficiency of various publications, radio and TV programmes. Ignore the National Readership Survey at your own peril.

NRSC

And now comes yet another body—the National Readership Studies Council. The other three bodies talked about earlier—AAAI, ABC and INS—came together to form

NRSC. What does it do? It provides, on a regular basis, audited data about the reach of publications, viewership of television channels and cinema as well as listenership of radio channels among different demographic groups in the form of the NRS.

Off the Record

A clever Public Relations man must prime his top management never to utter this, for it is an instant invitation to the not-so-conscientious journalist to go ahead and quote him on precisely that point which he wished to avoid making a public statement on. It is ultimately a matter of trust; a corporate head must tell no lies and media people must be responsible enough to stay within bounds of confidentiality if the request be so.

OTS

Not be confused with WYSIWYG—What you see is what you get. Opportunity to See means the average number of times a person gets exposed to a particular message, whether in the print media, television, radio, a poster or a hoarding. It is also a statistical means of selling poster advertising where other publications depend on circulation. The "showing" of brides for arranged marriages does not come under the OTS term.

A better word for OTS would be Frequent Focus.

Outdoor Site Rating

To reduce the guesswork involved in selecting hoarding sites by quantifying the exposure value of sites according to the number of people passing by and their profiles. The outdoor equivalent of readership studies. Portland Site Valuation Worldwide, which has global operations, provides data about 12 Indian towns and cities.

Palm

The greasing of palms has obvious connotations and is often pejoratively used for lobbyists who have to do this to gain business advantage. However, a cleaner version comes with the Palm hand-held computer. A neat device that is a new lifestyle product, with users growing daily. It could be a useful tool for the PR practitioner, individual affordability being the issue at the moment.

Propaganda, Persuasion, Puffery, Promotion

There is too much of an overlap in these terms.

With propaganda, it is the association with what happened during Hitler's regime that gives it a negative connotation. In its purest form, it is merely the act of influencing public opinion. Its methodology probably makes it suspect.

With persuasion, similar Pavlovian reaction works. The associate word that comes to mind immediately is "friendly". Which is what persuasion is all about— the gently coercive means of getting a person over to your way of thinking. Two communication experts, Winston Brembeck and William Howell, call persuasion "a communication to influence choices."

Puffery is Just Overblown Praise.

As for publicity, it is anything that brings an event, a person or a happening to public notice.

There is an anecdote which Wilcox, Ault and Agee's book on Public Relations carries, and which they reproduced from Reader's Digest. It is a very telling statement on the fine lines of distinction between Public Relations, Advertising, Promotion and Publicity.

"When I accepted a position in Public Relations, a friend remarked that the job would be a breeze for me with my advertising/promotion background. I explained that the areas are quite different, and I illustrated my point with this example. "If the circus is coming to town and you paint a sign saying, 'circus coming to fairground Saturday', that's advertising. If you put the sign on the back of an elephant and walk him through town, that's promotion. And if the elephant walks through the mayor's flowerbed, that's publicity. "And", he chimed in, "if you can get the mayor to laugh about it, that's Public Relations."

Printing

Some of the more commonly used processes are documented here.

Letterpress

Developed in the days of Gutenberg, most practitioners our country would probably agree that letterpress is still the simplest and most economical of all printing processes and the one that can be within personal control, somewhat like flying a Tiger Moth, as opposed to an FBW plane. Printing in letterpress is accomplished by pressing the surface to be printed onto a raised, inked surface, which may appear in a variety of combinations—line, tone and colour. Where letterpress loses out to its technologically more advanced counterparts is in speed and slickness.

Lithography

One of the more advanced and consequently more demanding processes, technologically speaking. Unlike letterpress, lithography involves transferring the matter to be printed onto a sensitized metal plate by a combination of optical and chemical processes, such that the plate will only ink in those areas from which an impression is desired.

Originally, the beauty of lithography was because the material was not metal, but a stone slab. It was used by artists who wanted to make limited edition prints. Their illustration would be put on the surface with a greasy material and then water and printing ink were successively applied.

Etching is a different process where a design is etched on to a metal plate and involves acidic action to eat away the portions not in the design.

Woodcuts and linocuts are other means of getting limited artistic prints, with many artists specializing in this area that requires a combination of creativity and technical competence.

Offset-litho

The offset process is the most popular today. The essence lies in the impression of the matter to be printed being transferred from the engraving plate to a rubber blanket which is in turn "offset" onto the printing surface, usually paper or paper board.

Offset works well for large runs, but some printing presses print small runs as well, although unit costs do seem much higher in the end for the consumer.

Rotogravure

The process is one in which the image is printed on a rotary press which uses copper cylinders etched from photographic plates. The impressions of photographs and illustrations are excellent by this process, which many newspapers use for their magazine sections. Also called intaglio, this process is suitable only for very large print quantities. Currency notes and postage stamps are usually printed by rotogravure.

Silkscreen Printing

Used for limited runs and also to get special effects with seemingly raised colour surfaces, to get non-tone, flat effects of a design. The cloth, which may or may not be silk, is stretched on to a frame and the parts of the design not to be printed are blocked out. Printing can be achieved on a variety of materials, from paper and board to metal, fabric, glass, plastic and wood.

Halftone Printing

In this process the artwork to be reproduced is photographed through a screen which separates the design into small-sized dots in various degrees of concentration, which, when printed, produces the required tonal variation.

Programming

The process of preparing a software or programme required to operate a computer, or other equipment such as mobile telephones, automatic washing machines or remote control devices on television receivers. See Software.

Proofs

Proofing is an essential part of printing. There are the first sets of galley proofs, followed by page proofs which show the form in which they will appear, page wise. Progressive proofs are essentially proofs of four-colour illustrations showing how the final result is made up in steps from and in combination with the four primary colours. Scan proofs can be invaluable in colour correction, before the final printing. (see Appendix 1 for proof reading marks)

Imposition

The process of arranging the typeset pages in a form, so that when folded, the pages are in the correct sequence.

Trim size

While not actually referring to the hour glass figure, the trim size of a publication is a measure of its final dimensions after it has been properly cut and bound.

Quidnunc

What a Public Relations practitioner ought to have—the sense of curiosity, not the variety that kills the feline species, but as in the who-what-why-where-how kind.

Quisling

Not the plural of anything, as is goose, gosling, neither to mean gender as in Sanskrit, not the prodigy offspring of a quizzer. A quisling, although a politically traitorous figure, can also be one in Ad and PR circles who promises the clients everything, but doesn't even deliver Arpege, not even a whiff of it.

RAM/ROM

See Memory

Readership

Not to be confused with circulation. When a newsmagazine like India Today tells you of a 50-lakh readership, it means the number of people who would are likely to read a particular edition, as opposed to the primary buyers of that publication—which is the circulation. A readership survey gives an insight into numbers, sex, age social standing and so on, of the reader. See I.R.S. and N.R.S.

Road Show

The new trapeze for corporate financial wizards to do a circus tour of important centres around the world to mop up big time funds. Several companies have had massive collections through their global issues. But now, some of the even more sophisticated companies are doing away with this huge waste of time and money on travel of the cream of the crop. They figure that since the offer of Global Depository Receipts is largely to institutional investors, why not get some pledges direct anyway with FIIs and save the bother.

Sales Promotion

The dictionary of Marketing spells out two distinct kinds of sales promotion activity. One is of the type when promotion involves the giving out of free samples, premium offers, money back deals, gifts and competitions. The other is more communication-related like product literature, exhibitions and sponsorship.

However, sales promotion is a separate discipline and one in which Public Relations can have a participative role as and when required.

SMS

Short Messaging Service. Mobile phone users find this to be the cheapest means of sending and receiving messages between any two points on the globe, without incurring huge bills on regular calls. Today, SMS is being used as a tool for Marketing and Advertising.

Features such as message storage, send notification and simultaneous transmission with voice and fax should ensure that SMS prospers. It has been around since 1992 and should continue, alongside such complementary services such as GPRS, UMTS and WAP.

Snail Mail

Conventional post. Compared to e-mail, which is transmitted instantly and may be received within moments, ordinary mail is much slower... hence the allusion. Post offices the world over hate the term, not without reason. See E-mail.

Soft copy

A copy of a document in digital form—not printed but stored on a device like a floppy or a hard disk or a CD that a computer can access. See hard copy.

Software

A series of coded instructions that make a computer work, also called programme. Computer hardware (or, for that matter, items like automatic washing machines or mobile phones) needs to be instructed to be able to work. Well known software include Windows, Word, Excel, Photoshop, PageMaker; Corel Draw etc. See Hardware.

Soliloquy

(also speech, dialogue, silence)

Normally not a trait associated with the PR professional, except when going over bills to be presented to the client and muttering damnations under his breath. The other extreme is speechifying, which emerges out of dialogue. The sound of silence can be welcome in all this, giving beauty and credibility to over communication, acting in the manner that white space does in layouts. Silence or white space scares the speaker and visualizer more than the listener and viewer.

Spam

The e-mail equivalent of junk direct mail, where hundreds or thousands of e-mail messages are sent out at random. Frowned upon by e-mail service providers as it congests the network, clutters up electronic mail boxes and is considered worse than a nuisance by receivers. Several organizations are engaged in tracking down senders of spam and shutting down their operations.

Sponsorships

Without patronage and sponsors, today's products, events, concepts cannot be promoted and launched in the kind of manner which can generate excitement, interest and coverage. It is a mega ballgame which will see even larger players in this millennium

TV Audience Measurement

Similar to readership surveys, these attempt to provide data on who's watching what. There are two sources of TV ratings in India—AC Nielson's TAM (Television Audience Measurement) and ORG-Marg's INTAM (Indian National Television Audience Measurement) which is more recent. The former is a joint effort of A C Nielsen and Kantor, in partnership with IMRB and represents the Joint Industry Board comprising members of AAAI, ISA and major television channel owners. Weekly data are made available to members, by conducting viewership studies across important towns and cities, through "peoplemeters" installed in homes. Invaluable for media planners and advertisers with large budgets for advertising on television.

At the time of going to press, the leak of the list of confidential respondents brought into focus a proposal by the Indian Broadcasting Foundation (IBF) representing 29 top broadcasting channels in India for a single ratings agency.

Teleconferencing

Saves time, and also travelling expenditure. Enables organization heads to talk to diverse groups and get an immediate feedback. See Videoconferencing.

URL

Uniform Resource Locator—a method of accessing Internet resources. Also called the address of the website. A sample URL might be http://www.ibm.com/search.

USP

A unique selling proposition is not only the prerogative of a product, but a person or a company can have a USP too, something that is, once more, a challenge for the corporate communicator. It is a term that was originally mooted by Rosser Reeves when talking about brand positioning.

In a multi-brand age, how USP is USP?

Videoconferencing

No flights to catch, no hotels to book... yet you see the person you're talking to. That's videoconferencing for you. Made possible by using microphones, video cameras and computers linked together so that groups of people scattered all over the globe may interact as if they were in the same location. Invaluable for saving time and money for companies, though the travel trade is understandably not too happy with this one. See Teleconferencing.

Videotex

Not videotext as many people misspell it. This is an

interactive technology which is cost-effective. Viewdata is its other name.

Video magazine

The new audio-visual house magazine route. Read about it under house journals.

Virtual Organizations

When a group of people operate from their own locations or homes, perhaps have never actually met, yet have a network of clients whom they service with their pool of wide resources. (see Back to the Future)

Virtual

Virtual agencies are the new ways of finding networked solutions to globalized clients. Not to be put in the same category of the new generation of Virtual computer-generated newscasters and brand ambassadors.

Virus

A malicious programme or computer code that spreads from one computer to another largely through the Internet, but may also spread through 'infected' floppy disks or CDs. There are thousands of computer viruses (and their cousins called Trojans and Worms) of which some may be just a nuisance while others destroy data or even damage hardware. To be safe, users should run anti-virus programmes that need updating very frequently because new viruses are being released almost every day by malevolent programmers.

Visitor

In the digital age, one who views, or visits, a website.

Wall Newspaper

If a steel company like Tata Steel can do it, which is not into selling anything to the general public, but does care enough for its employees to communicate with them daily, others should try it as well. DTP can be put to good use.

WAP-enabled telephones

WAP stands for 'Wireless Application Protocol', a technology that enables mobile telephones to receive e-mail and data from the Internet without using a computer. Very convenient, but slow due to technical limitations that have prevented WAP from becoming really popular.

Workaholic

Most advertising professionals are supposed to be this. But does it mean a person who is more addicted to the liquid than to solid work?

Web Edition

The Internet version of a printed newspaper or magazine, complete with photographs, text, moving pictures, hyperlinks, e-mail facilities for 'letters to the editor' and advertisements... in short, every thing that a printed publication offers. The great advantage is that it costs little to update; news can be posted as it happens and not once a day like in printed versions.

Website

See Homepage

Xerox

The photocopying device that has ensured there won't be paperless offices in the near future.

Yellow Journalism

That which makes you see the colour purple in prose.

Zero Price Advertising

Distribution of Advertising at a price which does not cover its costs. That is, a zero money price, while the advertised goods are marked up to finance the Advertising. The purchaser pays the cost of the Advertising.

Appendix 1

Instruction	Textual Mark	Marginal Mark
Insert matter indicaled in margin	⟨	⁄
Delete and leave space or insert space	Strike through letters, etc., to be deleted	⌀
Delete and close up	*I* above and below letters to be taken out	⌒
Leave as printed	– – – under letters or words to remain	stet
Change to italic	___ under letters or words to be altered	ital
Change to small (even) capitals	═ under letters or words to be altered	Sc
Change to capital letters	≡ under letters or words to be altered	Caps
Use capital letters for initial letters and small	≡ under initial letters and	C. & Sc.

Instruction	Mark in text	Mark in margin
capitals for rest of words	= under the rest of the words	
Change to bold type	under letters or words to be altered	Bold
Change to lower case	/ through letters to be altered	l.c.
Change to roman	Encircle words to be altered	Rom
(Wrong fount) Replace by letter of correct fount	Encircle letter to be altered	w.f.
Invert type	Encircle letter to be altered	
Change damaged letter(s)	Encircle letter(s) to be altered	×
Substitute or insert letters or signs under which this mark is placed in "superior" position	/ through character or ⟨ where required	⌐
Substitute or insert letters or signs over which this mark is placed, in "inferior" position	/ through character or ⟨ where required	⌐
Underline word or words	— under words affected	underline
Use ligature (e.g. ffi) or diphthong (e.g. œ)	⌣ enclosing letters to be altered	⌣ enclosing ligature or diphthong required

Close up—delete space between letters	⌒	linking words or letters	⌒
Insert space	⋏		#
Make space appear equal between words	/	between words	equal #
Reduce space between words	/	between words	less #
Transpose		between letters or words, numbered when necessary	trs.
Move matter to right	⊐	at left side of group to be moved	⊐
Move matter to left	⊏	at right side of group to be moved	⊏
Begin a new paragraph	⊏	before first word of new paragraph	n.p.
No fresh paragraph here		between paragraphs	run on
Insert omitted portion of copy	⋏		out, see copy
Substitute or insert comma	./ ⋏	through character or where required	,

Substitute or insert full-stop	/	through character	
	⋏	or where required	⊙
Insert hyphen	⋏		⏌-⏌
Insert apostrophe	⋏		ˀ
Insert double quotation mark	⋏		˝ ⫶

Appendix 2

Public Relations Society of India (PRSI)

The Public Relations Society of India (PRSI) is the national association of public relations practitioners and communication specialists in India. It functions primarily for professional development. It seeks to formulate and interpret the objectives and potential of public relations as a socially useful function and uphold its value as an integral part of management. It also maintains close links with academic bodies for promotion of public relations as a subject of management studies.

PRSI came into being as an informal body in 1958 with its headquarters in Mumbai. The genesis of the Society in Calcutta can be traced to 1965 when Sanat Lahari, Shankar Mitra, R.P.Gupta, Prasanta Sanyal, J.M.Kaul and other pioneers of the profession formed a nucleus, known as the Public Relations Circle. However, this was formally merged with the national body in 1968 to strengthen the public relations movement on all- India basis.

The National Council, the apex body of the PRSI, annually organises an All-India Public Relations Conference to highlight its contemporary relevance. It has a quarterly journal "Public Relations" which seeks to promote the case of public relations by bringing to its readers news and articles on public relations in India and abroad. The Society has 31 chapters spread all over the country. Members of the Society, numbering more than 3,000 are drawn from the private sector and public sector corporations as well as the Government, non-profit organizations and academic bodies.

All India PR Conferences

In 1968, the First All-India PR Conference was held in New Delhi. The subsequent Conferences were held as follows: (2) February, 1970 (Chennai)—Role of PR in Management, (3) March, 1972(Calcutta)-PR and the Changing Social Environment; (4) January, 1974 (Mumbai)-Towards More Responsible Citizenship; (5) March, 1976 (New Delhi)-Towards Greater Professionalism; (6) January, 1978(Cochin)-Public Relations in the Eighties, (7) January,1980(Calcutta)-New Dimensions in PR; (8) January, 1982 (Mumbai)-merged with the 9th PR World Congress. The Interdependent World; (9) February, 1984 (Bangalore)-Dynamics of Developmental Communications: PR Perspectives; (10) September, 1986(Delhi)-Changing Indian Scene; PR Challenges; (11) February, 1988 (Hyderabad)-One Country, One People; (12) June 1989 (Calcutta)- Public Relations-The State-of-the-Art; (13) June,1990 (Bangalore)-Change-A Challenge for Future, (14) October,1991 (Cochin)-Information Technology-A Challenge to Communicators; (15) November,1992 (New-Delhi)-India in the New World Order; (16) December,1993(Chennai)-Ushering in a New Era -PR Issues; (17) December,1994(Mumbai); (18) November,1995(Jaipur)-PR: The Decade Ahead; (19) February 1997(Ooty), Image Management, A Password to the 21st Century; (20) January,1998(Calcutta)-The Brave New World of PR (an Asia-Pacific Public Relations Conference); (21) April, 1999 (Chandigarh)-Image India: PR Strategies.

Bringing in a regional bias, and on a personal note, one can commend the initiatives taken in eastern India with several monographs published on subjects to grow the profession; the Sanat Lahiri Memorial Lecture on an annual basis which sees people prominent in business and industry and in Public Relations giving their state-of-the-art discourses and the growing camaraderie in making the association go beyond business into a culturally vibrant body of likeminded people.

International Public Relations Association (IPRA)

The concept of establishing an international public relations association first took concrete shape in November 1949 during a meeting in London between two Dutch and four British public relations practitioners. As they discussed their respective activities, the idea emerged of organizing public relations professionals into a transnational society, with the objective of raising standards of public relations practice in the various countries and improving the quality and efficiency of practitioners. The International Public Relations Association (IPRA) was formally established in London on May 1,1955.

Meetings World Wide

Reflecting a continued commitment to providing opportunities for international associations in public relations, the IPRA Council and its Board of Directors meet regularly to review the organisation's activities and future operations and to focus the attention of the membership on emerging issues in public relations practise. Council meetings are held normally in conjunction with an IPRA-sponsored public relations conference hosted by individual national public relations associations. Every three years IPRA sponsors a World Public Relations Congress, which brings together practitioners from all sectors of the profession to assess the latest standards and techniques of practice and to explore means of increasing co-operation.

Golden World Awards (GWA) For Excellence

In addition to promoting enhanced standards of ethics and social responsibility in public relations practise, IPRA also works to foster greater expertise and achievement at all levels of the profession. The IPRA Golden World Awards initiative, established in 1990, recognises excellence in public relations practice worldwide.

IPRA Today

Special emphasis continues to be laid on education and professional literature, though the scope of this activity has been increasingly expanded to include promotion of the profession in the developing countries and Eastern Europe and in addressing key issues such as the environment or the assessment of quality in public relations practice.

From its origins as a close-knit fellowship of public relations pioneers to its current status as the most representative international network, of top-level professionals in the field, IPRA has been the focus of an ever-evolving approach to business and social communications.

India played a prominent role in IPRA affairs, when Sanat Lahiri became the first international president; Anand Akerkar followed a few years later and then Zelma Lazarus kept the flag flying and even injected some funds into the organization.

Bibliography

Books:

Case Studies in Marketing, Advertising & Public Relations:
  Colin McIver

Effective Public Relations (Third Edition):
  Scott M. Cutlip & Center Alien H.

Handbook of Public Relations in India:
  D.S. Mehta

Introduction to Public Relations:
  Sam Black

Lesly's Public Relations Handbook (Second Edition):
  Edited by Lesly Philip

Managing for the Future: The 1990s and Beyond:
  Peter F. Drucker

*New Reporters & New Sources: Accomplices in shaping and misshaping
  the news* (Second Edition):
  Herbert Strentz

Profitable Public Relations:
  Aurthur R. Roalman

Public Relations: Strategies & Tactics:
  Dennis L. Wilcox, Philip H. Ault, Warren K. Agee

Public Relations Ideas in Action:
  Edited & Compiled by Allen H. Center

The Corporate Personality: An Inquiry into the nature of Corporate Identity:
  Wally Olins

The Public Affairs Handbook:
  Edited by Joseph S. Nagelschmidt

The Handbook of Public Relations (Third Edition):
  Chris Skinner & Llew Von Essen

The Role of Public Relations in Management:
  Sam Black

The Accidental Theorist:
  Paul Krugman

The Road Ahead:
  Bill Gates

Leading the Revolution:
  Gary Hamel

Losing My Virginity:
  Richard Branson

Leading Organizations:
  Editor, Gill Robinson Hickmann

Managing Radical Change: What Indian Companies Must do to become World Class:
  Sumantra Ghoshal, Gita Piramal, Christopher A. Bartlett

It was five past midnight in Bhopal:
  Dominique Lapierre & Javier Moro

Pentagram: The Compendium:
  Edited by David Gibbs

Ethics in Management: Vedantic Perspectives:
  S.K. Chakraborty

Is the Good Corporation Dead? Social Responsibility in a Global Economy:
Edited by John W. Houck & Oliver F. Williams

Publications and Monographs:

International Public Relations Review—Vol. 13 & Vol. 14.
IPRA XII Public Relations World Congress Proceedings.
Public Relations Case Studies (Indian Scene)—Vol. 1 (IFPR).
Twelfth all India Public Relations Conference (Extract from Speeches)

Ethical Dilemmas in Public Relations: A Pragmatic Examination:
John F. Budd, Jr. Gold Paper No. 8, June 1991 (IPRA).

Public Relations in India:
Sanat Lahiri.

Articles:

Washington and the World of Lobbying. By Chidanand Rajghatta:
The *Sunday Times of India*, Kolkata, August 26, 2001